"A disgrace to the profession"

THE WORLD'S SCIENTISTS
- *in their own words* -
ON MICHAEL E MANN,
HIS HOCKEY STICK,
AND THEIR DAMAGE TO SCIENCE

Volume I

"A disgrace to the profession"

THE WORLD'S SCIENTISTS
~ in their own words ~
ON MICHAEL E MANN,
HIS HOCKEY STICK,
AND THEIR DAMAGE TO SCIENCE

Volume I

compiled and edited by
MARK STEYN

illustrated by
JOSH

STOCKADE
BOOKS

Published in 2015 by Stockade Books
Box 30
Woodsville, New Hampshire
03785

Printed and bound in the Province of Québec, Canada

ISBN 978-0-9863983-3-9

If these scientists have done something wrong, it will be found out and their peers will determine it... Don't get your information from me, folks, or any newscaster. Get it from people with PhD after their names.

ED BEGLEY, JR
ACTOR AND ENVIRONMENTAL ACTIVIST IN TV INTERVIEW
WITH STUART VARNEY, NOVEMBER 24th 2009

Nullius in verba
MOTTO OF THE ROYAL SOCIETY
ADOPTED SHORTLY AFTER ITS FOUNDING IN NOVEMBER 1660

ABBREVIATIONS USED IN THE TEXT

AGU - American Geophysical Union

CRU - Climatic Research Unit at the University of East Anglia

EPA - US Environmental Protection Agency

GRL - The peer-reviewed journal *Geophysical Research Letters*

GST - ground surface temperature

HadCRUT - The instrumental temperature record combining sea surface temperatures from the UK Met Office's Hadley Centre and surface air temperatures from the CRU

IPCC - Intergovernmental Panel on Climate Change

LIA - Little Ice Age

MBH98 - 1998 Mann, Bradley and Hughes hockey stick

MBH99 - 1999 Mann, Bradley and Hughes hockey stick

MCO - Medieval Climate Optimum, a synonym for MWP

MWP - Medieval Warm Period

NH - Northern Hemisphere

NOAA - US National Oceanic and Atmospheric Administration

NRC - National Research Council of the US National Academy of Sciences

PCA - the statistical procedure of principal component analysis

SAT - surface air temperature

SPM - the IPCC's Summary for Policy Makers

SST - sea surface temperature

TAR - IPCC Third Assessment Report (2001)

WMO - World Meteorological Organization

CONTENTS

INTRODUCTION
by Mark Steyn

Climate of fear

Over the last 10,000 years it has been warmer than today 65 per cent of the time.[1]

PROFESSOR GERNOT PATZELT, PHD
THE INTERNATIONAL CLIMATE AND ENERGY CONFERENCE
MUNICH, 2011

Once upon a time there was a thing called "geologic time". It was a hell of a ride, as Professor Robert Laughlin of Stanford, summarizes:

Six million years ago the Mediterranean Sea dried up. Ninety million years ago alligators and turtles cavorted in the Arctic. One hundred fifty million years ago the oceans flooded the middle of North America and preserved dinosaur bones. Three hundred million years ago, northern Europe burned to a desert and coal formed in Antarctica.[2]

No humans were involved, nor a single SUV or air conditioner. There was no caveman Al Gore to distribute an awareness-raising poster of the last 'gator plashing merrily round the North Pole as the ice closes in. Hasta la vista, Arctic turtle! See you later, alligator!

Climate change... is a matter of geologic time, something that the earth routinely does on its own without asking anyone's

---

[1] http://notrickszone.com/2012/05/24/multiple-glacier-studies-show-wide-holocene-climate-variations-in-asia-and-europe/#sthash.wPO84Bvi.dpbs
[2] https://theamericanscholar.org/what-the-earth-knows/#.VTwQA5O4K_E

i

permission or explaining itself. The earth doesn't include the potentially catastrophic effects on civilization in its planning... Were the earth determined to freeze Canada again, for example, it's difficult to imagine doing anything except selling your real estate in Canada.

I doubt even Michael E Mann, the subject of this book and a man ever ready to pin the scarlet "D" to your chest, could get away with labeling Robert Laughlin a "climate denier". Professor Laughlin is a Nobel Laureate - a genuine one, that is, not a fake, self-conferred one like Mann. Professor Laughlin is less a climate denier than a climate insouciant: If God or Gaia decides to reset the global thermostat, you might as well relax, because there's not much you can do about it. Long after a dank Nordic chill settled on sun-drenched Scandinavia, and the American midwest emerged from underwater, and the polar bears hunted the Yukon alligator to extinction, and the Mediterranean bedouin on their annual desert trek from Tangiers to Monte Carlo said, "Hey, that oasis seems to be a lot bigger than it was last year", long after the upheavals of geologic time, man retained a certain humility before the awesome power of nature.

And then came the "hockey stick".

It was the single most influential graph in the history of climate science. It leapt from the pages of a scientific journal to the posters and slides of the transnational summits, to official government pamphlets selling the Kyoto Protocol, to a starring role on the big screen in an Oscar-winning movie, to the classrooms of every schoolhouse throughout the western world. At the turn of the 21st century it sold the simplest of propositions: This is the hottest year of the hottest decade of the hottest century of the millennium - which is, like, forever.

And suddenly no one remembered "geologic time" or "natural climate variability" anymore. In the history of Mann-made climate change, "nothing happened in the world before the 20th century" (as Oxford physicist Jonathan Jones put it) after which the mercury shot up and straight through the top of the thermometer: in other words, it's all your fault. As MIT's Richard Lindzen observed:

> *This is the problem. These guys think saying 'climate changes', saying it gets warmer or colder by a few tenths of a degree, should be taken as evidence that the end of the world is coming. And it completely ignores the fact that until this hysteria, climate scientists used to refer to the warm periods in our history as 'optima'.*[3]

He says that like it's a good thing.

In 2012 Michael E Mann sued me and various other parties in the District of Columbia Superior Court for "defamation of a Nobel Prize recipient"[4]. He was obliged to withdraw the false claim to be a Nobel Prize recipient, but not the defamation charge - over my description of his hockey stick as "fraudulent". I'll stand by that. It does not prove what it purports to prove. Whether or not Al Gore and the Intergovernmental Panel on Climate Change knew that, I doubt the schoolchildren to whom it has been force-fed for a generation ever did. I wonder how many of those who regard it as an authoritative graph of global climate across the centuries are aware that its hockey-stick shape for the entire hemisphere depends on two clumps of trees: some California bristlecones, and some

---

[3] http://www.climatedepot.com/2015/03/06/watch-mits-dr-richard-lindzen-on-fox-news-we-are-demonizing-a-chemical-a-molecule-essential-to-life-co2/#ixzz3dHHiZQdi

[4] http://legaltimes.typepad.com/files/michael-mann-complaint.pdf

cedars from the Gaspé Peninsula - or rather, for the years up to 1421, just *one* cedar from the Gaspé Peninsula. Quick, hands up, who knows where the Gaspé Peninsula is? I do, because I'm a Quebecker and I've been to the Gaspé dozens of times and regard it as one of my favorite places on earth. But it is not *the* earth. How many of us, on being assured that "the science is settled", are aware that it's been settled on the basis of one Québécois tree?

Two years after Mann launched his suit, in one of those procedural sideshows that encrust to the sclerotic and dysfunctional US court system like barnacles on the hulk of a rusting tugboat at the bottom of the Suez Canal, came the deadline for third parties to file "amicus briefs" with the courts. The American Civil Liberties Union, *The Washington Post*, NBC News, *The Los Angeles Times* and various other notorious right-wing climate deniers all filed amici briefs opposed to Michael Mann and his assault on free speech. They did this not because they have any great love for me or any of the other parties, but because their antipathy was outweighed by their appreciation of the First Amendment - and an understanding of the damage a Mann victory would inflict on it.

On the other hand, ever since this tedious suit was launched by Mann, his supporters had insisted that it's not about free speech at all. Instead, as they see it, it's about science finally fighting back against a sustained assault by Koch-funded "deniers". This sub-headline encapsulates the general line:

Michael Mann is taking a stand for science.[5]

Gotcha. Michael Mann is not doing this for Michael Mann, or even for Michael Mann's science, or even for climate science. He's doing it for science. Mann is science and science is Mann. In court his

---

[5] http://yalealumnimagazine.com/articles/3648

argument was a straightforward appeal to authority: Why, all these eminent acronymic bodies, from the EPA and NSF and NOAA even unto HMG in London, have proved that all criticisms of Mann are false and without merit. So I certainly expected them to file briefs on his behalf - and, given that Mann sees this as part of a broader "war on science" by well-funded "deniers", I also expected briefs from the various professional bodies: the National Academy of Sciences, the American Physical Society, the Royal Society, etc.

And yet the deadline came and passed, and not a single amicus brief was filed on behalf of Mann. Not one.

So Michael Mann is taking a stand for science. But evidently science is disinclined to take a stand for Michael Mann. The self-appointed captain of the hockey team is playing solo. As Dr Judith Curry of Georgia Tech wrote:

> The link between 'defending Michael Mann is defending climate science' seems to have been broken.[6]

Dr Curry has a point. If you're defending Michael Mann, you're not defending science, or defending climate science, or theories on global warming or anything else. Defending Michael Mann means defending Michael Mann - and it turns out not many people are willing to go there.

Mann had rested his case on an "appeal to authority" - to what eminent people say about him. I regard appeals to authority as somewhat unAmerican - but even for those of us born in lands less philosophically committed to egalitarianism they're a bit whiffy: a cat may look at a king, as they used to say in medieval Europe. So why can't a skeptic kitty look at a climate king? But Mann was taking his appeal to authority to the next level, appealing *falsely* to

---

[6] http://judithcurry.com/2014/08/14/mann-vs-steyn-et-al-discussion-thread/

authorities. Most of the official reports he claimed "exonerated" him had not a word to say about him. The Nobel Institute had nothing to say about him, other than that he had never won a Nobel Prize. And now the world's scientists he claimed to be taking a stand for had fallen deathly silent.

And so I started wondering what, in fact, do all these scientists think of Mann and his methods. Initially, I assumed it would be just the usual contrarians, the "skeptics", the "deniers". But then I discovered that around the world there are many, many scientists who, broadly speaking, believe in "anthropogenic global warming" but do not believe in Mann. We wound up with far more material than we could ever fit in one book, so this is Volume One, which I intended to confine to a nice round number of 100 scientists - ten scientists on ten aspects of Mann and his work - but it grew to 12 aspects, and we squeezed in a few more scientists in the introduction to each chapter. We'll try to hold it down to my planned 100-per-volume for the second instalment. Some of them are distinguished emeritus profs and Fellows of the Royal Society, but some are young up-and-comers. Many are from the heart of the Anglo-American climate establishment, but others are from Europe and elsewhere and don't quite understand why a small clique of outliers singlehandedly determines the "consensus" in the field. There are fewer women than one might wish, but it seems to be a male-dominated field and indeed there is a palpable misogyny in the way some of Mann's defenders attack his female critics.[7] Some are

---

[7]Diehard Manniac blogger "Tamino", for example, condescendingly refers to the aforementioned and distinguished Dr Judith Curry as "Aunt Judy" (see https://nigguraths.wordpress.com/2014/05/23/biotech-biostitutes/), which appears to be a derogatory porno term for an older woman one would be willing to have sex with if no one younger was to hand. Given that Mann enthusiastically facilitated the reduction of scientific dispute to name-calling, it would be

"climate scientists" (an extremely elastic term that has evolved considerably in recent decades) and some practice in related fields - but all know how science is meant to work and how in Mann's case it failed to work.

Oh, and one other ecumenical point: Mann told an Irish interviewer that "in the US, belief in climate change is about as good a predictor of party affiliation as anything in this country"[8] - in other words, only right-wing loons oppose him. But among the scientists you will hear from in these pages are men of the left - sometimes the Scandinavian social-democrat left, sometimes the hardcore Marxist left. Indeed, Mann's scourge Stephen McIntyre, the Toronto mining engineer who dismantled the hockey stick, is, I think it's fair to say, a fairly conventional Trudeaupian liberal in Canadian terms. Genuine Nobel Laureate Ivar Giaever voted for Obama as did fake Nobel Laureate Mann. Oxford University's Jerry Ravetz equates Climategate with Tony Blair's "sexed-up" dossier to justify invading Iraq.

One of Mann's more dull-witted partisans, Greg Laden of Science Blogs, noted the presence of Eduardo Zorita and Simon Tett on the list of scientists herein, and assumed I'd made a mistake - because these are "mainstream climate scientists" rather than deniers[9]. But I'm afraid poor Mr Laden is missing the point: as this book demonstrates, there is no contradiction between being "pro-science" and thinking Mann is full of it. For example, Michael Liebreich is a visiting professor at Imperial College, London and

---

unreasonable to expect his Mannboys to confine themselves to merely the Holocaust echoes of "denier".

[8] http://villagemagazine.ie/index.php/2014/04/5706/

[9] http://scienceblogs.com/gregladen/2015/06/22/mark-steyns-newest-attack-on-michael-mann-and-the-hockey-stick/

advisory board chairman of Bloomberg New Energy Finance, whose broad disposition you can adduce from its name. He's also on the World Economic Forum's Global Agenda Council on the New Energy Architecture and the UN Secretary General's High Level Group on Sustainable Energy for All. Get the picture? He believes in global warming. But he doesn't believe in Michael Mann. Invited by a Tweeter called Christian Thalacker to "Help Science Heroes Like Professor Michael Mann", Mr Liebreich replied coolly:

> *The @MichaelEMann who withheld data and conspired to exclude competing authors from journals is no science hero of mine.*[10]

Amid the groupthink that is Big Climate, this was not the response Christian Thalacker expected to receive. He was outraged, and Tweeted back that he would be taking it up with Liebreich's boss:

> *Fyi: i'm letting Mike Bloomberg know IDENTITY FRAUD-Twitter at Bloomberg New Energy Finance*[11]

And he did:

> *@MikeBloomberg@BloombergLP Michael Liebreich, NEF Chairman AGAINST climate science?*

Get that? If you're against Michael Mann you're against climate science. Mann's view is that *le climat, c'est moi.* And he means it. Nevertheless, Mr Liebreich pushed back at the charge that he was "AGAINST climate science":

> *Nope. I'm against abuse of academic power just as I am against abuse of any power. No exceptions, for any cause.*[12]

---

[10] https://twitter.com/MLiebreich/status/438430518791897088
[11] https://twitter.com/JP_Revere/status/438655764018626561

Mann himself decided to weigh in at this point and took time off from whining about all the one-star reviews of *The Hockey Stick and the Climate Wars* to recommend that Liebreich "should read my book"[13].

Mr Liebreich responded:

@MichaelEMann I've read #HSCW ...and #Climategate emails. I think you were sloppy and unethical. I also think #AGW is real. [14]

A few more from Liebreich?

Conflating climate science with @MichaelEMann discredits good climate science..!

Based on his indefensible methods and behaviour. He's going down, and taking a lot of good scientists with him...

The fact other scientists have found warming is profoundly different from them replicating his flawed work...

It has never been replicated because you can't without access to original data and algorithms. So it's junk. [15]

That's the dispute between the scientists in these pages: whether Mann's work is junk science, bad science, pseudo science, pathological science - or "brazen fraud". But there's not a lot of people willing to defend it as "good climate science".

As Michael Liebreich's Twitter feed suggests, it requires some energy and resilience to push back against Mann from within the global-warming establishment. I was struck by that, and a little

---

[12] https://twitter.com/MLiebreich/status/438657849653489664
[13] https://twitter.com/MichaelEMann/status/438757695248547840
[14] https://twitter.com/MLiebreich/status/438778296038588416
[15] https://twitter.com/MLiebreich/status/512491197479546880

disturbed. On the eve of publication of this book, *Esquire* ran a long article with a fey headline:

Ballad of the Sad Climatologists[16]

This was one of those pieces that now crops up every few months, about the way climate scientists are suffering from "pre-traumatic stress syndrome" - because they know the end of the world is nigh but nobody listens to them. Or as the even more overwrought sub-headline put it:

> *When the end of human civilization is your day job, it can be hard to sleep at night.*

Oh, get over yourself, you hysterical old queen. It's a grim reflection on American journalism that any self-respecting editor could type that with a straight face. The "pre-traumatic stress" thing is, aside from anything else, immensely trivializing of those suffering from real post-traumatic stress - from actual IEDs in Fallujah and suicide bombers in Helmand, rather than vague speculative concerns about sea levels in the Maldives a century hence. Even among scientists, Professor Tony Brown, whom we shall meet later, had the grim task of serving as "soil analyst" for the International Criminal Tribunal investigating war crimes in Bosnia, and surely has more claim to being stressed out by science.

Nevertheless, I turned the page and, inevitably, there he was: "Sad Climatologist" Numero Uno Michael E Mann, supposedly "the target of the most powerful deniers in the world", along with fellow data-hoarder and big-cheese butterfly ecologist Camille Parmesan[17], Mann's *Real Climate* colleague Gavin Schmidt and a

---

[16] *Esquire*, July 2015
[17] http://wattsupwiththat.com/2013/07/14/fabricating-climate-doom-part-1-parmesans-butterfly-effect/

couple of others to round out the numbers.

And not for the first time you wonder: If there's a 97 per cent consensus, why is it always the same handful of names in these pieces? Even amidst the somnolent drones of American magazine writing, does it never occur to anyone that maybe this time it would be nice to hear from someone other than Mann and the usual suspects? He may indeed be "the target of the most powerful deniers in the world" (the Koch brothers, me ...er, did we mention the Koch brothers?) but his unscientific science is also the target of Nobel Laureates, the President of the Royal Statistical Society, and the man who coined the term "global warming". He's also the target of significant numbers of Scandinavian climatologists who think that, instead of regarding "the end of human civilization" as his day job, Mann ought to concentrate on his actual day job and learn to handle their raw data with minimal competence.

Why do we never hear from them? Why is it always Mann and a handful of other ayatollahs of alarmism? Imagine how much more interesting the public discourse might be if the climate conversation expanded beyond the pre-stressed self-traumatized navel-gazers.

Come to think of it, how come they suck all the CO_2 out of the room anyway?

When you get embroiled in as many time-consuming legal matters as I do, it's always fun to have something bigger at stake than a mere courtroom victory. I find, otherwise, it's all a bit of a bore. When the Canadian "human rights" commissions came after me and *Maclean's* magazine, we turned the tables and put the "human rights" system itself on trial. The eventual repeal by Parliament of the disgusting and indefensible "hate speech" law was personally far more satisfying than the not-guilty verdict the British

Columbia "Human Rights" Tribunal graciously bestowed on me and *Maclean's*: By that stage, we had way bigger fish to fry.

In this case, Mann is suing me for defamation. I'd like to win that case - because losing it would be the worst setback for free speech in America in the half-century since *New York Times vs Sullivan*.

But as important a goal for me is lifting the climate of fear that Mann and his fellow enforcers have imposed on a critical field of science and in the broader sphere of public policy. The ugly retaliation that the climate mullahs use against anyone who steps out of line - as we'll see later in the hockey-sticking of distinguished Swedish scientist Lennart Bengtsson - ought to appall any real man of science. You shouldn't have to be a Nobel Laureate like Ivar Giaever or as well-connected as Michael Liebreich to be able to speak out without suffering bloody reprisals. So I'd like to end the protection racket of the Clime Syndicate and put them out of the intimidation business.

One quick bit of business: In the pages that follow, the source for each scientist's quotation is footnoted. However, because of the extraordinary level of paranoia about "doctored quotes" that attends the climate debate, we've retained the various spellings - British, American or the often charming English of Swedes and Finns - and made only a few punctuation changes. Each scientist is introduced by a brief recap of his curriculum vitae. As I said above, a cat may look at a king, but the position of Emperor Mike's courtiers is that only a cat with a PhD may gaze upon His Tree-Ringed Majesty. So we've also stuck all those in: As a fellow with not a single letter after my name, I have never typed so many post-nominals in my life.

That said, what follows would not have been possible without the sterling work of Stephen McIntyre and Ross McKitrick or without A W Montford's invaluable book *The Hockey Stick Illusion*. These men did the real peer review that *Nature*, the CRU, the IPCC and Mann's professional colleagues all balked at.

Just to recap, these scientists have all manner of views on climate change, CO_2, the warming pause, etc. But their words on Michael Mann deserve to be more widely known. The truth about the hockey stick was always obvious to anyone who looked at it coolly and objectively.

On Sunday January 26th 2003 at 10.27pm on a Yahoo discussion forum for climate skeptics, a Dutch doctorandus called Hans Erren posted a short note pointing out a few curiosities in Mann's method:

Dear Forum,

Mann et al did the following: They compared North american treelines and the Principal component #1 of North American Treerings for the period 1400-1980. This was matched. Then they correlated North american tree rings with Northern hemisphere temperatures 1860-1980.

How well does Northern hemisphere temperature correlate with North american temperature? Actually it doesn't. EG for the 48 USA states the 1930s were comparable to the 1990s

The logical conclusion is that Northamerican trees respond better to global average temperatures than to local temperatures.

My Big question Why did MBH1999 not use North american temperatures to calibrate north american tree ring data??

Then the following jump was made: the ITRDB Principal component#1 doesn't show a medieaval warm period therefore

the average northern hemisphere (average globe) must not show a MWP. And the hockestick [sic] was born.
Hans E[18]

And so it began.

~Mark Steyn is the author of the international bestsellers America Alone *and* After America, *as well as the acclaimed theatrical classic* Broadway Babies Say Goodnight. *His latest book is* The [Un]documented Mark Steyn, *and his latest album is* Goldfinger, *which includes what Ted Nugent calls Steyn's "killer" version of "Cat Scratch Fever".*

---

[18] https://groups.yahoo.com/neo/groups/climatesceptics/info

PROLOGUE

"A colossal mistake"

DR JERRY D MAHLMAN, PhD (1940-2012)

Director of the National Oceanic and Atmospheric Administration's Geophysical Fluid Dynamics Laboratory and Professor of Atmospheric and Oceanic Sciences at Princeton. Senior Research Associate at the National Center for Atmospheric Research. Pioneer in the use of computational models to examine the interactions between atmospheric chemistry and physics, and one of the first scientists to raise concerns about ozone depletion. Recipient of the Rossby Research Medal of the American Meteorology Society, the US Government's Presidential Rank Award of Distinguished Executive and the Gold Medal of the US Department of Commerce.

One day toward the end of the last millennium a young scientist called Michael Mann went to give a talk at the Geophysical Fluid Dynamics Laboratory, one of America's premier climate research institutions. Among his audience was the lab's director, Dr Mahlman, who, upon seeing Mann's latest temperature reconstruction, observed that it looked like a "hockey stick" - a long 900-year shaft of steady, slight cooling and then a short, sharp blade of rising 20th-century temperatures.

Almost 70 years earlier, Margaret Herrick of the Academy of Motion Picture Arts and Sciences had cast an eye on the statuette for the organization's awards night and said, "He looks like my Uncle Oscar." The name stuck. And so it was with Dr Mahlman's aside: The stick stuck. It was catchier than the formal title - "Northern Hemisphere temperatures during the past millennium: inferences, uncertainties, and limitations" - and its very name would lead to many more streamlined and thus more stick-like versions of the graph by the World Meteorological Organization and other bodies who should have known better.

Dr Mahlman was a serious believer in global warming: He scoffed at the Kyoto Protocol because everyone knows "it would take 40

1

Kyotos to actually stop the increase"[1]. He told a peer-reviewed journal that Stephen McIntyre and Ross McKitrick, the two Canadians who had the nerve to criticize Mann's science, were mere "quacks"[2].

And yet Dr Mahlman came to see that the hockey stick he helped loose upon the world had done grievous harm. As The Chronicle of Higher Education *reported in 2006, re the Intergovernmental Panel on Climate Change's Third Assessment[3]:*

> In the first figure of the summary, the authors chose to highlight only one of the long-term temperature reconstructions: the hockey-stick curve from Mr Mann's group. When Sir John T Houghton, leader of the IPCC's scientific working group, appeared before the television cameras to unveil his committee's long-awaited report, he had a poster behind him bearing a large image of the hockey stick.
>
> For many in the news media and the general public, that graph appeared to be the star witness in the IPCC's case that humans were warming the globe, when in fact that argument actually rested on a mass of other evidence unrelated to the curve.
>
> The panel's decision to emphasize the hockey stick so strongly "was a colossal mistake, just as **it was a mistake for the climate-science-writing press to amplify it**," says Mr Mahlman, the scientist who named the curve. "In other words, was that the smoking gun for global warming? It's not the smoking gun. That's the data we've had for the past 150 years."

Too late. Sir John and the IPCC had decided to take a flyer on Mann's cartoon climatology, and all science could do was hang on and enjoy the ride.

---

[1] http://www.tysknews.com/Depts/Environment/new_climate.htm

[2] Mann: *The Hockey Stick and the Climate Wars* (Columbia, 2012) page 127

[3] http://chronicle.texterity.com/chronicle/20060908a?pg=12

I

Mann is an island

TRUST ME, I'M A SCIENTIST

*We need to remember what science is - it is not a compilation of facts. Rather it is a set of processes used to gather relatively reliable information about the world we live in, our societies and ourselves. It is the formality of these processes that gives science its privilege and validity over other claims to knowledge about our world that can only come from belief, received wisdom, or anecdote. When this formality is broken - whether by **unsupported claims**, **hidden biases**, **lack of reproducibility**, and **inadequate peer review** - public trust in science is harmed and its privilege is undermined.[1]*

PROFESSOR SIR PETER GLUCKMAN, ONZ, KNZM, FRS, FMEDSCI, FRSNZ

ARTHUR E MILLS MEMORIAL ORATION TO

THE ROYAL AUSTRALASIAN COLLEGE OF PHYSICIANS, MAY 18th 2014

---

[1] http://www.pmcsa.org.nz/wp-content/uploads/Arthur-E-Mills-Memorial-Oration-to-RACP.pdf

PETER GLUCKMAN is the Chief Scientific Advisor to the Government of New Zealand, and broadly supportive of the general line on "climate change". His emphasis on the formality of scientific processes is not contentious, and his list of breaches in that formality and their harm to public trust is worth considering with respect to Michael E Mann and his work:

1) Unsupported claims

In the Summary for Policy Makers of its Third Assessment Review, the Intergovernmental Panel on Climate Change made the single most dramatic assertion in the history of the global-warming movement:

> *The increase in temperature in the 20th century is likely to have been the largest of any century during the past 1,000 years. It is also likely that, in the Northern Hemisphere, the 1990s was the warmest decade and 1998 the warmest year.* [2]

The only evidence offered in support of this statement was Michael Mann's hockey stick. Does it, indeed, support such a claim? Not according to many of the scientists in these pages. The Danish climatologist Bo Christiansen examined nine Mann "hockey sticks" and says it is "almost impossible to conclude" from any of them that "the present period is warmer than any period in the reconstructed period". Professor David Legates writes that "one can have no confidence in the claim that the 1990s are the warmest decade of the last two millennia" (by then Mann had extended his flexi-shaft back another millennium.) Almost every other serious reconstruction shows much greater natural climate variability, and the 1990s within the bounds of that. And, as Professors McShane and Wyner point out, most of these reconstructions look nothing like hockey sticks.

---

[2] http://www.ipcc.ch/ipccreports/tar/wg1/005.htm

Indeed, it remains an open question whether what his oeuvre purports to divine - a "global temperature" - is in a scientific sense "supportable". In the absence of reliable tropical data, says Dr David Rind, "we have no way of knowing how cold (or warm) the globe actually got".

So unsupported claims: yes.

2) Hidden biases

Later in this book, Nobel Prize winner Ivar Giaever reminds us that "in pseudoscience you begin with a hypothesis which is very appealing to you, and then you only look for things which confirm the hypothesis". Mann began with a hypothesis that the global temperature record had been pretty stable for 900 years and then in the 20th century it soared up and out the roof. And so he looked for "things which confirm the hypothesis": As Mann put it, "one set of tree-ring records" was "of critical importance" in conjuring his stick[3]. So his hypothesis that it looks like a hockey stick is confirmed only because a tree ring that produces a hockey-stick shape is given 390 times the weight of a tree ring that does not. That tells you nothing about what the temperature was in the 15th century, but a lot about Mann's biases. He chose a statistical method that, as the US National Research Council noted rather primly, "tends to bias the shape of the reconstructions". Furthermore, the scientists who actually collected the tree-ring data that Mann cannibalized insist they're primarily an indicator of CO_2 fertilization, not temperature.

At the IPCC level, he maintained his bias against anything that contradicted his hypothesis. As Professor John Christy testified to Congress, Mann "misrepresented the temperature record of the past thousand years by (a) promoting his own result as the best estimate, (b) neglecting studies that contradicted his, and (c)

---

[3] Mann: *The Hockey Stick and the Climate Wars* (2012) page 51

amputating another's result so as to eliminate conflicting data".

Hidden biases: yes.

3) Lack of reproducibility

Is Mann's work "reproducible"? They gave it a go in Berlin. "She came to the conclusion that she cannot reproduce his diagram," says Professor Ulrich Cubasch. "The real problem in this case, in my view, is that Michael Mann does not disclose his data." Except for a small trusted coterie, Mann declined - for years - to release the elements needed to reproduce his stick. In evidence before the House of Commons in London, Professor Darrel Ince noted Mann's refusal to cough up his computer code, and said that he would "regard any papers based on the software as null and void". His stick could be neither proved nor disproved - and, as Professor Vincent Courtillot reminded European climatologists, if "it's not falsifiable, it's not science".

Lack of reproducibility: yup. So three strikes, he's out. No, wait, that's another sport entirely. For hockey, you need four.

4) Inadequate peer review

"The hockey stick is an extraordinary claim which requires extraordinary evidence," wrote Oxford physicist Jonathan Jones. *Nature* never asked for any and, when it fell to others to demonstrate the flaws of the stick, the journal declined to share their findings with its readers. Mann and a few close allies controlled the fora that mattered, and banished any dissidents. "It's a completely rigged peer-review system," concluded CalTech's Dr David Rutledge.

Fourth strike. The unsupported claims, hidden biases, lack of reproducibility and inadequate peer review of Mann have surely harmed "public trust in science". What follows is one scientist and his science, by those who know both the work and the man.

1

"Today most scientists dismiss the hockey stick."

DR MADHAV KHANDEKAR, PHD

Meteorologist and climatologist. Research Scientist with Environment Canada for 25 years. Editorial board member of *The Journal of Natural Hazards*, and former editor of *Climate Research*. Member of the American Geophysical Union, the Canadian Meteorological and Oceanographic Society, and the American Meteorological Society. Former World Meteorological Organization lecturer in meteorology. MSc in Statistics from Pune University, PhD in Meteorology from Florida State University.

Before the hockey stick, climate science was a complicated business: a vast Amazonian river (as Professor Kiminori Itoh of Yokohama National University characterized it[1]) with many tributaries - from aerosols and volcanoes to solar variations and land surface modifications. What if all that complexity could be simplified? Really *simplified - into "a nice tidy story" (in Professor Keith Briffa's words) about "unprecedented warming in a thousand years"[2].*

    In 2009 Dr Khandekar was interviewed by Canada's Frontier Centre for Public Policy. Asked whether Michael E Mann's hockey stick was "a smoking gun that proves the alarmists right", he replied[3]:

The hockey stick was a graph constructed by some scientists

---

[1] https://pielkeclimatesci.wordpress.com/2012/05/18/guest-post-by-kiminori-itoh-what-is-the-psychological-origin-of-the-narrow-view-of-the-ipcc-socio-psychological-aspect-of-the-climate-change/

[2] http://www.di2.nu/foia/0938031546.txt

[3] https://fcpp.org/files/9/122%20Madhav%20Khandekar.pdf

about ten years ago. What it was meant to show was that the earth's temperature from about 1080 till about 1850 remained essentially constant and then it started to shoot up. Lots of problems have been found out in the graph. The most glaring error in the hockey stick was that it did not show the Little Ice Age, which was significant. It did not show the Medieval Warm Period from the 8th to 12th century, which was also significant. There were errors in the use of the tree-ring data and also other errors. So today, most scientists dismiss the hockey stick. **They do not consider the hockey stick graph to be a correct representation of the global mean temperature.**

Can that really be true - that most scientists "dismiss" the hockey stick? As we shall see in the pages that follow, many scientists from around the world disagree with Mann's science, and sometimes very forcefully - and they include not only "deniers" but full-scale "alarmists" and all points on the spectrum in between. These people reject not only his science but his style - the peculiarly vicious yet self-defeating "climate war" mentality so unsuited to a great grey blur of contradictory uncertainties. You can believe in anthropogenic global warming, an impending ice age, solar heating, natural variability or no big deal whatever happens, and still regret the appalling damage done to climate science by Mann's total war in service of a piece of cartoon climatology by a one-stick pony.

Yet the real question is not whether "most scientists" dismiss the hockey stock today, but why more scientists didn't denounce it back then. Too many people who should have known better sat idly by as an obscure researcher, with the ink barely dry on his PhD, overturned the accumulated scientific wisdom of centuries - because it was convenient to the political goals of activists, bureaucrats, politicians - and above all an ambitious new transnational bureaucracy, the Intergovernmental Panel on Climate Change.

2

"The whole hockey-stick episode reminds me of the motto of Orwell's Ministry of Information."

PROFESSOR WILLIAM HAPPER, PHD

Cyrus Fogg Brackett Professor of Physics at Princeton University and a member of the US Government's group of independent scientific advisors JASON, for whom he pioneered the development of adaptive optics. Recipient of the Davisson-Germer Prize in Atomic or Surface Physics, the Herbert P Broida Prize, and a Thomas Alva Edison patent award. Fellow of the American Physical Society and of the American Association for the Advancement of Science.

On February 25th 2009, Professor Happer testified before the US Senate's Environment and Public Works Committee[1]:

The existence of climate variability in the past has long been an embarrassment to those who claim that all climate change is due to man and that man can control it. When I was a schoolboy, my textbooks on earth science showed a prominent "Medieval Warm Period" at the time the Vikings settled Greenland, followed by a vicious "Little Ice Age" that drove them out. So I was very surprised when I first saw the celebrated "hockey stick curve," in the Third Assessment Report of the IPCC. **I could hardly believe my eyes.** Both the Little Ice Age and the Medieval Warm Period were gone, and the newly revised temperature of the world since the year 1000 had suddenly become absolutely flat until the last hundred years when it shot up like the blade on a

---

[1] http://www.hatch.senate.gov/public/_files/ProfessorWilliamHapper.pdf

hockey stick... **The hockey stick was trumpeted around the world as evidence that the end was near.** The hockey stick **has nothing to do with reality** but was the result of incorrect handling of proxy temperature records and incorrect statistical analysis. There really was a Little Ice Age and there really was a Medieval Warm Period that was as warm or warmer than today.

I bring up the hockey stick as a particularly clear example that the IPCC Summaries for Policy Makers are not dispassionate statements of the facts... The whole hockey-stick episode reminds me of the motto of Orwell's Ministry of Information in the novel *1984*: **"He who controls the present controls the past. He who controls the past controls the future."**

In 2011, Will Happer expanded his thoughts on "controlling the past"[2]:

This *damnatia memoriae* of inconvenient facts was simply expunged from the 2001 IPCC report, much as Trotsky and Yezhov were removed from Stalin's photographs by dark-room specialists in the later years of the dictator's reign. There was no explanation of why both the Medieval Warm Period and the Little Ice Age, very clearly shown in the 1990 report, had simply disappeared eleven years later.

The IPCC and its worshipful supporters did their best to promote the hockey-stick temperature curve. But as John Adams remarked, "Facts are stubborn things, and whatever may be our wishes, our inclinations, or the dictates of our passion, they cannot alter the state of facts and evidence."

Maybe not. But the hockey stick certainly took "facts and evidence" on a wild ride. In order to control the future, the IPCC had to take control of the past - and Mann's graph was their way to do that.

---

[2] http://www.firstthings.com/article/2011/06/the-truth-about-greenhouse-gases

3

"The blade of the hockey stick could not be reproduced using either the same techniques as Mann and Jones or other common statistical techniques."

PROFESSOR DAVID R LEGATES, PHD

Professor of Geography and former Director of the Center for Climatic Research at the University of Delaware. Former Delaware State Climatologist, Coordinator of the Delaware Geographic Alliance and Associate Director of the Delaware Space Grant Consortium. Author of peer-reviewed papers published in *The International Journal of Climatology, The Bulletin of the American Meteorological Society* and other journals.

After taking control of the past - the shaft of the hockey stick - it was necessary to clarify the present - the blade - with a clear, simple message: This is the hottest year of the hottest decade of the hottest century, like, forever! Following the publication of his 2004 paper "Estimation and representation of long-term (>40 year) trends of Northern-Hemisphere-gridded surface temperature: A note of caution[1]" Dr Legates wrote[2]:

Recently, my colleagues and I closely examined the "blade" of Mann's latest temperature reconstruction (*Geophysical Research Letters*, February 2004). According to the IPCC (2001) and

---

[1] http://onlinelibrary.wiley.com/doi/10.1029/2003GL019141/full
[2] http://www.ncpa.org/pub/ba478/

many other published sources, the earth warmed only 0.6°C (1°F) during the 20th century. However, that contrasts sharply with the most recent reconstruction by Mann and Jones, which shows warming over the last century of 0.95°C (1.5°F) - a temperature rise more than 50 percent larger than the IPCC claims. Mann's warming estimate has grown substantially over the last couple of years, apparently to accommodate his continuing claim that the 1990s were the warmest decade of the last two millennia, but we found that the blade of the hockey stick could not be reproduced using either the same techniques as Mann and Jones or other common statistical techniques. **Since reproducibility is a hallmark of scientific inquiry and the blade does not represent the observed climate record, it is unreliable...**

Dr Legates noted that the IPCC was now using Mann's work to claim that 1998 was the warmest year and the 1990s the warmest decade of the last millennium. He continued:

But a review of the data shows that these claims are untenable. **Mann's research is clearly the outlier.**

Consider that if 1) the amount of uncertainty is doubled (an appropriate representation of the "sheath"), 2) appropriate 20th century increases in observed air temperature are applied (a correct representation of the "blade"), or 3) the period from AD 200 to 1900 correctly reproduces millennial-scale variability (a reliable representation of the "shaft"), then **one can have no confidence in the claim that the 1990s are the warmest decade of the last two millennia.** The assertions of Mann and his colleagues - and, consequently, the IPCC - are open to question if even one component of their temperature reconstruction is in error, let alone all three!

4

"If you want to claim that you are engaging in science, the programs are in your possession and you will not release them, then you are not a scientist."

PROFESSOR DARREL INCE, PHD

Professor of Computing at the Open University's Centre for Research in Computing in the United Kingdom. Author of peer-reviewed papers published by *Empirical Software Engineering* and other journals.

Until global warming came along, climate science was a comparatively obscure interdisciplinary backwater and many other scientists paid it little heed. So it took a while for the scale of the hockey stick's audacity to manifest itself: A single graph by an unknown researcher had entirely overturned the conventional wisdom - and nobody had bothered to check how he did it. In 2010, Professor Ince wrote in The Guardian[1]:

One of the key features of science is deniability: if you erect a theory and someone produces evidence that it is wrong, then it falls. This is how science works: by openness, by publishing minute details of an experiment, some mathematical equations or a simulation; by doing this you embrace deniability. This does

---

[1] http://www.theguardian.com/technology/2010/feb/05/science-climate-emails-code-release

not seem to have happened in climate research. Many researchers have refused to release their computer programs — even though they are still in existence and not subject to commercial agreements. An example is **Professor Mann's initial refusal to give up the code that was used to construct the 1999 "hockey stick" model** that demonstrated that human-made global warming is a unique artefact of the last few decades. (He did finally release it in 2005.)

A few days later, Professor Ince expanded on his remarks about Mann in evidence before the British House of Commons[2]:

The situation is by no means bad across academia: most academics release code and data. Also, a number of journals, for example those in the area of economics and econometrics, insist on an author lodging both the data and the programs with the journal before publication... I believe that, if you are publishing research articles that use computer programs, if you want to claim that you are engaging in science, the programs are in your possession and you will not release them, then you are not a scientist; **I would also regard any papers based on the software as null and void.**

Instead of that, the climate-industrial complex doubled down on Mann and his hockey stick. As Professor Marcel Leroux would write[3]:

The curve by Mann et al (1998, 1999) 'miraculous' indeed for the IPCC, did away in one fell swoop with the MWP and the LIA... **We are certainly no longer moving in the realms of science here!**

---

[2] http://www.publications.parliament.uk/pa/cm200910/cmselect/cmsctech/387b/387we36.htm

[3] Leroux: *Global Warming: Myth or Reality?* (Springer-Praxis, 2005) pp208-209

5

"The behavior of Michael Mann is a disgrace to the profession."

DR HENDRIK TENNEKES, PHD

Former Director of Research at the Royal Dutch Meteorological Institute and member of the Royal Netherlands Academy of Arts and Science. Former Professor of Aeronautical Engineering at Pennsylvania State University (now Michael E Mann's employer). Author of *The Simple Science Of Flight - From Insects To Jumbo Jets* (MIT Press, 1997) and co-author of the classic *A First Course In Turbulence* (MIT Press, 1972).

Long before Climategate, a few principled scientists had spoken up against Mann and an IPCC that put all its eggs in his basket. As Dr Tennekes said[1]:

We only understand ten per cent of the climate issue. That is not enough to wreck the world economy with Kyoto-like measures.

Henk Tennekes is one of the most far-sighted men in his field - that's to say, in a famous speech on climate science in 1987 he predicted the limits of our ability to predict. No one familiar with Tennekes would have bet the farm on those turn-of-the-century climate models.

On February 22nd 2005 Dr Tennekes sent the following email to Stephen McIntyre in Toronto[2]:

1) The IPCC review process is fatally flawed.

---

[1] http://www.nationalpost.com/story.html?id=9bc9a7c6-2729-4d07-9629-807f1dee479f&k=0

[2] http://climateaudit.org/2005/02/22/hendrik-tennekes-retired-director-of-research-royal-netherlands-meteorological-institute/

2) IPCC willfully ignores the paradigm shift created by the foremost meteorologist of the twentieth century, Edward Lorenz.

3) The behavior of Michael Mann is a disgrace to the profession.

4) Hans von Storch and Steve McIntyre have shown the courage of their convictions.

The names Dr Tennekes mentions may not be known to all:

Stephen McIntyre is the Toronto mining engineer who received, as did every Canadian, a pamphlet from the government with a prominent reproduction of Mann's graph. To Ottawa, the hockey stick was the easiest way to sell Canadians on the need for the Kyoto Accord. When Mr McIntyre saw it, it reminded him of the type of prospectus he'd seen many times in the mining industry, and which often turned out to be too good to be true. And he wondered whether this might also turn out to be too good to be true.

And then he put his statistician's hat on and got to work...

Hans von Storch, by contrast, is a climate scientist who has long been "convinced that we are facing anthropogenic climate change brought about by the emission of greenhouse gases", as he told the US Congress in 2006. But, among such believers, he was one of the first to be not quite so "convinced" by Mann's hockey stick...

And Edward Lorenz? Not so long ago, he was all the rage. Lorenz (1917-2008) was dubious of linear statistical models in meteorology and pioneered "chaos theory". He was the first to use the term "butterfly effect", and not just his fellow scientists but the general public picked it up, too. But "chaos theory" faded quickly in a world in which almost everyone who mattered assumed that governments could restore the climate of the planet to some Edenic idyll if only they were permitted to tax and regulate us enough. And the surest marketing gimmick for that proposition was the antithesis of "chaos theory" and the "butterfly effect" - Michael Mann's hockey stick.

16

6

"We now know that the hockey stick graph is fraudulent."

DR MICHAEL R FOX, PHD (1936-2011)

Nuclear scientist, Professor of Chemistry at Idaho State University and researcher at the National Engineering Laboratory. Chairman of the American Nuclear Society's Public Information Committee.

In 2008, in evidence submitted to the Environmental Protection Agency, Dr Fox said the following[1]:

The hockey stick is a name given to a graph of reconstructed temperature data... The "handle" of the hockey stick graph is intended to portray rather flat, constant global temperatures extending from about 1000 AD to about 1900. At this time the global temperatures turn sharply upward indicating the "blade"...

The overall message is/was that after about a 900 year period of constant temperatures, the global temperatures rose sharply upward beginning around 1900, allegedly. This is often assumed to be the beginning of the industrial age, and therefore the presumed beginning of significant man-made CO_2 emissions. This is incorrect...

This hockey stick graph has been featured prominently and globally in a major scientific journal... It has been given pivotal importance in several of the IPCC assessment reports, and featured prominently in Al Gore's documentary *An Inconvenient Truth*, which now is discredited too.

---

[1] https://www.heartland.org/sites/all/modules/custom/heartland_migration/files/pdfs/23818.pdf

17

This section of Dr Fox's remarks is a useful précis of how the hockey stick was wafted up on ever wider circles of deceit:

It is useful to list some of the approval processes which led to **this global deception**. The authors, scientists themselves, obviously approved of their own creation. The peer reviewers assigned by the science journal approved it, the editors of the science journal who reviewed, checked, and approved it, and the reviewers of the IPCC reports, the editors of the IPCC documents. The producers of Gore's documentary approved it, presumably Mr Gore himself, and the thousands of school teachers around the world who required millions of students to view and analyze it. **The extent of global fear inspired by the educational systems around the world is incalculable.**

We now know that the hockey stick graph is fraudulent. How should we treat those who approved it? What should the EPA do now proposing to adopt rule making for CO_2 mitigation? To do so they must embrace **the underlying fraudulent science**, and the terrible harm it will bring.

EPA action seems simple: do not proceed with the rule making for greenhouse gas mitigation. Have the courage not to mitigate man-made CO_2 and avoid joining with the scientific deceptions.

Close analyses of the hockey stick scandal are essential for policy makers, educators, media, and many scientific institutions and their PhD staffers. **All of them played a role in creating and/or spreading the deceptions.** It has shaken the pillars of institutional science to its foundation and undermined the public trust science once had. **We are either dealing with willful scientific deceptions or woeful and lazy scientific mediocrity** from PhDs themselves.

7

"Mann's 'hockey stick' has indeed been substantively discredited."

DR HAMISH CAMPBELL, PHD

Geologist and paleontologist with New Zealand's Institute of Geological and Nuclear Sciences (GNS Science), and scientist in residence at Te Papa Tongarewa, the national museum of New Zealand. Former President of the New Zealand Association of Scientists, Companion of the Royal Society of New Zealand, and Member of the Geological Society of New Zealand.

Once the hockey stick had been taken up by the IPCC and Al Gore, it departed, as Professor Marcel Leroux said, "the realm of science" and became an instrument of propaganda - and one so effective that politicians, activists and, alas, even school teachers were reluctant to abandon it. Visiting Te Papa, New Zealand's national museum, in November 2011, the writer Tony Thomas was surprised to see, prominently displayed, a large blown-up copy of Mann's stick. His concerns were brought to the attention of Dr Campbell, who responded[1]:

You are perfectly correct: Mann's "hockey stick" has indeed been substantively discredited.

I remember at the time [of helping to design the exhibit] that **I was very uncomfortable with so-called predictions based on models of an inherently chaotic system that surely were a far cry from any representative simulation of nature.**

---

[1] https://tthomas061.wordpress.com/2013/09/21/wanted-remedial-education-for-museum-curators/

However, part of Te Papa's role/function is to provoke or stimulate thought. I let it go with the proviso that the graph was properly referenced ...and it is.

Dr Campbell conceded that, hockey-wise, it was no longer 2001[2]:

Things have changed and we at Te Papa have not made any effort to respond to those changes. Now is the time to do so...

We shall revisit this exhibit in the next few weeks and see what we can do.

With his graph assiduously promoted to every corner of the earth, Mann's self-regard shot up as dramatically as his hockey stick. One of the most bizarre aspects of his personality is his apparent belief that he is a Nobel Laureate, as boldly declared in his press materials, his book jackets, and even in the court filings of his current libel suit, where he accuses the defendants of the hitherto unknown crime of "defamation of a Nobel Prize recipient"[3].

So what Nobel Prize did Michael Mann win?

What happened is that in 2007 Al Gore and the IPCC were jointly awarded the Nobel Peace Prize. Mann was one of thousands of contributors to IPCC reports over the years, but he genuinely seems to think that his association with the organization entitles him to market himself as a "Nobel Prize winner" - and not just of a crappy old Peace Prize like Gore and Yasser Arafat but, by implication, one of the real ones - for science.

So what does a genuine Nobel Laureate make of the work of a fake Nobel Laureate? We shall hear from one over the page.

---

[2] http://quadrant.org.au/opinion/doomed-planet/2012/11/land-of-the-long-white-hockey-stick/

[3] http://legaltimes.typepad.com/files/michael-mann-complaint.pdf

8

"We come to the hockey-stick graph... the Emperor's new clothes."

PROFESSOR IVAR GIAEVER, PHD

Winner of the 1973 Nobel Prize in Physics, with Leo Esaki and Brian Josephson, "for their discoveries regarding tunnelling phenomena in solids". Professor-at-large at the University of Oslo, and Professor Emeritus at the Rensselaer Polytechnic Institute. Recipient of the Oliver E Buckley Condensed Matter Prize from the American Physical Society and the Zworykin Award from the National Academy of Engineering. Member of the Norwegian Academy of Science and Letters.

Since 1951 Nobel Laureates have gathered in the German town of Lindau each year to share their thoughts on various issues. Mann does not get to attend these meetings because, despite his apparently indestructible belief to the contrary, he has not won a Nobel Prize, and so is ineligible. But Dr Giaever does, and at the 2012 meeting he said the following[1]:

I am not really terribly interested in global warming. Like most physicists, I really don't think much about it. But in 2008 I was on a panel here about global warming and I had to learn something about it, and I spent a day or so - half a day maybe - on Google. And I was horrified by what I learned... Global warming has become a new religion - because you can't discuss it, and that's not right...

Pseudoscience is a very strange thing, because **in**

---

[1] http://www.mediatheque.lindau-nobel.org/videos/31259/the-strange-case-of-global-warming-2012

21

pseudoscience you begin with a hypothesis which is very appealing to you, and then you only look for things which confirm the hypothesis. You don't look for other things. And so the question then... is global warming a pseudoscience..?

We come to the hockey-stick graph - which the previous speaker showed in a little different manner - and I have to say I have to rely on HC Anderson and the Emperor's new clothes. The little boy was innocent: he didn't see that the Emperor had clothes on. And I am the little boy here: I don't see that the CO_2 is the cause of all these problems.

But, if you believe the stick, then the matter of the Emperor's splendid robes is, as they say, settled. And so settled that it is beyond debate. Professor Giaever was one of the most distinguished members of the American Physical Society, but he did not want to be told that hockey-stick pseudoscience cannot be questioned:

As you heard, I resigned from the American Physical Society because of this statement: "The evidence is incontrovertible." The American Physical Society discussed the mass of the proton: The mass of the proton is not incontrovertible... But the global warming is. See, that's a religion. That's a religious statement, like the Catholic Church says the earth is not round, and the American Physical Society says that the global warming occurs. I mean, that's a terrible thing. So I resigned from the Physical Society and I hope I can get one or two of you to resign as well...

In the last 150 years, the Earth has got warmer according to these people. But the human health has got better, the social system is better, everything is better. The Earth is much better now than it was 150 years ago... Why is it suddenly getting "worse"?

9

"Michael Mann, Phil Jones and Stefan Rahmstorf should be barred ...because the scientific assessments in which they may take part are not credible anymore."

DR EDUARDO ZORITA, PHD

Senior Scientist at the Institute for Coastal Research in Germany. Former Head of the Department of Paleoclimate at the GKSS Research Centre, and Associate Researcher at the Laboratory of Dynamic Oceanography and Climatology at Pierre and Marie Curie University. Author of peer-reviewed papers published in *Science*, *Nature Climate Change*, *The Holocene*, *The Journal of Climate* and other journals, and member of the editorial boards of *Climate Change*, *Climate of the Past* and *Climate Research*. IPCC contributing author.

If global warming is, as Dr Giaever says, a religion, then Mann is the world's least infallible pontiff. After Stephen McIntyre & Ross McKitrick's attempts to reproduce the hockey stick, and Mann's refusal to release his data, and two major investigations that found severe problems with his methods, it was still just about possible to believe that the creator of the hockey stick was an ethical scientist who was simply in way over his head. The release of the Climategate emails in November 2009 made the theory that Mann was a naïf with a propensity for major errors harder to credit. The correspondence exposed a malevolent clique at the highest levels of climate science determined to prevent any

23

dissenters getting a foot in the door.

Perhaps the most obvious question, after Climategate, is why anybody still pays any attention to these guys. On November 27th Dr Zorita wrote on the GKSS website a piece with an arresting headline[1]:

Why I Think That Michael Mann, Phil Jones and Stefan Rahmstorf[2] Should be Barred from the IPCC Process

Short answer: because the scientific assessments in which they may take part are not credible anymore...

These words do not mean that I think anthropogenic climate change is a hoax. On the contrary, it is a question which we have to be very well aware of. But I am also aware that in this thick atmosphere - and I am not speaking of greenhouse gases now - editors, reviewers and authors of alternative studies, analysis, interpretations, even based on the same data we have at our disposal, have been bullied and subtly blackmailed. In this atmosphere, PhD students are often tempted to tweak their data so as to fit the "politically correct picture". Some, or many, issues about climate change are still not well known. Policy makers should be aware of the attempts to hide these uncertainties under a unified picture. I had the "pleasure" to experience all this in my area of research.

Dr Zorita had eschewed the "pleasure" of the Hockey Team as best he could. In 2005 he co-wrote a piece for Nature *called "The Decay of the Hockey Stick"[3]. Decaying maybe, but like a Gay Nineties boulevardier with advanced syphilis it staggered on.*

---

[1] http://wattsupwiththat.com/2009/11/27/zorita-calls-for-barring-phil-jones-michael-mann-and-stefan-rahmstorf-from-further-ipcc-participation/
[2] Professors Jones and Rahmstorf are both close collaborators of Mann's.
[3] http://blogs.nature.com/climatefeedback/2007/05/the_decay_of_the_hockey_stick.html

10

"If we mistakenly took the hockey stick seriously..."

PROFESSOR RICHARD MULLER, PHD

Professor Emeritus in the Department of Physics at the University of California at Berkeley, and Faculty Senior Scientist at the Lawrence Berkeley National Laboratory and Institute for Nuclear and Particle Astrophysics. Founder of the Berkeley Earth Surface Temperature project. Co-creator of accelerator mass spectrometry and one of the first scientists to measure anisotropy in the cosmic microwave background. Proponent of the Nemesis hypothesis, which argues that the Sun could have a so far undetected dwarf star. Recipient of the Alan T Waterman Award from the National Science Foundation.

For many years, Richard Muller was a columnist for the Massachusetts Institute of Technology's Technology Review. *He was one of the first to recognize that McIntyre & McKitrick had dealt the hockey stick's credibility a fatal blow. In his column of October 15th 2004, Professor Muller wrote, with remarkable prescience[1]:*

If you are concerned about global warming (as I am) and think that human-created carbon dioxide may contribute (as I do), then you still should agree that **we are much better off having broken the hockey stick.** Misinformation can do real harm, because it distorts predictions. Suppose, for example, that future measurements in the years 2005-2015 show a clear and distinct global cooling trend. (It could happen.) If we mistakenly took the hockey stick seriously – that is, if we believed that natural fluctuations in climate are small – then we might conclude

---

[1] http://www.technologyreview.com/news/403256/global-warming-bombshell/

(mistakenly) that the cooling could not be just a random fluctuation on top of a long-term warming trend, since according to the hockey stick, such fluctuations are negligible. And that might lead in turn to the mistaken conclusion that global warming predictions are a lot of hooey. If, on the other hand, we reject the hockey stick, and recognize that natural fluctuations can be large, then we will not be misled by a few years of random cooling.

A phony hockey stick is more dangerous than a broken one – if we know it is broken. It is our responsibility as scientists to look at the data in an unbiased way, and draw whatever conclusions follow. When we discover a mistake, we admit it.

As noted above, that column was amazingly prescient. In the years that followed, there was, indeed, a "pause" in global warming, which the climate-change industry has struggled to explain precisely because it chose not to "reject the hockey stick" - and, as a result, has it hanging round its neck, rotten and maggot-ridden, like the Ancient Mariner's albatross.

What Professor Muller could not have foreseen was that hockey-stick science was not just "phony" but corrupt. Six years later he wrote[2]:

What they did was, and there's a quote... "Let's use Mike's trick to hide the decline." Mike, who's Michael Mann, said "Hey, 'trick' just means mathematical trick, that's all." My response is: I'm not worried about the word "trick", I *am* worried about the "decline"... What they did is they took the data from 1961 onward, from this peak, and erased it... The justification would not have survived peer review in any journal that I'm willing to publish in. But they had it well hidden and they erased that... Frankly, as a scientist I now have a list of people whose papers I won't read anymore. **You're not allowed to do this in science.**

---

[2] https://www.youtube.com/watch?v=8BQpciw8suk

II

Mann of the past

ONE TREE-RING TO RULE THEM ALL

It is difficult to avoid the impression that the IPCC uncritically accepted scientific work that "repealed" the Medieval Warm Period and the Little Ice Age because these two well-known features of the climate record placed Global Warming Theory in doubt, at least for the global public.[1]

DR JEFFREY E FOSS, PhD
BEYOND ENVIRONMENTALISM: A PHILOSOPHY OF NATURE
(2009)

---

[1] Foss: *Beyond Environmentalism* (Wiley, 2009) page 125

T HE HOCKEY stick is what's known as a "proxy reconstruction". There's only two things wrong with it - the proxies and the reconstruction. Other than that, you can take it to the bank.

First, the proxies:

The hockey stick is generally believed to show global (actually Northern Hemisphere) temperatures for the last millennium. But Mann does not, in fact, have any temperature readings for, say, the year 1143. That's because your average medieval peasant village did not have a weather station, and neither Daniel Gabriel Fahrenheit nor Anders Celsius had yet been born. So Mann has to divine his 12th century thermometer readings from "proxy data".

What is a proxy? Well, it's something like an ocean coral or an ice core or some lake sediment from which one can "reconstruct" the temperature history. In Mann's case, it was mostly tree rings. Much of the world isn't terribly forested, and most of the parts that are can't tell you the temperature for 1143. For a shot at that, you need a thousand-year-old tree, and there are only a few of those around, here and there - in Siberia, in parts of Canada, in California.

That was his first mistake: His proxy reconstruction uses the wrong proxy. To a kid, a tree ring is simple: Jack counts in and finds out whether his tree is older than Jill's. But, if you're trying to figure out the temperature, it's more fraught. "The original 'hockey stick' graph figured strongly in the IPCC 2000," Professor Anthony Trewavas told the British House of Commons. "But it is an artifice... The size of the tree ring is determined by everything that affects all aspects of plant development. These are: soil nutrients and structure; light variations; carbon dioxide; competition from other trees; disease; predators; age; rainfall; previous developmental activity as well as temperature. Temperature, for which it supposedly acts as a proxy, is just one contributor amongst many and of course reflects local conditions only. Mann's 'hockey stick' failed," he continued, because "tree rings on their own are not a reliable proxy."[2]

Oddly enough, boreholes and other proxies disagree with tree-rings when it comes to the temperature record. Mann had a few alternative proxies in his mix, but just a *soupçon*, so he could claim to have included them if anybody asked.

And then he further refined the process: Having chosen the wrong proxy - trees - he took the additional precaution of using the wrong kind of tree. Those ones in the American west, for example, are bristlecone pines. They're certainly old: There's a bristlecone pine in California's White Mountains that has been precisely dated - 5,064 years old in 2015 - and is believed to be the oldest tree on earth. Unfortunately, the guys who know bristlecones - including the very scientists who collected the data Mann used - say they're unreliable as thermometers. Those California bristlecones are sensitive to higher atmospheric CO_2 concentration, regardless of whether the temperature's going up or down.

Mann knew this. As Hans Erren observed, Mann's North American trees did not match the North American temperature record. Yet he decided that, even if they couldn't reliably tell you the temperature for the bit of sod they were planted in, they could reliably tell you the temperature for the entire Northern Hemisphere. Even the National Research Council of the National Academy of Sciences bristled at the cones:

> *For the earliest part of the 1999 analysis, Mr Mann's group relied heavily on bristlecone pines from western North America. The original study noted that there were some difficulties in using such trees because of peculiarities in their*

---

[2] http://www.publications.parliament.uk/pa/cm201314/cmselect/cmsctech/254/254vw13.htm

recent growth, but Mr Mann and his group attempted to quantify those problems and to work around them. The National Research Council suggested that researchers avoid using trees that are the most difficult to interpret[3].

The NRC can "suggest" all they want: for years, Mann and his Hockey Team continued to rely on bristlecones as failsafe treemometers. Yet, even when you decide to apply the wrong example of the wrong proxy to the wrong part of the planet, repealing the Medieval Warm Period is harder than you think. So Mann additionally decided to apply the wrong weighting to his wrong example of the wrong proxy to the wrong part of the planet - by giving tree-ring data that produced a hockey-stick curve over 300 times the value of tree-ring data that didn't.

Wrong proxy, wrong tree, wrong location... But what else do we need? Ah, yes, the wrong method. Put aside the bristlecones in MBH98 and Mann's hockey-stick curve for the entire Northern Hemisphere up to 1421 comes from just one tree, and from thereafter to 1447 from just two trees - both from Québec's Gaspé Peninsula[4]. (And from 1400 to 1403 from zero trees: he just extrapolated the 1404 reading.) By contrast, reputable dendrochronologists won't use data sets with fewer than five trees - on the grounds that one or two (never mind zero trees) might not be *that* representative.

But Mann did - and then he made them even more mega-representative by double-counting that pair of Gaspé trees in two separate data sets. And suddenly you can't see the Little Ice Age or the Medieval Warm Period for the trees - or tree.

Wrong proxy, wrong tree, wrong location, wrong method = right answer: LIA MIA. MWP RIP.

---

[3] http://chronicle.com/article/Inside-the-Hockey-Stick/14125
[4] http://www.geo.utexas.edu/courses/387h/PAPERS/conf05mckitrick.pdf

11

"Do I expect you to publicly denounce the hockey stick as obvious drivel? Well, yes."

PROFESSOR JONATHAN JONES, DPHIL

Professor of Physics at Oxford University's Department of Atomic and Laser Physics, and Lecturer and Tutorial Fellow in Physics at Brasenose College. Specialist in Nuclear Magnetic Resonance who performed the first NMR implementation of a quantum algorithm in 1997. Recipient of the Marlow Medal from the Royal Society of Chemistry. Author of peer-reviewed papers published in *Nature*, *Science* and other journals.

On December 3rd 2011, at the Bishop Hill website, Professor Jones responded to a query from UK Met Office scientist Richard Betts as to why nuclear magnetic resonance types and other chaps were so interested in climate science[1]:

My whole involvement has always been driven by concerns about the corruption of science.

Like many people I was dragged into this by the Hockey Stick. I was looking up some minor detail about the Medieval Warm Period and discovered **this weird parallel universe** of people who apparently didn't believe it had happened, and even more bizarrely appeared to believe that **essentially nothing had happened in the world before the 20th century**. The Hockey

---

[1] http://www.bishop-hill.net/blog/2011/12/2/tim-barnett-on-the-hockey-stick.html

Stick is an extraordinary claim which requires extraordinary evidence, so I started reading round the subject. And it soon became clear that the first extraordinary thing about the evidence for the Hockey Stick was how extraordinarily weak it was, and the second extraordinary thing was how desperate its defenders were to hide this fact. I'd always had an interest in pathological science, and it looked like I might have stumbled across a really good modern example.

As to when he'd be done with climate science, Professor Jones didn't mince words. He'd go back to his own field when climate "stops being a pathological science" and resumes acting according to scientific norms. He called on Dr Betts to "stand up against the all too obvious stench emanating from some of your colleagues":

The Hockey Stick is obviously wrong. Everybody knows it is obviously wrong. Climategate 2011 shows that even many of its most outspoken public defenders know it is obviously wrong. And yet it goes on being published and defended year after year.

Do I expect you to publicly denounce the Hockey Stick as obvious drivel? Well yes, that's what you should do. **It is the job of scientists of integrity to expose pathological science... It is a litmus test of whether climate scientists are prepared to stand up against the bullying defenders of pathology in their midst.** So, Richard, can I look forward to returning back to my proper work on the application of composite rotations to the performance of error-tolerant unitary transformations? Or will we all be let down again?

By those criteria, it's fair to say that Professor Jones remains let down.

12

"The work of Mann and his colleagues was initially accepted uncritically, even though it contradicted the results of more than 100 previous studies."

DR DAVID DEMING, PHD

Geologist, geophysicist and associate professor at the University of Oklahoma. Associate Editor of *Petroleum Geoscience* and *Ground Water*. Author of peer-reviewed papers published by *Science* and other journals, and of "Global warming, the politicization of science, and Michael Crichton's *State of Fear*", published in *The Journal of Scientific Exploration*.

The Medieval Warm Period - when Greenland got its name and was extensively farmed, and vineyards flourished in much of England - was a matter of uncontroversial historical record. But, once you've decided to "repeal" it, it's amazing how easy it is. On December 6th 2006 Dr Deming testified before the United States Senate Committee on Environment and Public Works[1]:

I had another interesting experience around the time my paper in *Science* was published. I received an astonishing email from a major researcher in the area of climate change. He said, "We have

---

[1] http://www.epw.senate.gov/public/index.cfm?FuseAction=Hearings.
Testimony&Hearing_ID=bfe4d91d-802a-23ad-4306-
b4121bf7eced&Witness_ID=6b57de26-7884-47a3-83a9-5f3a85e8a07e

to get rid of the Medieval Warm Period.[2]"

The Medieval Warm Period (MWP) was a time of unusually warm weather that began around 1000 AD and persisted until a cold period known as the Little Ice Age took hold in the 14th century. Warmer climate brought a remarkable flowering of prosperity, knowledge, and art to Europe during the High Middle Ages. The existence of the MWP had been recognized in the scientific literature for decades. But now it was a major embarrassment to those maintaining that the 20th century warming was truly anomalous. It had to be "gotten rid of."

In 1769, Joseph Priestley warned that scientists overly attached to a favorite hypothesis would not hesitate to "warp the whole course of nature." In 1999, Michael Mann and his colleagues published a reconstruction of past temperature in which the MWP simply vanished. This unique estimate became known as the "hockey stick," because of the shape of the temperature graph.

Normally in science, **when you have a novel result that appears to overturn previous work, you have to demonstrate why the earlier work was wrong.** But the work of Mann and his colleagues was initially accepted uncritically, even though it contradicted the results of more than 100 previous studies. Other researchers have since reaffirmed that the Medieval Warm Period was both warm and global in its extent.

No matter. By 1998 a "favorite hypothesis" was on its way to "warp the whole course of nature".

---

[2] The identity of this person is usually assumed to be Jonathan Overpeck (see http://wattsupwiththat.com/2013/12/08/the-truth-about-we-have-to-get-rid-of-the-medieval-warm-period/). Dr Overpeck has denied it, although he has not denied a very similar email (http://di2.nu/foia/1105670738.txt).

13

"The 'hockey stick'
...was at best bad science. "

DR LEE C GERHARD, PHD

Principal geologist of the Kansas Geological Survey. Senior editor of *Geological Perspectives of Global Climate Change* (2001). Former state geologist of North Dakota and honorary member of the Association of American State Geologists. Former co-chair of the American Association of Petroleum Geologists Climate Change Issues Committee.

In 2009, Dr Gerhard wrote[1]:

Voluminous historic records demonstrate the Medieval Climate Optimum (MCO) was real and that the "hockey stick" graphic that attempted to deny that fact was at best bad science. The MCO was considerably warmer than the end of the 20th century.

During the last 100 years, temperature has both risen and fallen, including the present cooling. **All the changes in temperature of the last 100 years are in normal historic ranges,** both in absolute value and, most importantly, rate of change.

That would have been an uncontentious statement in the pre-Mann era. But his hockey stick singlehandedly overthrew the ancien régime. *Before Mann, the late Hubert Lamb was regarded by many as the greatest climatologist of the 20th century. He was the founder of East Anglia's Climatic Research Unit, and the scientist whose chart (showing the Medieval Warm Period and the Little Ice Age) had appeared in the very first IPCC report in 1990. In 2011, Professor Tony Brown (of whom*

---

[1] https://www.heartland.org/policy-documents/fact-based-climate-debate

more over the page) contrasted the differing views of climate variability of Lamb and Mann[2]:

> So we have two competing climate history stories - one developed over a lifetime of academic research mostly before the computer era, and the other derived from a scientist using modern statistical techniques and **the extensive use of novel proxies interpreted in a highly sophisticated manner** using computers.
>
> The "hockey stick" and Lamb's graph remain potent symbols to this day, and have created two vociferous climate camps, as the reconstructions seem to tell very different stories...
>
> In the Mann version of historic climate there is very limited variation either side of a mean anomaly, which gave rise to a limited MWP, generally substantially cooler than today, with gently declining temperatures throughout the period from 1400 to 1900, coupled with a lesser impact of the "Little Ice Age" than had previously been accepted. Most controversial of all is the very dramatic uptick from the 1902 instrumental temperature records...

The important and influential part of Mann's hockey stick is not the blade (very few people dispute that it's warmer now than 200 years ago) but the shaft. In abolishing the Medieval Warm Period and the Little Ice Age, Dr Mann wound up abolishing the very concept of "natural climate variability" - to the point where all his rube celebrity pals believe there was a millennium-long stable climate until industrial, consumerist humans came along and broiled the planet.

They believe that because that's what the hockey stick told them.

---

[2] http://judithcurry.com/2011/12/01/the-long-slow-thaw/

14

"The hockey stick remains a potent icon to this day. However the gradual decline in temperatures over the centuries that it depicts cannot be detected, nor the lack of variability of the climate over the same time scales."

PROFESSOR TONY BROWN, PHD

Professor of Physical Geography, GeoData Research Director and Group Leader at the University of Southampton's Palaeoenvironmental Laboratory. Former General Secretary of the International Union for Quaternary Research's Global Palaeohydrology Subcommission. Former geological expert and soil analyst for the International Criminal Tribunal investigation into war crimes in Bosnia. Fellow of the Geological Society, and of the Society of Antiquaries. Co-founder and editor of *The Journal of Wetland Archaeology*, and author of peer-reviewed papers published by *The Journal of Quaternary Science*, *The Holocene* and other journals.

Among Professor Brown's conclusions on the hockey stick are these[1]:

3) Any attempt to construct a single global or even Northern Hemisphere temperature covering many centuries will encounter substantial difficulties, as incomplete information from novel proxies will probably not adequately represent the extremes that are experienced at either end of the temperature spectrum, so

---

[1] http://judithcurry.com/2011/12/01/the-long-slow-thaw/

37

what is considered the "average" is possibly representative of **no climate state that actually ever existed...**

Noting that "tree rings have an inability to adequately represent the conditions of the entire year", he continued:

4) The nature of the proxies used in MBH98 and 99 have inherent problems and have proved very controversial... Mixing proxies also causes their own problems. Taken in total, the data used in such studies is unlikely to accurately represent the climates prevailing at the time back to 1400AD and 1000AD. **Carrying out complex statistical analysis on questionable data does not render the initial data any more meaningful...** Paleo reconstructions as a whole should be treated with caution when it relates to precise representations of temperature...

6) The hockey stick remains a potent icon to this day. However the gradual decline in temperatures over the centuries that it depicts cannot be detected, nor the lack of variability of the climate over the same time scales. The sharp uptick in temperatures from the start of the 20th century is **a likely artifact of computer modeling through over complex statistical interpretation of inadequate proxies.** Modern warming needs to be put into its historic context with the patterns of considerable natural climatic variability that can be observed from the past.

7) The available information seems to demonstrate that there is a long established warming trend dating back some 350 years to 1660...

8) When viewed from a 1538 perspective **the warming trend becomes imperceptible.** That period seems to have been around as warm as today and there are others that also seem to exhibit notable warmth to levels not dissimilar to today's.

15

"All of these observations are at odds with what is portrayed in the thousand-year Northern Hemispheric hockey-stick temperature history of Mann."

DR CRAIG D IDSO, PHD, DR SHERWOOD B IDSO, PHD, AND DR KEITH E IDSO, PHD

Sherwood Idso is a former research physicist with the US Department of Agriculture's Agricultural Research Service and adjunct professor at Arizona State University. He is a recipient of the Arthur S Flemming Award and Petr Beckman Award, and ranks as one of the Institute for Scientific Information's highly cited researchers. With his sons Craig and Keith Idso, he is a founder of the Center for the Study of Carbon Dioxide and Global Change. Idso tree-ring studies are part of the data that make up Mann's original hockey sticks.

The doctors Idso maintain an updated, extensive summary of evidence for the Medieval Warm Period at their online magazine CO_2 *Science. In a round-up of recent papers[1], this comment on Naurzbaev et al (2002) could stand for all[2]:*

With respect to the second of these periods, they emphasize that "the warmth of the two centuries AD 1058-1157 and 950-1049

---

[1] http://www.co2science.org/subject/m/summaries/mwparctic.php
[2] http://www.co2science.org/articles/V7/N43/C2.php

attests to the reality of relative mediaeval warmth in this region." Their data also reveal three other important pieces of information: (1) **the Roman and Medieval Warm Periods were both warmer than the Current Warm Period has been to date**, (2) the "beginning of the end" of the Little Ice Age was somewhere in the vicinity of 1830, and (3) the Current Warm Period peaked somewhere in the vicinity of 1940.

All of these observations are at odds with what is portrayed in the thousand-year Northern Hemispheric hockey-stick temperature history of Mann et al (1998, 1999) and its thousand-year global extension developed by Mann and Jones (2003), wherein (1) the Current Warm Period is depicted as the warmest such era of the past two millennia, (2) recovery from the Little Ice Age does not begin until after 1910, and (3) the Current Warm Period experiences it highest temperatures in the latter part of the 20th century's final decade.

Once again, we note that these results apply to but the specific portion of the planet studied by Naurzbaev et al, but that **there are many such "specific portions of the planet" that tell the same story.** Hence, we continue to describe the unique but similar temperature records of these numerous locations, as new studies become available and we discover older studies we have not previously reviewed. **All of them will someday have to be recognized as carrying considerably more weight, in their totality, than the controversial and highly-debated hockey stick record, which is beginning to look more and more questionable with each passing week.**

16

"That was a mistake and it made tree-ring people angry."

DR GORDON JACOBY, PHD (1934-2014)

A pioneer in dendrochronology, and founder and Senior Research Scientist of the Tree-Ring Laboratory of the Lamont-Doherty Earth Observatory. Founder of tree labs in Mongolia and Russia, and sampler of trees in Alaska, Siberia, Thailand and Australia. Member of the American Geophysical Union, the Committee on Environmental Global Change, and the American Association for the Advancement of Science. Leader of the Tree-Ring Analysis Group at the International Union of Forestry Research Organizations. Member of the editorial board of *Geology*. Research Hydrogeologist at the Institute of Geophysics and Planetary Physics at the University of California Los Angeles.

Professor Brown said that Mann's reconstructed planetary "average" is "possibly representative of no climate state that actually ever existed". That's not just because of averaging. When you're divining the planet's temperature from as few proxies as Mann had, the uses you put them to can be creative. In 2006 The Guardian's *Fred Pearce interviewed Dr Jacoby about the hockey stick[1]:*

Reconstructing past temperatures from proxy data is fraught with danger. Tree ring records, the biggest component of the hockey stick record, sometimes reflect rain or drought rather than temperature. When I investigated the continuing row surrounding the graph in 2006, Gordon Jacoby of Columbia University in New York, said: "Mann has a series from central

---

[1] http://www.theguardian.com/environment/2010/feb/09/hockey-stick-graph-ipcc-report

China that we believe is more a moisture signal than a temperature signal... He included it because he had a gap. That was a mistake and it made tree-ring people angry." A large data set he used from bristlecone pines in the American west has attracted similar concern.

Pearce's book With Speed and Violence *contains more of his talk with Dr Jacoby[2]:*

The world of proxy data trends is a statistical minefield. This is partly because the physical material that shows past climate loses detail with time. Tree rings, for instance, get smaller as the tree gets older, so annual and even decadal detail gets lost. "You lose roughly 40 per cent of the amplitude of changes," says the tree-ring specialist Gordon Jacoby, of Lamont-Doherty. But it goes far beyond that. To make any sense, analysis of a single data set - for instance, from the tree rings in a forest - involves smoothing out the data from individual trees to reveal a "signal" behind the "noise" of short-term and random change. The kind of analysis pioneered by Mann, in which a series of different data sets are merged involves further sorting and aggregating these independently derived signals, and smoothing the result. And Mann's work involves a further stage: meshing that proxy synthesis with the current instrumental record.

Some, including Jacoby, complain that **by combining smoothed-out proxy data from past centuries with the recent instrumental record, which preserves many more short-term trends, Mann created a false impression of anomalous recent change.** "You just can't do that if you are losing so much of the amplitude of change in the rest of the data," Jacoby told me.

---

[2] Pearce: *With Speed and Violence: Why Scientists Fear Tipping Points in Climate Change* (Beacon Press, 2007)

17

"A lot of the data sets he uses are sh*tty."

PROFESSOR WALLACE SMITH BROECKER, PhD

Newberry Professor in Columbia University's Department of Earth and Environmental Sciences and a scientist at the Lamont-Doherty Earth Observatory. Fellow of the American Academy of Arts and Sciences, the National Academy of Sciences, the American Geophysical Union, and the European Geophysical Union. Foreign Member of the Royal Society. He has been honored with the Ewing Medal, the Agassiz Medal, the Urey Medal from the European Association of Geochemistry, the Goldschmidt Award from the Geochemical Society, the Wollaston Medal of the Geological Society of London, the Benjamin Franklin Medal and the Balzan Prize.

Dr Jacoby states his disagreements with Mann in very moderate language. Not all scientists are so discreet. Professor Broecker is the man who in 1975 coined the phrase "global warming". In 2010, in an interview with The Guardian*'s Fred Pearce, he gave a frank estimation of Mann and his science[1]:*

"The goddam guy is a slick talker and super-confident. He won't listen to anyone else," one of climate science's most senior figures, Wally Broecker of the Lamont-Doherty Earth Observatory at Columbia University in New York, told me. "I don't trust people like that. A lot of the data sets he uses are shitty, you know. They are just not up to what he is trying to do.... If anyone deserves to get hit it is goddam Mann."

---

[1] http://www.theguardian.com/environment/2010/feb/09/hockey-stick-michael-mann-steve-mcintyre

Professor Broecker exercised more restraint in a paper he wrote for the journal Science *in February 2001, shortly after the appearance of Mann's first two but already "widely cited" hockey sticks[2]:*

A recent, widely cited reconstruction leaves the impression that the 20th century warming was unique during the last millennium. It shows no hint of the Medieval Warm Period ...suggesting that this warm event was regional rather than global. It also remains unclear why just at the dawn of the Industrial Revolution and before the emission of substantial amounts of anthropogenic greenhouse gases, Earth's temperature began to rise steeply.

Was it a coincidence? I do not think so. Rather, I suspect that the post-1860 natural warming was the most recent in a series of similar warmings spaced at roughly 1,500-year intervals throughout the present interglacial, the Holocene...

One difficulty encountered when trying to reconstruct Holocene temperature fluctuations is that they were probably less than 1°C. In my estimation, at least for time scales greater than a century or two, only two proxies can yield temperatures that are accurate to 0.5°C: the reconstruction of temperatures from the elevation of mountain snowlines and borehole thermometry. **Tree ring records are useful for measuring temperature fluctuations over short time periods but cannot pick up long-term trends....** Corals also are not accurate enough, especially because few records extend back a thousand years. The accuracy of the temperature estimates based on floral or faunal remains from lake and bog sediments is likely no better than ±1.3°C and hence not sufficiently sensitive for Holocene thermometry.

---

[2] http://www.jstor.org/discover/10.2307/3082492?uid=3739688&uid=2&uid=4&uid=3739256&sid=21106345064551

18

"The hockey stick was a sham even allowing for statistical ignorance regarding the instrumental temperature record."

DR DENIS RANCOURT, PHD

Former Professor of Physics at the University of Ottawa, and member of the Ottawa-Carleton Institute for Physics and the Ottawa-Carleton Geoscience Centre. First scientist to describe the phenomenon of superferromagnetism, and developer of a landmark spectral lineshape analysis algorithm. Former host of film series Cinema Politica and author of *Hierarchy* and *Free Expression in the Fight Against Racism.*

Unlike many "deniers", who lean right, Dr Rancourt is a man of the left, and ferociously so. But he has no time for Mann's science. In 2007 he explained some of the problems with tree-ring proxies[1]:

When one uses a temperature proxy, such as the most popular tree ring proxy, instead of a physical thermometer, one has the significant problem of calibrating the proxy. With tree rings from a given preferred species of tree, there are all kinds of unavoidable artefacts related to wood density, wood water content, wood petrifaction processes, season duration effects, forest fire effects, extra-temperature biotic stress effects (such as recurring insect infestations), etc. Each proxy has its own calibration and preservation problems that are not fully understood.

---

[1] http://activistteacher.blogspot.com/2007/02/global-warming-truth-or-dare.html

45

The reported temperature curves should therefore be seen as tentative suggestions that the authors hope will catalyze more study and debate, not reliable results that one should use in guiding management practice or in deducing actual planetary trends. In addition, the original temperature or proxy data is usually not available to other research scientists who could critically examine the data treatment methods; nor are the data treatment methods spelled out in enough detail. Instead, **the same massaged data is reproduced from report to report** rather than re-examined.

Indeed - because the hockey stick's promoters were never interested in "tentative suggestions" that might "catalyze more study and debate". The past was reconstructed not because anyone was interested in (as Mann's friend Gavin Schmidt would subsequently sneer) what the weather was like a thousand years ago, but in order to yoke it to a stark, terrifying tag-line about the here-and-now. As Dr Rancourt wrote in 2011[2]:

This all occurred after **the ludicrous "hottest year in the hottest decade of the last thousand years" madness of the 1990s, now politely referred to as the "hockey stick controversy".** And recently Climategate has conclusively settled the latter controversy: The hockey stick was a sham even allowing for statistical ignorance regarding the instrumental temperature record...

Climate change "science" is part of just another screw-the-brown-people scam... Or is the societal goal to use the fabricated sanitized problem of CO_2 in order to mask the real problems and to shield us from our responsibilities as influential First Worlders?

---

[2] http://activistteacher.blogspot.com/2011/03/on-gargantuan-lie-of-climate-change.html

19

"It is precip that is the driver"

PROFESSOR TOM WIGLEY'S SON EIRIK

Eirik Wigley is the son of Tom Wigley, Professorial Fellow at the University of Adelaide and former head of the Climatic Research Unit at the University of East Anglia.

If you were at school in the pre-Mann era, you'll have a vague recollection that, before their new eminence as precision treemometers, tree rings were something to do with rainfall. In 2003 doctors Willie Soon and Sallie Baliunas of the Harvard-Smithsonian Center for Astrophysics published one of the first papers challenging the hockey stick[1], and restoring a Medieval Warm Period warmer than the late 20th century. In public, the Hockey Team were dismissive of the paper. In private, they were less so. On June 5th Tom Wigley emailed Mann[2]:

Mike,

Well put! By chance SB03 [the Soon & Baliunas paper] may have got some of these precip[3] things right, but **we don't want to give them any way to claim credit.**

Also, stationarity[4] is the key. Let me tell you a story. A few years back, my son Eirik did a tree-ring science fair project using trees behind NCAR[5]. He found that widths correlated with both

---

[1] http://www.atmos.washington.edu/2006Q2/211/articles_optional/ Soon2003_paleorecord.pdf
[2] http://di2.nu/foia/foia2011/mail/0682.txt
[3] Precipitation - ie, rain.
[4] A statistical concept: A common assumption in time-series techniques is that the data are stationary. Parameters such as mean, variance and autocorrelation structure do not change over time and do not follow any trends.
[5] The National Center for Atmospheric Research in Boulder, Colorado

temp and precip. However, temp and precip also correlate. There is much other evidence that it is precip that is the driver, and that the temp/width correlation arises via the temp/precip correlation. Interestingly, **the temp correlations are much more ephemeral**, so the complexities conspire to make this linkage nonstationary.

I have not seen any papers in the literature demonstrating this - but, as you point out Mike, it is a crucial issue.

Tom

So some schoolkid's science project understood the problem with treemometers, but the self-garlanded Nobel Laureate never gave it a thought. Given Mann's usual reaction to criticism, Professor Wigley is lucky the guy didn't go to the School Board and have his kid expelled as a Koch-funded denier.

Scientists who work with actual trees were as wary as Wigley fils about their new eminence as millennial temperature gauges. One of the Climategate emails includes this from Rod Savidge, Professor of Tree Physiology and Biochemistry at the University of New Brunswick[6]:

There are bounds to dendrochronology ...and the discipline has spilled over way outside of those bounds, to the point of absurdity. There is uncertainty associated with estimating an accurate age for even a living tree that you cut down today, and much more when you try to make chronological sense out of pieces of trees of uncertain origin. **What troubles me even more than the inexactness attending chronological estimates is how much absolute nonsense - really nothing but imaginative speculation - about the environment of the past is being deduced from tree rings.**

---

[6] http://www.ecowho.com/foia.php?file=1738.txt

20

"We conclude unequivocally that the evidence for a 'long-handled' hockey stick ...is lacking in the data."

DR BLAKELEY B MCSHANE, PHD
& DR ABRAHAM J WYNER, PHD

Blakeley B McShane is Associate Professor of Marketing at Northwestern University's Kellogg School of Management, and a former editor of *The Journal of the American Statistical Association*. His areas of expertise are data analysis and statistical modeling. Abraham J Wyner is Professor of Statistics at the University of Pennsylvania's Wharton School and an expert on probability models.

In March 2011 Professors McShane and Wyner published in The Annals of Applied Statistics *a paper called "A statistical analysis of multiple temperature proxies: Are reconstructions of surface temperatures over the last 1,000 years reliable?" Their answer was blunt*[1]:

We find that **the proxies do not predict temperature significantly better than random series generated independently of temperature**... The proxies seem unable to forecast the high levels of and sharp run-up in temperature in the 1990s ...thus **casting doubt on their ability to predict such phenomena** if in fact they occurred several hundred years ago...

Research on multi-proxy temperature reconstructions of

---

[1] http://www.e-publications.org/ims/submission/index.php/AOAS/user/submissionFile/6695?confirm=63ebfddf

the earth's temperature is now entering its second decade. While the literature is large, **there has been very little collaboration with university-level, professional statisticians...** Our paper is an effort to apply some modern statistical methods to these problems.

And long overdue. Their findings:

We conclude unequivocally that the evidence for a "long-handled" hockey stick (where the shaft of the hockey stick extends to the year 1000 AD) is lacking in the data. The fundamental problem is that there is a limited amount of proxy data which dates back to 1000 AD; what is available is **weakly predictive of global annual temperature.** Our backcasting methods, which track quite closely the methods applied most recently in Mann (2008) to the same data, are unable to catch the sharp run up in temperatures recorded in the 1990s... Consequently, the long flat handle of the hockey stick is best understood to be a feature of regression and less a reflection of our knowledge of the truth.

While agreeing that "the temperatures of the last few decades have been relatively warm", the authors conclude that the number of genuinely independent proxies "may be just too small for accurate reconstruction":

Climate scientists have greatly underestimated the uncertainty of proxy-based reconstructions and hence have been overconfident in their models... Even proxy-based models with approximately the same amount of reconstructive skill, produce strikingly dissimilar historical backcasts; **some of these look like hockey sticks but most do not.** Natural climate variability is not well understood and is probably quite large. It is not clear that the proxies currently used to predict temperature are even predictive of it at the scale of several decades let alone over many centuries.

III
Mann of the present
THE END JUSTIFIES THE MEANS

An article about computational science in a scientific publication is not *the scholarship itself, it is merely* advertising *of the scholarship. The actual scholarship is the complete software development environment and the complete set of instructions which generated the figures.*[1]

"CLAERBOUT'S PRINCIPLE", AFTER JON CLAERBOUT
CECIL GREEN PROFESSOR EMERITUS OF GEOPHYSICS AT STANFORD
"WAVELAB AND REPRODUCIBLE RESEARCH"
LECTURE NOTES IN STATISTICS VOLUME 103, 1995

---

[1] http://statweb.stanford.edu/~donoho/Reports/1995/wavelab.pdf

A S DISCUSSED in the previous chapter, the only two things wrong with Mann's proxy reconstruction are the proxies and the reconstruction. His chosen proxies were unreliable California bristlecones and a couple of highly influential Gaspé cedars. The reconstruction is the use he made of them. So, if you remove the bristlecones, the hockey-stick shape goes away.

Where once paleoclimatologists pottered around their own area of expertise working with their own data, Mann took everybody else's data from everybody else's area and claimed to be able to handle it with a pan-global expertise all his own. But he was engaging in an ambitious statistical exercise for which he was way out of his league and for which he sought no assistance from actual statisticians - as we'll hear. The healthy reaction to the hockey stick is "Wow! How'd he do that?" It's not clear anybody did say that - or, at any rate, not anyone who mattered at *Nature* or the IPCC. Because the problem with Mann's reconstruction is very basic:

The hockey stick is so called because it divides neatly into two parts: a long flat "handle" for the first nine centuries followed by a 20th century "blade" that shoots straight up. The takeaway - the one that Mann, Al Gore and the IPCC marketed to such effect - is that the earth was hotter in the late 20th century than at any time in the previous millennium.

But the science underpinning the graph is also made up of two elements: actual recorded temperatures, and proxies - or temperatures derived from the aforementioned tree rings. So what matters is how these two elements are "spliced" together. If, for example, the hockey stick simply used tree rings for the flat handle and temperature readings for the vertical blade, it would perhaps be a bit too crude even for the alarmists. On the other hand, that in turn raises a more obvious question: If tree rings are such a reliable guide to the 11th century, and the 13th century, and the 16th century, surely they're also accurate for the 20th century. So why not just do a straight tree-ring graph of the last millennium?

Ah, well. That's because most of the tree-ring data used by Mann only go up to 1980. When asked why these series hadn't been updated, he responded:

> *Most reconstructions only extend through about 1980 because the vast majority of tree-ring, coral, and ice core records currently available in the public domain do not extend into the most recent decades. While paleoclimatologists are attempting to update many important proxy records to the present, this is a costly, and labor-intensive activity, often requiring expensive field campaigns that involve traveling with heavy equipment to difficult-to-reach locations (such as high-elevation or remote polar sites).[2]*

"Costly"? Compared to what? Kyoto? A carbon tax? As Stephen McIntyre responded:

> *Think about the billions spent on climate research and then try to explain to me why we need to rely on "important records" obtained in the 1970s. Far more money has been spent on climate research in the last decade than in the 1970s. Why are we still relying on obsolete proxy data?[3]*

Because, as eventually emerged in 2014[4], when you update the tree rings, the hockey stick collapses - as Mann knew all along. He folded in the real-world temperature data because, by the mid-20th century, the proxies don't tell the story that Mann et al wanted to sell, and certainly don't produce anything that looks like a hockey

---

[2] http://www.realclimate.org/index.php?p=11#comments
[3] http://climateaudit.org/2005/02/20/bring-the-proxies-up-to-date/
[4] http://climateaudit.org/2014/12/04/sheep-mountain-update/

stick. From the 1940s on, the tree rings head south, and fail to show the late 20th-century warming that the thermometers do. So for Mann the actual temperatures become more useful than the proxies.

The hockey stick thus requires you to believe that:

a) The tree rings are reliable proxies in the pre-thermometer era;

b) They remain reliable in the age of thermometers as long as both the thermometer and the tree ring are going up;

c) If the thermometer's going up but the tree ring's going down, then it's the thermometer that's accurate and the tree ring that's junk.

This is what became known as the "divergence problem" - which in turn led to the catchphrase of Climategate: "hide the decline" - ie, the decline in temperature as determined by tree rings. As Professor Jonathan Jones wrote:

> *'Hide the decline...' is not a complicated technical matter on which reasonable people can disagree: it is a straightforward and blatant breach of the fundamental principles of honesty and self-criticism that lie at the heart of all true science. The significance of the divergence problem is immediately obvious, and seeking to hide it is quite simply wrong. The recent public statements by supposed leaders of UK science, declaring that hiding the decline is standard scientific practice are on a par with declarations that black is white and up is down.*[5]

And few of those science "leaders" wanted to address the most basic question: If the tree rings can't read the 1960s correctly, why should we believe what they tell us about the 1560s or the 1260s?

---

[5] http://bishophill.squarespace.com/blog/2011/2/23/the-beddington-challenge.html?currentPage=2#comments

21

"A case of Michael Mann …sticking an apple on the end of a banana."

DR JENNIFER MAROHASY, PHD

Adjunct Research Fellow at Central Queensland University's Centre for Plant and Water Science. Formerly a field researcher in continental Africa and Madagascar, and a scientist for the Government of Queensland. Author of peer-reviewed papers published in *The International Journal of Sustainable Development and Planning*, *Wetland Ecology and Management*, *Atmospheric Research*, *Environmental Law and Management*, *Advances in Atmospheric Sciences* and *Human and Ecological Risk Assessment*.

In 2013 Dr Marohasy provided a very clear explanation of why she found Mann's famous graph such an unlikely proposition[1]:

My key problem with the "the hockey stick" has always been that the upward spike representing runaway global warming in the 20th century was never of the same stuff as the rest of the chart. That is the spike is largely based on the instrumental temperature record - i.e. the thermometer record - while the downward trending line that it was grafted on to is based on proxies, in particular estimates of temperature derived from studies of tree rings.

It has always, for me, been a case of Michael Mann comparing apples and oranges, or to put it another way sticking an apple on the end of a banana.

---

[1] http://jennifermarohasy.com/2013/04/the-apple-on-the-banana-again-marcott-admits-temperature-spike-not-robust/

- the banana being the long gradual 900-year decline, with an apple core grafted onto the end and pointing upward as the latter-day spike.

But why was Mann obliged to do this? Dr Marohasy explains:

The grafting was necessary because the proxy record, i.e. the tree ring record, shows that global temperatures have declined since about 1960.

Of course we know that global temperature haven't declined since 1960, or thereabout, so there must be something wrong with the proxy record. This is known as "the divergence problem" and it is a problem, because **if tree rings are not a good indicator of global temperature after 1960, how can they be a good indicator of global temperature prior to 1960?**

Indeed there doesn't appear to be a reliable method for reconstructing the last 100 or so years based on the standard techniques used to reconstruct the last 2,000, 4,000 and even 11,000 years of global temperature.

So when someone claims the past ten years have been hotter than the past 11,300 years, as the Australian Broadcasting Commission did recently, there is good reason to cringe.

This is the hockey stick's double deformity: The shaft used a novel and bizarre formula to re-make the past ...but, if you were to apply the same method to the 20th and 21st century, the result would look nothing like the observed temperature record. In other words, Mann's "reconstruction" method can't accurately reconstruct today's climate. So, if his method is a flopperoo for telling you what, say, the 1970s were like, why should it be any more reliable for the 1470s?

22

"Any scientist ought to know that you just can't mix and match proxy and actual data... Yet that's exactly what he did."

PROFESSOR PHILIP STOTT, PHD

Professor Emeritus of Biogeography at the University of London's School of Oriental and African Studies. Co-author of *Global Environmental Change* and *Political Ecology: Science, Myth And Power*. Former editor of *The Journal of Biogeography*. Chairman of the Anglo-Thai Society.

For his part, Philip Stott eschewed bananas in favor of the traditional apples and oranges. In 2009, in the wake of the Climategate emails about "hide the decline" and "Mike's Nature trick", Professor Stott spoke to Britain's Mail *on* Sunday *about the way the World Meteorological Organization hockey stick co-authored by Mann truncates the tree-rings in 1960 - because after that date they cease to be useful to what Mann calls "the cause"[1]:*

On the [WMO] hockey stick graph, his line is abruptly terminated - but the end of the line is obscured by the other lines.

"Any scientist ought to know that you just can't mix and match proxy and actual data," said Philip Stott... "They're apples and oranges. Yet that's exactly what he did."

---

[1] http://www.dailymail.co.uk/news/article-1235395/SPECIAL-INVESTIGATION-Climate-change-emails-row-deepens--Russians-admit-DID-send-them.html

Five years earlier, Professor Stott had been among the first scientists to note the hockey stick had been "unmasked"[2]:

The recent temperature "spike", known as "the hockey stick", has been **unmasked as a statistical artefact**, while the Medieval Warm Period and the Little Ice Age have been statistically rediscovered. Moreover, the latest research has shown that there has probably been no real warming, except that which is surface-driven. And in Russia, global warming has been likened to Lysenkoism.

Lysenkoism refers to the system of ruthless central control over science by Comrade Lysenko in the Soviet Union, in which the scientific method was perverted to meet political needs. This ideologically-settled science led to the starvation of millions. Professor Stott argues that ideologically-settled climate science is a form of "neo-colonialism" that will keep 1.6 billion people in the less developed world in lifelong poverty. Given what Big Climate is asking of us, there is a lot at stake. Yet the same misgivings he had about "mixing and matching" tree rings and temperature records were (privately) expressed far closer to home. Mann's Penn State colleague Professor Richard Alley[3]:

The performance of the tree-ring paleo-thermometry is central. Taking the recent instrumental record and the tree-ring record and joining them yields a dramatic picture, with rather high confidence that recent times are anomalously warm. Taking strictly the tree-ring record and omitting the instrumental record yields a less dramatic picture and a lower confidence that the recent temperatures are anomalous.

---

[2] http://www.spiked-online.com/newsite/article/2417#.VWYId0a4K_F
[3] http://di2.nu/foia/foia2011/mail/3234.txt

23

"The comparison between tree rings from a millennium ago and instrumental records from the last decades does not seem to be justified... This is about icons, not science."

DR RICHARD ALLEY, PHD

Evan Pugh Professor of Geosciences at Pennsylvania State University. Recipient of the Seligman Crystal for "his prodigious contribution to our understanding of the stability of the ice sheets and glaciers of Antarctica and Greenland", and of the Louis Agassiz Medal. Chair of the National Research Council on Abrupt Climate Change. Fellow of the American Academy of Arts and Sciences, Foreign Member of the Royal Society, and member of the National Academy of Sciences. Invited to testify on climate change by the US Senate, House of Representatives, and then Vice-President Al Gore. Author of peer-reviewed papers published by *Nature*, *Science* and other journals. IPCC lead author.

Dr Alley, like Mann, is a Penn State climate scientist, and in 2014 shared the "Friend of the Planet" Award with him. Nevertheless, in March 2006, he wrote to fellow scientists Keith Briffa, Edward Cook and Jonathan Overpeck about the imminent National Research Council investigation of Mann's stick. He did not expect the NRC to "provide a strong endorsement of the tree-ring based millennial reconstructions"[1]:

Despite assurances from Ed and Keith, I must admit that **I still**

---

[1] http://di2.nu/foia/foia2011/mail/3234.txt

don't get it. The NRC committee is looking at a number of issues, but the one that is most publicly noted is to determine whether, and with what confidence, we can say that recent temperatures have emerged from the band of natural variability over the last millennium or two...

The problem is the post-1960 "divergence". The thermometer heads north but the tree rings head south - which is why they had to "hide the decline":

Unless the "divergence problem" can be confidently ascribed to some cause that was not active a millennium ago, then the comparison between tree rings from a millennium ago and instrumental records from the last decades does not seem to be justified, and the confidence level in the anomalous nature of the recent warmth is lowered...

Dr Alley dismissed what he called "the relative scientific unimportance" of the hockey stick - "this is about icons, not science" - but returned to his central point: How can you yoke tree rings to the temperature record as if they're compatible when you know *they're not?*

If some of the records, or some other records such as Rosanne's new ones, show "divergence", then I believe **it casts doubt on the use of joined tree-ring/instrumental records**, and I don't believe that I have yet heard why this interpretation is wrong...

I'd rather go back to teaching and research and raising money and advising students and all of that, but I'm trying to be helpful. Casting aspersions on Rosanne, on the NRC panel, or on me for that matter is not going to solve the underlying problem.

Regards,
Richard

24

"The hockey stick is broken."

DR BO CHRISTIANSEN, PHD

Climate scientist at the Danish Meteorological Institute. Author of peer-reviewed papers in *Geophysical Research Letters*, *The Journal of Climate*, *The Journal of Geophysical Research: Atmospheres*, *Advances in Geosciences*, *Surveys in Geophysics*, *Journal of the Atmospheric Sciences*, *Atmospheric Chemistry and Physics*, and *The Quarterly Journal of the Royal Meteorological Society*.

Despite the concerns of even his closest colleagues, by the early years of the century Mann's "mix and match" model was the principal evidence driving calls for sweeping, unprecedented changes in public policy across the western world. In 2009 Dr Christiansen published a new paper in The Journal of Climate[1]. *On March 2nd the Danish Meteorological Institute announced that "the hockey stick is broken"[2]:*

It has been the icon of what's gone wrong with the climate since preindustrial times. In the case of the so-called Mann hockey-stick curve, which shows the evolution of the Northern Hemisphere surface temperature over the past 600 years, a new Danish study breaks the foundations of the curve.

"**The hockey-stick curve does not stand,**" says climate researcher Bo Christiansen from the Danish Meteorological Institure, and adds: "It does not mean that we cancel the man-made greenhouse effect, but the causes have become more nuanced...

"Popularly, it can be said that **the flat piece on the**

---

[1] http://journals.ametsoc.org/doi/abs/10.1175/2008JCLI2301.1
[2] https://web.archive.org/web/20090304223434/http://www.dmi.dk/dmi/
klimaets_hockeystav_er_braekket

hockey stick is too flat. The earlier part of the reconstructions underestimates the potency of natural climate variations," says Bo Christiansen and adds. "In addition, **their method contains a large element of randomness...**"

It is the statistical methods which the Danish researchers have looked at more closely... They have tested seven different reconstructive methods and all seven exhibit the same weaknesses. "We have therefore encountered a fundamental problem that limits the value of reconstruction studies," says Bo Christiansen.

On March 16th Dr Christiansen wrote to many of the Hockey Team summarizing his paper's findings[3]:

It is almost **impossible to conclude from reconstruction studies that the present period is warmer** than any period in the reconstructed period.

In the paper itself, Dr Christiansen and his colleagues from the Danish Meteorological Institute, Dr Torben Schmith and Dr Peter Thejil, examined multiple Mann reconstructions - Mann et al (1998), Mann and Rutherford (2002), Rutherford et al (2003), Jones and Mann (2004), Mann et al (2004), Mann et al (2005), Rutherford et al (2005), Mann et al (2007a), Mann et al (2007b) - as well as other reconstructions. Their conclusion was devastating:

The underestimation of the amplitude of the low-frequency variability demonstrated for all of the seven methods **discourage the use of reconstructions to estimate the rareness of the recent warming.** That this underestimation is found for all the reconstruction methods is rather depressing.

---

[3] http://di2.nu/foia/foia2011/mail/0300.txt

25

"He only put a lot of numbers into his computer, played with statistical subroutines for a while and wow, headline-breaking results popped up!"

DR JARL AHLBECK, PHD

Lecturer in Environmental Technology at Åbo Akademi. Author of more than 200 papers published in scientific journals, and holder of four patents. Former member of the Finnish Parliament's energy expert commission. Expert in water treatment and creator of clean-water supply systems for poor people in China, India and Bangladesh. Expert on the CO_2 cycle and the benefits of CO_2 for food production and economic growth. Former member of Greenpeace.

Even without the "divergence", with a large-scale reconstruction from multiple elements, what matters is how you put it together. Jarl Ahlbeck was on to Mann very early, and understood very clearly his approach to the tree-ring data he threw in his magic woodchipper. On October 7th 2004 Dr Ahlbeck summarized it thus (in English)[1]:

Well, I don't think Dr Mann came up with his Hockey Stick just because he first discovered MW and LI in the data and then wanted to prove that there were no MW or LI at all. He only put a lot of numbers into his computer, played with statistical

---

[1] http://meteo.lcd.lu/globalwarming/Ahlbeck/071004.html

subroutines for a while and wow, headline-breaking results popped up! **Of course he was excited and happy of becoming the man who was able to create a radical shift of paradigm!**

Good old Bert Bolin[2] was almost dancing of joy when he presented the Hockey Stick for the first time.

The problem was that nobody could repeat the calculations because Dr Mann did not provide exact information about the data files and computing procedures. So much for the referee process, the referees judge the quality of the work according to their personal opinions about what may be true or not, not by double-checking the calculations because it was not possible. How can Dr Mann claim that his greenhouse-believer fellow Dr Storch has made flawed calculations if he cannot repeat them..?

The downplaying of the Hockey Stick is nice but the way it was done may simply be bad science due to the fact that the climate models do not reliably model the real climate. I have seen (and made) so much junk science during my 30 years of work with chemical process analysis by statistical methods and process simulations so I have became typical sceptic on almost anything. My processes usually offered a lot of surprises that were never modelled. And they were very simple compared to the World Climate. **(Of course I don't believe in the Hockey Stick.)**

In fact, global and NH mean temperatures are not very interesting. Nobody lives in the mean temperature, it is the local temperature at a certain time that matters.

Greenhouse religion is a funny thing. There are so much feelings and aggressions in it. Just as in classical religions.

---

[2] Dr Bolin (1925-2007) was the first chairman of the IPCC.

26

"Mann (and maybe Steig) are examples of how NOT to proceed..."

NEAL J KING, MA (PHYSICS)
Physics graduate from the University of California, and contributor to John Cook's pro-Mann anti-denier website Skeptical Science.

What do you do if you believe global warming is a crisis for the planet but you suspect - or know - that the best known evidence for that argument is a crock? In public, Mann's enforcers insisted the science was settled. In private, it was a different story. Skeptical Science is a very Mann-friendly website. (Its material turns up in his legal pleadings.) But, behind the scenes, Skeptical Science operated a private forum in which their disquiet over Mann's methods and their distaste at feeling obliged to defend him is palpable. In 2011, Neal King wrote[1]:

My impression is that **Mann and buddies have sometimes gone out on a limb** when that was unnecessary and ill-advised... Mann, for all his technical ability, is sometimes his own worst enemy.

Similarly, with regard to "hiding the decline" in Climategate, I am left with the impression that the real question is, Why would you believe the tree-ring proxies at earlier times when you KNOW that they didn't work properly in the 1990s? I guess there is a good answer to that, but no one has ever given it to me.

I believe a good 50 per cent of the game is being able to avoid booby traps... I think Mann (and maybe Steig[2]) are

---

[1] http://climateaudit.org/2013/11/20/behind-the-sks-curtain/
[2] Eric Steig is a fellow contributor at Mann's website RealClimate.org.

examples of how NOT to proceed.

Mr King later added[3]:

Mann et al spent too much time defendinig [sic] what was incorrect, and allowed the totality of the argument to become "infected" by the fight.

Agreeing with King, his colleague Robert Way quoted a "denier":

'Assume you start with 1000 sets of random very noisy set of data which swings up and down by 4°C and you average them. You should get a relatively flat line with wiggles of a magnitude much smaller than any of the individual peaks.

'If you take the same random data, calibrate its endpoint to today's temperature (offset it so the end matches today's temperature) and then sort it (throw data out) so that only data which correlate to a temperature rise at the end 5 per cent of the dataset remains. Then you average the remaining data you would get a relatively flat line with an upward spike at the end. The averaged data would have an end spike which would almost certainly be of greater magnitude than the rest of the curve.'

This is from Jeff Id's site[4] and although I do think he's a douche he does bring up a good point. Even with a hockey stick in the dataset **the method will result in excluding datasets which support the hockey stick the least.**

The douche shall set you free!

---

[3] http://www.hi-izuru.org/forum/General%20Chat/2011-09-29-McIntyre%27s%20new%20target.html

[4] https://noconsensus.wordpress.com/2008/09/04/how-to-make-a-hockey-stick-paleoclimatology-what-they-dont-want-you-to-know/

27

"How such an expensive project was launched and collected so much data without having statisticians on board is a mystery."

PROFESSOR JAMES V ZIDEK, PHD

Professor Emeritus in the Department of Statistics at the University of British Columbia. Former President of the Statistical Society of Canada, and recipient of its Gold Medal. Fellow of the Royal Society of Canada, and member of the Royal Statistical Society, and the International Statistical Institute. Member of the American Statistic Association and recipient of its Distinguished Achievement Medal in Environmental Statistics. Member of the Scientific Advisory Committee of the US National Center for Atmospheric Research, and of the US National Science Foundation Statistics Panel. Former Senior Research Scientist at the Commonwealth Scientific and Industrial Research Organization. Editor of *The Encyclopedia of Environmental Statistics*, and Associate Editor of *The Journal of Agricultural, Biological and Environmental Statistics*.

When something bears the imprimatur of science, the public assumes it's, well, scientific. But the hockey stick is essentially a statistical creation - and yet no statisticians were involved at any point of the process. In November 2010, Professor Zidek was interviewed by Y K Leong for Imprints, *the newsletter of the National University of Singapore's Institute for Mathematical Sciences. He was asked what he thought, as a statistical scientist, of the case for anthropogenic climate change[1]:*

PROFESSOR ZIDEK: From the statistical perspective, I think what

---

[1] http://www2.ims.nus.edu.sg/imprints/imprints-17-2010.pdf

is interesting is the great uncertainty that abounds in that field. A lot of discussion at our workshop has been around the question of which model to use, for example, how you plug-in the uncertainty about these models, which kind of scenarios to use, and so on. There is a healthy recognition that there is a lot of uncertainty about this whole question of climate change. In particular, there is a lot of uncertainty about how much is exactly due to anthropogenic causes, how much is due to natural process. I know that the International Panel on Climate Change has come down saying it is very likely that climate change is, to a substantial extent, due to anthropogenic causes, but trying to figure out how much seems quite a challenge... It's an important opportunity for statisticians to get involved in what is arguably the most important issue of our age...

IMPRINTS: Were there any statisticians on the Panel itself?

ZIDEK: Hardly any, Peter Guttorp being the only one I know. But I was involved in the early 1990s, thanks to the International Statistical Institute, in trying to get ourselves as statisticians on that Panel, and we did not succeed. I don't know why. At the same time I do know that these scientists do know a lot of statistics, so I'm not saying their work is flawed. On the other hand, there's a lot of discussion recently about something called a "hockey stick", with a blade that rises steeply from the handle and tells us that the climate changed, tentatively anyway, a lot over the last century. There has been a lot of controversy about that stick among non-statisticians, as to what that really represents and there is an argument that it is flawed. That analysis anyway might have benefitted from some input by statisticians. How such an expensive project was launched and collected so much data without having statisticians on board is a mystery.

28
"Tree rings with a hockey stick shape dominate the PCA with this method."

DR MIA HUBERT, PHD

Head of the Statistics Section and Professor in the Faculty of Science at the Catholic University Leuven. Author of peer-reviewed papers in *Computational Statistics & Data Analysis, Statistical Methods and Applications, Statistical Papers, The Journal of Quality Technology, The Journal of the American Statistical Association* and many more.

In the end it was two Torontonians, Stephen McIntyre and Ross McKitrick, who launched the most forensic critique of Mann's hockey stick - and especially of what statisticians call the principal component analysis (PCA). They discovered that Mann used an algorithm that looked for hockey-stick shapes and then overstated their dominance in the resulting patterns - thereby dramatically understating all the uncertainties of his climate reconstruction. In February 2005, Marcel Crok was one of the first environmental journalists to investigate seriously McIntyre & McKitrick's claims against the hockey stick. In his report for the Dutch magazine Natuurwetenschap & Techniek, *Mr Crok quoted Mr McIntyre as follows[1]:*

> The effect is that tree ring series with a hockey stick shape no longer have a mean of zero and end up dominating the first principal component (PC1); in effect, **Mann's program mines for series with a hockey stick shape.** In

---

[1] http://www.uoguelph.ca/~rmckitri/research/Climate_H.pdf

the crucial period of 1400-1450, in the critical PC1 of the North American network, the top-weighted Sheep Mountain series, with a hockey stick shape gets over 390 times the weight of the least weighted series, which does not have a hockey stick shape.

The layman tends to think of "statistics" as averaging: If you examine ten trees, and two have dramatic hockey sticks but eight show no curve at all, the combined graph would show a very slight rise. But, under Mann's weighting, the graph of all ten trees would still be rocketing into the stratosphere.

Mr Crok understood that this would be an astounding indictment of Mann if true. So he sought confirmation:

At our request, Dr Mia Hubert of the Katholieke Universiteit Leuven in Belgium, who specializes in robust statistics, checked to see if Mann's unusual standardization influenced the climate reconstruction. She confirms: "Tree rings with a hockey stick shape dominate the PCA with this method."

What was astonishing - given the promotion of the stick by the IPCC and western governments - was that until Mr McIntyre prompted Mr Crok to ask Dr Hubert, no serious statistician had attempted to verify Mann's findings. As the Canadian told the Dutchman:

McIntyre has growing doubts about the other studies as well. His initial impression is that they are also dubious. It is almost certain, or so he states, that the other studies have not been checked either. McIntyre: "...Mann speaks of independent studies, but they are not independent in any usual sense. Most of the studies involve Mann, Jones, Briffa and/or Bradley. Some datasets are used in nearly every study. Bristlecone pine series look like they affect a number of other studies as well."

29
"They used a brand new statistical technique that they made up."

ROBERT WAY, MSc

PhD student in permafrost science and physical geography at the University of Ottawa. Recipient of the W Garfield Weston Award for Northern Research. Fellow of the School of Graduate Studies and Master of Science in Glaciology and Physical Geography at Memorial University of Newfoundland. Author of peer-reviewed papers published by *The Quarterly Journal of the Royal Meteorological Society*, *Atmospheric Science Letters*, *Quaternary Science Reviews*, *Ecological Modelling* and other journals.

As noted earlier, Skeptical Science is a Mann-friendly website. They defend him in public, but backstage, in an in-house comments forum, the authors' misgivings about his work are more openly expressed. In 2011, Robert Way wrote[1]:

I don't mean to be the pessimist of the group here but Mc[2] brought up some very good points about the original hockey stick... The statistical methodology used by Mann did rely too much on tree rings which still are in debate over their usefulness to reconstruct temperature and particularly their ability to record low-frequency temperature variations. **I've personally seen work that is unpublished that challenges every single one of his reconstructions** because they all either understate or overstate low-frequency variations... That's why I don't like to talk the HS stuff, because **I know a lot of people who have doubts about**

---

[1] http://climateaudit.org/2013/11/20/behind-the-sks-curtain/
[2] Stephen McIntyre, Mann's nemesis

the accuracy of the original HS.

Just like we complain about skeptics like Pielke and Christy etc letting their work be misconstrued, Mann et al stood by after their original HS and let others treat it with the confidence that they themselves couldn't assign to it.

Mr Way globally warmed to his theme:

Even his newest reconstruction doesn't validate past 1400 if you don't include disputed series (which I have no idea why he's including them at all). Let's make this clear. There is a hockey stick shape in the data, but the original hockey stick still used the wrong methods and **these methods were defended over and over despite being wrong... He fought like a dog to discredit and argue with those on the other side that his method was not flawed.** And in the end he never admitted that the entire method was a mistake. Saying "I was wrong but when done right it gives close to the same answer" is no excuse... What happened was they used a brand new statistical technique that they made up and that there was no rationalization in the literature for using it... They then let this HS be used in every way possible (including during the Kyoto protocol lead-up that resulted in Canadian Parliament signing the deal with many people ascribing their final belief in climate change being assured by the HS) despite knowing the stats behind it weren't rock solid.

But who cares about the science? Mann defender Julian Brimelow, who presented a paper on "Hydroclimatological aspects of the extreme 2011 Assiniboine River Basin flood" at the 2014 American Geophysical Union meeting, cuts to the chase:

McIntyre need [sic] to go down, it is quite that simple.

30

"It therefore seems crazy that the MBH hockey stick has been given such prominence and that a group of influential climate scientists have doggedly defended a piece of dubious statistics."

PROFESSOR IAN JOLLIFFE, PHD

Professor Emeritus of Statistics at the University of Aberdeen and Honorary Visiting Professor at the University of Exeter's College of Engineering, Mathematics and Physical Sciences. Author of *Principal Component Analysis* (Springer, New York, 2002), regarded as the most authoritative text in its field, and of the entry on the same subject in *The International Encyclopedia of Statistical Science* (Springer, New York, 2011).

In response to criticisms of his statistics, Mann asserted that he was simply following one of the most respected statisticians on earth, Professor Jolliffe. Diehard Manniac Grant Foster, who blogs as "Tamino", repeated this defense on his website "Open Mind" - to which Professor Jolliffe responded as follows[1]:

It has recently come to my notice that on the following website, my views have been misrepresented, and I would therefore like to correct any wrong impression that has been given. An apology

---

[1] http://climateaudit.org/2008/09/08/ian-jolliffe-comments-at-tamino/

from the person who wrote the page would be nice.

In reacting to Wegman[2]'s criticism of "decentred" PCA, the author says that Wegman is "just plain wrong" and goes on to say "You shouldn't just take my word for it, but you *should* take the word of Ian Jolliffe, one of the world's foremost experts on PCA, author of a seminal book on the subject. He takes an interesting look at the centering issue in this presentation[3]." It is flattering to be recognised as a world expert, and I'd like to think that the final sentence is true, though only "toy" examples were given. However there is a strong implication that I have endorsed "decentred PCA". This is "just plain wrong"...

The talk... certainly does not endorse decentred PCA. Indeed I had not understood what MBH had done until a few months ago. Furthermore, the talk is distinctly cool about anything other than the usual column-centred version of PCA...

I am by no means a climate change denier. My strong impressive [sic] is that the evidence rests on much much more than the hockey stick. It therefore seems crazy that the MBH hockey stick has been given such prominence and that a group of influential climate scientists have doggedly defended a piece of dubious statistics. Misrepresenting the views of an independent scientist does little for their case either...

Ian Jolliffe

As the aforementioned Robert Way remarked[4]:

This is the epitome of how I feel.

---

[2] Professor Edward Wegman et al's report on the hockey stick for the US House of Representatives

[3] http://empslocal.ex.ac.uk/people/staff/itj201/RecentTalks.html

[4] http://www.hi-izuru.org/forum/General%20Chat/2011-09-29-McIntyre%27s%20new%20target.html

IV

Mann of the hour
EMPIRE OF THE STICK

The most famous example of what I consider outright cheating was Michael Mann's famous "Hockey Stick" graph...

This graph has had an amazing existence, rising from the ashes each time someone points out a fatal flaw. Why? Because the UN IPCC desperately needs this graph.[1]

DR GORDON J FULKS, PHD
SPEECH TO THE OREGON CHAPTER OF THE AMERICAN
METEOROLOGICAL SOCIETY, JANUARY 25th 2012

---

[1]http://www.ametsoc.org/chapters/oregon/Minutes/2012/2012_1_25_Meeting/
2012_1_25_Presentations/2012_1_25_GordonFulksTranscripts.pdf

THE INTERGOVERNMENTAL Panel on Climate Change was born in 1988. It enjoyed the unlikely support of Mrs Thatcher, in defiance of her usual rule that, if you set up a bureaucracy to fix a problem, then you'll never be rid of the problem. And so the IPCC is not a general science body or a general climate-science body, but a bureaucracy whose only business is "climate change". The thing about saving the planet is that the planet's a complicated thing. Its climate involves many factors, including water vapor, the sun, ocean currents, bovine flatulence, all interacting with each other. If you show the layman a graph of any of the preceding, he'll have no idea what it means: is it good or bad? But the public does understand temperature: It knows that if it's 75 you put on shorts and T-shirt, but if it's 35 you button up your overcoat. The thermometer is one of the few climate-related instruments everyone can grasp. MIT's Richard Lindzen:

> *Thermometric measurements ...is something people can understand. They can understand a temperature series and they can understand there's a connection between the word 'warming' and temperature change.*[2]

To the public, "climate" means "weather" and "weather" is measured in temperature. So, if you're the IPCC and you want a shorthand for catastrophe that can be sold to bureaucrats, politicians and citizens, the dream ticket is a big scary temperature graph.

The IPCC has never had a hit like its Third Assessment Report. Their first two did the boring scientific thing and considered all the uncertainties, and the fourth and fifth were comparatively *sotto voce* after the headline-grabbing hockey stick. But the TAR is the IPCC's pop smash, the one that broke through

---

[2] http://video.mit.edu/watch/the-great-climategate-debate-9529/

to become the Big Climate boy-band's "Livin' La Vida Loca", a veritable "Candle In The Wind Turbine". Mann's temperature graph accomplished even more than the IPCC were looking for. Discussing "that unknown fraction of warming since 1950 that can be attributed to humans", Dr Judith Curry cautioned that it's important to include the A (for "anthropogenic") in AGW:

If you leave out the 'A', people are misled into thinking that all warming for the past 1,000 years is caused by humans (the 'hockey stick' argument).[3]

She's right. Mann's hockey stick showed that there was no such thing as "global warming" until the Industrial Revolution took off. So, in Mannworld, 100 per cent of "global warming" is anthropogenic. How did the IPCC come to promote an "outlier" (as Dr Curtis Covey described the stick) by an obscure individual of no previous distinction as the consensus of the world's scientists?

As Professor John Christy, a former IPCC "Lead Author" himself, told the US Congress, Lead Authors are nominated by their countries but ultimately selected by a somewhat inscrutable IPCC bureaucracy. They are supposed to represent "the highest level of expertise in particular fields" and in practice have "virtually total control over the material" - which means there is a strong temptation to "cite their own work heavily and neglect or belittle contradictory evidence". In most areas of life, "this would be called a conflict of interest", but not at the IPCC. Enter Mann:

Add to this situation the rather unusual fact that the LA of this particular section had been awarded a PhD only a few months before his selection by the IPCC.[4]

---

[3] http://judithcurry.com/2014/06/01/global-warming-versus-climate-change/
[4] http://science.house.gov/sites/republicans.science.house.gov/files/documents/hearings/ChristyJR_written_110331_all.pdf

How could such a thing happen? A one-paper nobody with the ink still wet on his diploma suddenly becomes the voice of the IPCC?

But his patron was Britain's IPCC honcho John Houghton. Sir John immediately recognized the potential of Mann's stick and decided to make it *the* poster for global warming. Paleoclimatology had once been an obscure discipline; Mann made it an applied science: Its purpose is to tell us what we should do *now*.

Having buried "the divergence problem" in his own work, was it ever likely that Mann would want to address it from his new seat of power? As Dr Judith Curry would later write:

> *There is no question that the diagrams and accompanying text in the IPCC TAR, AR4 and WMO 1999 are misleading. I was misled. Upon considering the material presented in these reports, it did not occur to me that recent paleo data was not consistent with the historical record...*
>
> *Not only is this misleading, but it is dishonest... The authors defend themselves by stating that there has been no attempt to hide the divergence problem in the literature... I infer then that there is something in the IPCC process or the authors' interpretation of the IPCC process (i.e. don't dilute the message) that resulted in the scientists deleting the adverse data in these diagrams.* [5]

In the words of Dr Gordon Fulks:

> *The mismatched data should have told Mann that his data were not reliable. But instead, they provided him exactly the result he wanted* and *worldwide acclaim*[6].

---

[5] http://judithcurry.com/2011/02/22/hiding-the-decline/
[6] http://www.ametsoc.org/chapters/oregon/Minutes/2012/2012_1_25_Meeting/2012_1_25_Presentations/2012_1_25_GordonFulksTranscripts.pdf

31

"The statistical analysis underlying the hockey stick was thoroughly trashed."

PROFESSOR G KORNELIS VAN KOOTEN, PHD

Professor and Senior Canada Research Chair in Environmental Studies and Climate and Adjunct Professor of the Institute for Integrated Energy Systems at the University of Victoria's Department of Economics. Former Chair of the Department of Applied Economics and Statistics at the University of Nevada. Co-author of *The Economics of Nature* (Blackwell, Oxford, 2000). IPCC reviewer and contributing author.

Professor van Kooten has never been under any illusions about the hockey stick[1]:

Scientists manipulated paleoclimatic data and the peer-review process to make the case that average global temperatures had been stable for a thousand years or more... Despite efforts to block access to data and attempts to prevent critics from publishing their research, **the "hockey stick" story has now been thoroughly discredited. There is no scientific basis to support this view of the world.** Today's temperatures are no different than those experienced in the past two millennia.

But, if there is "no scientific basis to support this view of the world", how did it become the world's best-known scientific graph? Nature *is a prestigious scientific journal, but it is, in the end, only a journal. What*

---

[1] https://www.heartland.org/policy-documents/climate-change-and-poverty

catapulted Michael E Mann to global celebrity was the 2001 Third Assessment Report by the Intergovernmental Panel on Climate Change. As Professor van Kooten wrote in December 2012[2]:

> After having been a reviewer of the Third Report, putting in quite a bit of time and then totally ignored, I viewed the process as nothing more than a sham... The IPCC's Third Assessment Report basically relied on the hockey stick to make the case that current temperatures were higher than those experienced by humans in the last 1,500 to 2,000 years... Subsequently, the statistical analysis underlying the hockey stick was thoroughly trashed, but there are some who continue to think otherwise (which is disappointing). The hockey stick was such a nice device for showing the supposed link between CO_2 and temperatures – the concentration of CO_2 in the atmosphere was flat until it began to rise at the time of the industrial revolution in Europe. If temperatures could be shown to follow the same trend – presto!

Presto indeed. The Third Assessment Report made the hockey stick a household name - in that western governments sent it to every household in the land in order to sell the Kyoto Accord. Because it was so successful at selling Kyoto (in pretty much the entire developed world except the United States), Al Gore put it in his movie An Inconvenient Truth. *Because* An Inconvenient Truth *was a box-office hit and an Oscar winner, education departments around the globe began showing it to schoolchildren. And soon the hockey stick became the easiest shorthand for every slacktivist who wanted to get a swig of the planet-saving juice without having to plough through a lot of boring peer-reviewed papers.*

The hockey stick was no longer science, it was an icon of the new millennium's new religion.

---

[2] http://web.uvic.ca/~kooten/Commentary/ClimateConfusion.pdf

32

"Common sense in science tells you to be a bit skeptic about any investigation which throws old truths away and gives a completely new picture... Not so in this case."

DR LARS KAMÉL, PHD

Former professor in the University of Uppsala's Department of Astronomy and Space Physics.

Why was the hockey stick so valuable to the IPCC? Because the easiest riposte to Big Climate alarmism is "natural variability": If the planet was as warm as this a few centuries back and things worked out fine, then what's the big deal? Thus, Mann's great gift to the "climate catastrophists" is that he abolished the very idea of natural variability. In Mannworld, nothing much happened to the climate for 900 years and then it leapt in the air like a startled cat. In 2003 Dr Kamél wrote[1]:

That the climate could vary so much by natural means was a problem for the climate catastrophists, who wanted to claim that (almost) all of the climate change of the 20th century was due to man. If natural variations could do this before 1850, maybe they were responsible also for changes after 1850..? To the relief of the catastrophists, a new study, which questioned the old view (Mann et al 1999), was published. According to this new study,

---

[1] http://sciliterature.50webs.com/Climate/klipseue.html

the world was somewhat colder 1,000 years ago than it is today. Then followed 850 years of almost linear and slow cooling. In the middle of the 19th century this was abruptly switched to a warming...

Common sense in science tells you to be a bit skeptic about any investigation which throws old truths away and gives a completely new picture. Preferably, scientists wait for more research, which either supports or disproves the new view, before they decide what to think about the new investigation. Not so in this case. **IPCC immediately adopted Mann's reconstruction as the truth about the past climate of the world...** The politicians and laymen should be in no doubt that **the evolution of the world's climate in the past 1,000 years was decided once and for all...**

A closer inspection of the study in question shows some peculiarities. The temperature indicators, which were used, in fact end in 1980, when the temperature is a little bit colder than in 1940. To give the impression of a rapid warming in the end of the 20th century, the calculations from the weather stations have been added to the diagram.

As Dr Kamél wrote in "The Rise and Fall of a Hockey Stick"[2]:

It came as no surprise to me when **several new investigations showed that the Hockey Stick analyses was full of faults and errors.** In 2003, I considered the immediate acceptance of the Hockey Stick by IPCC as the scientific truth to be pseudo scientific. Soon thereafter, it turned out that **the Hockey Stick itself may well be an example of pseudo science...**

There could be no doubt that the Hockey Stick is broken. It was, at best, the result of bad science and a programming error.

---

[2] http://sciliterature.50webs.com/Climate/HockeyStick.html

33

"It is strange that the climate reconstruction of Mann passed both peer review rounds of the IPCC without anyone ever really having checked it."

DR ROB VAN DORLAND, PHD
Researcher at KNMI, the Royal Netherlands Meteorological Institute.
IPCC lead author.

The IPCC Assessment Reports run to thousands of pages, far too many for the average government minister, or even his flunkeys. So what matters is the so-called SPM, the concise "Summary for Policy Makers". In 2001 the hockey stick graph was the only climate reconstruction to make it to the SPM, and the only "proof" offered of the Summary's most dramatic assertion[1]:

> The increase in temperature in the 20th century is likely to have been the largest of any century during the past 1,000 years. It is also likely that, in the Northern Hemisphere, the 1990s was the warmest decade and 1998 the warmest year.

The graph and its stark conclusion would prove invaluable when it came to marketing Kyoto - because Mann's stick was the most graspable

---

[1] http://www.ipcc.ch/ipccreports/tar/wg1/005.htm

visualization of the urgency. As Professor Wallace Smith Broecker told The Wall Street Journal[2]*:*

> Because the graph so neatly strengthened the case for man-made warming, Dr Broecker says, '**a lot of people grabbed that hockey stick.**'

Broecker, the man who coined the term "global warming", was now watching Mann reduce it to a cartoon. As Dr van Dorland commented in 2005[3]:

> It's really too definitive a statement. Truthfully, we are far from knowing with certainty how natural climate factors, such as volcanic eruptions and solar activity, affect the earth's climate. **The IPCC made a mistake by only including Mann's reconstruction and not those of other researchers...**"
>
> For now, I will consider it an isolated incident, but it is strange that the climate reconstruction of Mann has passed both peer review rounds of the IPCC without anyone ever really having checked it. I think this issue will be on the agenda of the next IPCC meeting in Peking this May.

Oddly enough it wasn't. But what exactly did Dr van Dorland mean by "peer review" in the context of the IPCC? "Peer review" at scientific journals means that every paper submitted gets reviewed by (generally) anonymous referees with expertise in the field. "Peer review" at the IPCC means something quite different: Reviewers propose changes and clarifications, which can be accepted or rejected. But control remains within a tight group under the charge of each chapter's "lead authors". In this case it meant that Contributing Author Mann got peer-reviewed by Lead Author Mann, which worked out swell for both of them.

---

[2] http://www.wsj.com/articles/SB110834031507653590
[3] http://www.uoguelph.ca/~rmckitri/research/Climate_H.pdf

34

"A reconstruction of the climate which Mr Mann created and which distorted too many people's views on climate."

PROFESSOR WIBJÖRN KARLÉN, PHD

Professor Emeritus of Physical Geography and Quaternary Geology at Stockholm University. Member of the Royal Swedish Academy of Sciences.

In 2011 Professor Karlén observed[1]:

The first of Mann's reconstructions of the temperature, which covered the period from the 15th century and up to 1980, were based on relatively few tree-ring series... The hockey stick was an important argument in the IPCC report, and Mann was given the responsibility for the paleoclimatology chapter of the IPCCs 2001 report. Of course, Mann's views on climate dominated it.

In "peer review" terms, it's as if Mann were simultaneously the author of the paper, the anonymous reviewer, and the editor-in-chief of Nature. He had never contributed to the IPCC reports before: indeed, at the time of the Second Assessment Report (1995), he did not yet have his PhD and was an unknown student. Yet, from never having served as a co-author or reviewer, Mann was instantly appointed to the most senior level of IPCC contributor. Great consequences flowed from this decision.

---

[1] http://old.theclimatescam.se/2011/11/02/the-hockey-stick-illusion/

Professor Karlén made his remarks above in the context of a review of A W Montford's exposé The Hockey Stick Illusion:

> This book provides a detailed picture of the efforts a large team of researchers put into defending the "hockey stick", a reconstruction of the climate which Mr Mann created and which distorted too many people's views on climate... The climate reconstruction has resulted in a number of policy decisions that are not justified.

The public - and even many political leaders - think the IPCC reports represent the "consensus" of thousands of experts compressed into one balanced overview. Not in the case of Mann's chapter. Ten years later Professor John Christy explained[2]:

> Regarding the Hockey Stick of IPCC 2001 evidence now indicates, in my view, that an IPCC Lead Author, working with a small cohort of scientists, **misrepresented the temperature record of the past thousand years** by (a) **promoting his own result** as the best estimate, (b) **neglecting studies that contradicted his**, and (c) **amputating another's result** so as to eliminate conflicting data and limit any serious attempt to expose the real uncertainties of these data.

The Lead Author in question was Michael E Mann.
     Who?
     "The rather unusual fact", as Christy put it, was that for the first time in IPCC history a critical chapter was under the control of a Lead Author who "had been awarded a PhD only a few months before".

---

[2] https://science.house.gov/sites/republicans.science.house.gov/files/documents/hearings/ChristyJR_written_110331_all.pdf

35

"[Mann] misrepresented the temperature record of the past 1,000 years."

PROFESSOR JOHN CHRISTY, PHD

Distinguished Professor of Atmospheric Science and Director of the Earth System Science Center at the University of Alabama in Huntsville. Recipient of NASA's Medal for Exceptional Scientific Achievement and the American Meteorological Society's Special Award for his role in developing the first successful satellite temperature record.

On March 31st 2011 Professor Christy testified before Congress and gave a glimpse of how Mann, as a "Lead Author" of the IPCC report that was to make him a star, "misrepresented the temperature record of the past thousand years" in order to promote his hockey stick[1]:

In our September 1999 meeting (Arusha, Tanzania) we were shown a plot containing more temperature curves than just the Hockey Stick including one from K Briffa that diverged significantly from the others, showing a sharp cooling trend after 1960. It raised the obvious problem that if tree rings were not detecting the modern warming trend, they might also have missed comparable warming episodes in the past. In other words, absence of the Medieval warming in the Hockey Stick graph might simply mean tree ring proxies are unreliable, not that the climate really was relatively cooler.

---

[1] https://science.house.gov/sites/republicans.science.house.gov/files/documents/hearings/ChristyJR_written_110331_all.pdf

The Briffa curve created disappointment for those who wanted "a nice tidy story"[2]... The LA [Michael E Mann] remarked in emails that he did not want to cast "doubt on our ability to understand factors that influence these estimates"... which would provide "fodder" to "skeptics"[3]... **One may interpret this to imply that being open and honest about uncertainties was not the purpose of this IPCC section.** Between this email (22 Sep 1999) and the next draft... two things happened: (a) the email referring to a "trick" to "hide the decline" for the preparation of report by the World Meteorological Organization was sent[4] (...referring to a splicing technique used by the LA [Mann] in which non-paleo data were merged to massage away a cooling dip at the last decades of the original Hockey Stick) and (b) the cooling portion of Briffa's curve had been truncated for the IPCC report (it is unclear as to who performed the truncation...)

So... data which contradicted the Hockey Stick, whose creator was the LA [Mann], had been eliminated. No one seemed to be alarmed (or in my case aware) that this had been done.

Procedures to guard against such manipulation of evidence are supposed to be in place whenever biases and conflicts of interest interfere with duties to report the whole truth, especially in assessments that have such potentially drastic policy implications.

Mann has never responded directly to Professor Christy's critique, but does like to sneer at him[5]:

> It takes some real hutzpah [sic] for John Christy to be criticizing other scientists.

---

[2] http://www.di2.nu/foia/0938031546.txt
[3] http://www.di2.nu/foia/0938018124.txt
[4] http://www.di2.nu/foia/0942777075.txt
[5] http://thinkprogress.org/climate/2014/07/17/3461320/john-christy-climate-change-dick-cheney-iraq/

36

"I never liked it that the 2001 IPCC report pictured Mann's without showing alternates... Mann is an outlier."

DR CURTIS C COVEY, PHD

Research Scientist at the Program for Climate Model Diagnosis and Intercomparison at the Lawrence Livermore National Laboratory. Author of "Vertical correlations of water vapor in GCMs" and "Intercomparison of climate data sets as a measure of observational uncertainty".

Not all climate scientists were happy with the prominence given to the hockey stick - or at least that's what they claimed with hindsight. On February 5th 2007 Dr Covey responded to an email from A-list "deniers" Viscount Monckton and Professor Fred Singer as follows[1]:

Re high-resolution paleodata, I never liked it that the 2001 IPCC report pictured Mann's without showing alternates. Phil's [sic] Jones' data was also available at the time. Focusing so exclusively on Mann was unfair in particular to Mann himself, who thereby became the sole target of criticism in *The Wall Street Journal*, etc.

It now seems clear from looking at all the different analyses (e.g. as summarized in last year's NRC review by North et al[2]) that Mann is an outlier though not egregiously so. Of course, like

---

[1] http://www.assassinationscience.com/climategate/1/FOIA/mail/1170724434.txt
[2] See page 151

any good scientist Mann argues that his methods get you closer to the truth than anyone else. But the bottom line for me is simply that all the different studies find that the rate of warming over the last 50-100 years is unusually high...

If you want to discuss any of this further, let me know. I attach my latest presentation - and would appreciate seeing both Christopher's report mentioned in the *Journal* editorial and Fred's comment on Rahmstorf's article published in *Science*...

Best regards,

Curt

Nothing wrong with a polite exchange with the other side is there?

Oh, dear. Having been copied on the above, Mann was not happy - and didn't stop to spell-check[3]:

Curt, I can't believe the nonsense you are spouting, and I furthermore cannot imagine why you would be so presumptuous as to entrain me into an exchange with these charlatans. What ib [sic] earth are you thinking? You're not even remotely correct in your reading of the report...

I find it terribly irresponsible for you to be sending messages like this to Singer and Monckton. You are speaking from ignorance here, and you must further know how your statements are going to be used. You could have sought some feedback from others who would have told you that you are speaking out of your depth on this. By instead simply blurting all of this nonsense out in an email to these sorts charlatans [sic] you've done some irreversible damage. **Shame on you for such irresponsible behavior!**

Mike Mann

---

[3] http://www.assassinationscience.com/climategate/1/FOIA/mail/1170724434.txt

37
"Even I fell for this hockey stick."

PROFESSOR FRITZ VAHRENHOLT, PHD

Professor of Chemistry at the University of Hamburg. Member of the Sustainability Advisory Board to Chancellors Angela Merkel and Gerhard Schröder. Former Principal of the City of Hamburg Environmental Ministry, Head of the Department of Environmental Policy, Waste Management and Air Pollution Control at the Hessian Ministry of Regional Development. Former researcher at the University of Munster, the Max Planck Institute for Carbon Research, and the German Federal Environmental Agency.

On June 13th 2012, at the Royal Society in London, Professor Vahrenholt delivered the annual Global Warming Policy Foundation lecture. He described well the spectacular rise of Mann's stick[1]:

How often has this hockey stick been used as proof for the anthropogenic causes of climate change in recent years! Al Gore used the hockey stick in his infamous film *The Inconvenient Truth*. Thousands of copies of this film were bought by the German Environment Minister to be shown to school children. Countless school children have been dragged into cinemas to watch this film. And even I fell for this hockey stick.

We now know, thanks to Steve McIntyre and Ross McKitrick, that the statistical methods used by Michael Mann were flawed, and that many of the used tree-ring data were questionable. The hockey stick had only one goal: to show that the temperature was flat - as the handle of a hockey stick - for centuries and only rose steeply because of the CO_2 emissions of the industrial age.

---

[1] http://kaltesonne.de/wp-content/uploads/2012/10/vahrenholt-2012-annual-gwpf-lecture_new.pdf

We all should have been more sceptical. Where in the hockey stick was the Little Ice Age of the 16th to 18th centuries, when it was bitterly cold in Europe and the successors of the Swedish king, Gustav Adolf, could carry out their conquests by marching on foot across the frozen Baltic Sea to Denmark..? Famines dominated Europe, and on the frozen Thames winter fairs took place. The Breughelschen pictures of Dutch winters are evidence of this. We know today that it must have been as much as 2 ° Celsius colder than currently.

And where in the hockey stick graph was the Medieval Warm Period, when Erik the Red settled Greenland ...and for 100 years a high culture developed? Recently, the retreating glaciers have released the remains of the bishop's see of that time. And Norwegian scientists told me that recently drinking water wells from that period have been found which are frozen in the lower part. It must therefore have been warmer in Greenland 1,000 years ago than today.

At the 2012 Swiss Energy & Climate Summit in Bern, Professor Vahrenholt debated Thomas Stocker[2]. As Pierre L Gosselin reported it[3]:

Vahrenholt presents the infamous Michael Mann hockey stick graph and says **"this graphic has been shown to be false, and was even in part faked..."**

When asked why he went from being a warmist to a skeptic, Vahrenholt said he found too many things that didn't fit and was surprised to discover that **Mann's stick was phony.** Examining the science more closely, he found that many things just didn't add up.

---

[2] https://www.youtube.com/watch?feature=player_embedded&v=OrGNh4JEBb0
[3] http://notrickszone.com/2012/09/18/vahrenholt-provokes-stocker-by-calling-manns-hockey-stick-a-fake/#sthash.i3e9UC90.9980PhdR.dpbs

38

"What Mike Mann continually fails to understand ...is that there is practically no reliable tropical data... We have no way of knowing how cold (or warm) the globe actually got."

DR DAVID H RIND, PHD

Emeritus Professor at NASA's Goddard Institute for Space Studies. Adjunct Senior Research Scientist at Columbia University's Center for Climate Systems Research. Author of peer-reviewed papers published by *Nature*, *Science* and other journals.

Professor Tony Brown said that Mann's reconstructed planetary "average" is "possibly representative of no climate state that actually ever existed". As a general rule, whenever a paper sets out to reconstruct the climate in an actual, specific place it finds proof of a Medieval Warm Period. Yet Mann declared on the basis of a couple of proxies here and there that it was not a "global" phenomenon. Nor, in fact, was his hockey stick. It was a Northern Hemisphere reconstruction, although it was assumed to be (and not so subtly promoted as) a representation of "global" warming. Yet even his colleagues knew that, for many parts of the world, it stated something that could not be known. On April 27th 2005, Dr Rind emailed fellow climate scientists Jonathan Overpeck and Eystein Jansen re the upcoming IPCC Fourth Assessment Review[1]:

---

[1] http://di2.nu/foia/foia2011/mail/4133.txt

Hi Jonathan and Eystein...

Concerning the hockey stick (which took up probably three-quarters of the review pages!): what Mike Mann continually fails to understand, and no amount of references will solve, is that there is practically no reliable tropical data for most of the time period, and without knowing the tropical sensitivity, we have no way of knowing how cold (or warm) the globe actually got... Therefore the detailed comments Mike provides concerning the extratropical issues - how much does snow cover alter the ground temperature versus the surface air temperature - are to some extent beside the point. **I've made the comment to Mike several times, but it doesn't seem to get across** - during the 20th century, according to Jim Hansen's temperature reconstruction, the tropical warming has been 60 per cent of that in the extra-tropics (and that includes the amplifying AO/NAO extra-tropical change). I believe that in Mike's reconstruction, it averages about 30 per cent. How well we know the numbers for the first part of this century is also somewhat uncertain, so I can't say Mike is wrong - but the point is, I don't know that he's right, nor do I think anybody else knows either.

So what should we do about it? Basically I think we should indicate that there are conflicting views concerning the actual global climate change during this time period - quote the references (including the ones Mike provides), note that there are uncertainties concerning the magnitude of the extratropical response, and that there is a paucity of tropical data - and leave it at that. Unsatisfying, perhaps, since people will want to know whether 1200 AD was warmer than today, but **if the data doesn't exist, the question can't yet be answered.** A good topic for needed future work.

39

"Why did the IPCC so quickly and uncritically accept the hockey stick..? Because they wanted to believe it."

DR ROY SPENCER, PHD

Principal Research Scientist at the University of Alabama in Huntsville and US Science Team leader for the Advanced Microwave Scanning Radiometer on NASA's Aqua satellite. Recipient (with John Christy) of the Exceptional Scientific Achievement Award from NASA and the American Meteorological Society's Special Award for his work in satellite-based temperature monitoring. Formerly Senior Scientist for Climate Studies at NASA's Marshall Space Flight Center.

So, if "we have no way of knowing how cold (or warm) the globe actually got", how did the IPCC know it's hotter than it's been for a thousand years? On January 27th 2005 Dr Spencer wrote[1]:

As you might imagine, it's a little difficult to construct a temperature history for a period of record that, for the most part, had no reliable thermometer measurements. Since good thermometer measurements extend back to only around the mid-1800s, "proxy" measurements, primarily tree ring data, have been used to extend the temperature record back additional centuries... The claim of unprecedented warmth and the hockey stick shape appear to hinge on the treatment of one species of tree, the bristlecone pine, from North America in the 1400s. Further

---

[1] http://www.sepp.org/twtwfiles/2005/Feb.%2012.htm

statistical tests showed that this critical signal in the early 15th century lacked statistical significance. This suggests that **the results of Mann et al were simply a statistical fluke**, which greatly exaggerated a characteristic of the bristlecone pines, which may or may not be related to global temperatures.

The original Mann et al article has had huge repercussions. The hockey stick, along with the "warmest in 1,000 years" argument, has become a central theme of debates over the Kyoto Protocol, a treaty to limit emissions of greenhouse gases, in governments around the world. The question begging to be answered is: Why did the IPCC so quickly and uncritically accept the Mann et al hockey stick analysis when it first appeared? I cannot help but conclude that it's because they wanted to believe it.

Dr Spencer pointed out what should have been obvious - that the hockey stick had never been subjected to one of the most basic tests of science:

Unusual claims in science should be met with unusual skepticism, and this did not happen with the Mann et al study. An increasing number of researchers have anecdotal evidence that the science tabloids, *Nature* and *Science*, select reviewers of some manuscripts based upon whether they want those papers to be accepted or rejected. In other words, it seems like the conclusions of a paper are sometimes more important that the scientific basis for those conclusions. Since those periodicals have profit and popularity motives that normal scientific journals do not, maybe the time has come to downgrade the scientific weight of publications in those journals, at least for some purposes...

It will be interesting to see if the IPCC, and its member countries, continue to rally around the hockey stick, or discard it.

40

"Environment Canada and others continue to use this graph as if it were still valid. It is not."

DR TIM PATTERSON, PHD

Professor of Geology at Carleton University's Department of Earth Sciences and International Fellow in the School of Geography, Archaeology and Palaeoecology at Queen's University, Belfast. Chairman of the International Climate Science Coalition. Former Canadian leader of the International Geological Correlation Programme. Former associate editor of *The Journal of Foraminiferal Research* and of *Micropaleontology*, and founding editor of *Palaeontologia Electronica*.

"Discarding" the hockey stick, as Dr Spencer put it, was easier said than done. The activists and the politicians and the bureaucrats loved it. On February 10th 2005 Professor Patterson gave evidence to the Standing Committee on Environment and Sustainable Development of the Canadian House of Commons, and said this about Mann's iconic graph[1]:

The Intergovernmental Panel on Climate Change, the IPCC, used this study as a major prop. Now that prop is gone, yet Environment Canada and others continue to use this graph as if it were still valid. It is not...

The blue line is one of the primary pieces of evidence used by the IPCC to promote the idea that the 20th century warming

[1] http://www.parl.gc.ca/HousePublications/Publication.aspx?DocId=
1623904&Language=E&Mode=1&Parl=38&Ses=1

was unprecedented in the past millennium. This line has become known as the hockey stick. The shaft of the stick is the supposedly relatively lower temperatures for the first 900 years of the period, and the blade of the stick is the reputed sudden temperature rise of the past century. The red line in figure 1 is **the result you get when the data and the methodology used to produce the hockey stick are applied correctly.** As you can see, there's an enormous difference between the two curves prior to about 1500 AD.

If Canada's government is to base climate policy on real science, then it must accept that its policy decisions should be changeable as climate science advances. Otherwise, policy becomes disconnected from science, and we may waste billions of dollars going in entirely the wrong direction.

Until we have a far better understanding of the underlying science, the government should cancel funding allocated to stopping climate change, which is ridiculous. The only constant about climate is change. Instead, we should be preparing for whatever nature throws at us next, as well as continuing to fund research that will help us to eventually understand our planet's complex climate system.

Thank you, Mr Chairman and committee members. I look forward to answering any questions you may have.

But weaning governments and bureaucracies off Mann's invalid graph was easier said than done. As far as the hockey stick was concerned, the science wasn't just settled, it was frozen - in place.

V

Mann of integrity

THE ABOLITION OF UNCERTAINTY

Be wary of any science that loathes statistics or resents external investigation. That's the start of rot.[1]
DR BARRY COOKE, PHD
EMAIL TO DR MARYANNE NEWTON OF CORNELL UNIVERSITY'S
WIENER LABORATORY FOR AEGEAN AND NEAR EASTERN
DENDROCHRONOLOGY AT CORNELL UNIVERSITY (2006)

---

[1] http://www.ecowho.com/foia.php?file=1153172761.txt

FOR THE FIRST few years, everything went swimmingly. And then the hockey stick caught the eye of a mining engineer fiendishly good at statistics. The rap on Stephen McIntyre is that he's "not a climate scientist". As Dr Lars Kamél observes mordantly, "In the infected science of climate research, this may be an advantage rather than a disadvantage."[2]

Besides, Mr McIntyre is a citizen and taxpayer of Canada, and Her Majesty's Government in Ottawa was proposing to alter significantly the economic landscape of the nation by signing up to Kyoto. In free societies, the people bear the ultimate responsibility for public policy, and, when that policy is being determined by what purports to be "science", they certainly have the right to examine that science - especially when, as with the hockey stick, the science is promoted largely because of its potential public-policy impact.

Nevertheless, one shares the concern of the climate-science peer-review fetishists that it should require two Torontonian dilettantes to speak truth to hockey-stick power. Where was everybody else? As we shall see, the doubts, suspicions and even specific criticisms of McIntyre & McKitrick were shared by many of Mann's closest colleagues. As Dr David Rind put it:

> *When something is uncertain we should say it. I know uncertainty lies in the eyes of the beholder, but I think it will also be found in the eyes of the reviewers, and here I would suggest a democratic approach -* **let's not use one person's dogmatic view***, but by quoting what the community thinks (as in the case of solar forcing), let the uncertainty be made apparent[3].*

---

[2] http://sciliterature.50webs.com/Climate/HockeyStick.html
[3] http://di2.nu/foia/foia2011/mail/4133.txt

Mann and the Hockey Team were in no mood for that. So "one person's dogmatic view" prevailed.

Yet from the earliest days even core members of the Hockey Team never subscribed to Mann's grotesque simplification. That Medieval Warm Period he got rid of? Ask Professor Keith Briffa:

> *I believe that* **the recent warmth was probably matched about 1000 years ago.** *I do not believe that global mean annual temperatures have simply cooled progressively over thousands of years as Mike appears to.*[4]

Briffa, like most of Mann's early collaborators, was older and more experienced. But his "uncertainties" about the hockey stick's central conclusions counted for naught in the face of the younger man's sudden eminence. An even closer colleague, and co-author of Mann's first two hockey sticks, Malcolm Bradley was also concerned about "uncertainties":

> *All of our attempts, so far, to estimate hemisphere-scale temperatures for the period around 1000 years ago are based on* **far fewer data than any of us would like.** *None of the datasets used so far has anything like the geographical distribution that experience with recent centuries indicates we need, and no one has yet found a convincing way of validating the lower-frequency components of them against independent data. As Ed wrote, in the tree-ring records that form the backbone of most of the published estimates, the problem of* **poor replication** *near the beginnings of records is particularly acute, and ubiquitous. I would suggest that this problem probably cuts in closer to 1600 than 1400 in the several*

---

[4] http://www.ecowho.com/foia.php?file=4872.txt&search=rather+self-indulgent+ramble

*published series. Therefore, I accept that **everything we are doing is preliminary**, and should be treated with considerable caution.*[5]

Mann didn't need these complications and wasn't interested in them. The point of his work was to bolster the IPCC's takeaway: This is the hottest year of the hottest decade of the hottest century since centuries were invented - and he didn't want any dithering about "uncertainties" getting in the way.

Instead, what got in the way were Steve McIntyre and Ross McKitrick. In the Climategate correspondence, the obsession with the dogged but affable and unfailingly polite McIntyre is bizarre - if, that is, Mann et al had been confident in their science. Mr McIntyre lives in the same Toronto neighborhood as Rachel McAdams[6], co-star of *Mean Girls*, and a whiff of high-school mean-girliness permeates the East Anglia emails: McIntyre wants to bust into the cool girls' club, but they think his weird obsession with PCA and stuff is so not fetch.

Other parties were less dismissive. On its face, the McIntyre & McKitrick case had merit, and at the senior levels of the Big Climate bureaucracy - both scientific and governmental - key figures demanded to know from the climatologists whether Mann had got it wrong.

The answers were revealing - if only they'd thought to share them with us.

And so Dr Barry Cooke was right. Mann's resentment and obstruction of external investigation was, indeed, "the start of rot" - for climate science, and beyond.

---

[5] http://junkscience.com/2011/12/02/climategate-2-0-hughes-hokey-stick-should-be-treated-with-considerable-caution/

[6] See his letter here: http://www.steynonline.com/6724/the-limitations-of-lawyers

41

"I don't think they are scientifically inadequate or stupid. I think they are dishonest."

DR EUGENE I GORDON, PHD

Physicist, and former director of the Lightwaves Devices Laboratory of Bell Labs. Fellow of the Institute of Electrical and Electronics Engineers, and recipient of its Edison Medal and Vladimir K Zworykin Award. Founder of the IEEE Quantum Electronics Council and *The Journal of Quantum Electronics*. Inventor of the continuous argon ion laser. Member of the National Academy of Engineering.

Climate science decided to take a wild ride on the hockey stick, and for a while it worked. But it was never likely that a hitherto obscure researcher could "repeal the Medieval Warm Period" (and, indeed, the very concept of natural variability) and that somebody someday wouldn't be sufficiently curious as to try to figure out how he did it. When the questions began, the core "climate community" made the worst decision in its relatively brief history and decided to dig in.

Since then, the broader realm of science has been divided over whether the hockey team were simply foolish and insecure, or not very good at their jobs ...or duplicitous skunks. Dr Gordon was in no doubt where he came down. On October 4th 2009, a few weeks before *the Climategate leaks, he received an email from Alan White detailing more shenanigans around what he called the "hokey hockey sticks". Dr Gordon replied[1]:*

---

[1] https://groups.google.com/forum/#!topic/geoengineering/8SGhSo8mLhM

Alan:

Thanks for the extensive and detailed e-mail. This is terrible but not surprising. Obviously I do not know what gives with these guys. However, I have my own suspicions and hypothesis. I don't think they are scientifically inadequate or stupid. I think they are dishonest and members of a club that has much to gain by practicing and perpetuating global warming scare tactics. That is not to say that global warming is not occurring to some extent since it would be even without CO_2 emissions. The CO_2 emissions only accelerate the warming and there are other factors controlling climate. As a result, the entire process may be going slower than the powers that be would like. Hence, (I postulate) the global warming contingent has **substantial motivation to be dishonest or seriously biased**, and to be loyal to their equally dishonest club members. Among the motivations are increased and continued grant funding, university advancement, job advancement, profits and payoffs from carbon control advocates such as Gore, being in the limelight, and other motivating factors I am too inexperienced to identify.

Alan, this is nothing new... Humans are hardly perfect creations. I am never surprised at what they can do. I am perpetually grateful for those who are honest and fair and thankfully there is a goodly share of those.

-gene

One can have different views on whether Mann and his colleagues were "scientifically inadequate or stupid" or simply "dishonest". But, from the first attempt by outsiders to "replicate" the stick, they were obstructive and abusive to a degree rarely seen in science.

42

"You're on very dodgy ground with this long-term decline in temperatures."

PROFESSOR PHIL JONES, PHD

Director of the Climatic Research Unit and Professor in the School of Environmental Sciences at the University of East Anglia. Fellow of the American Meteorological Society and the American Geophysical Union. Member of the editorial board of *Climatic Change* and formerly of *The International Journal of Climatology*. Recipient of the Royal Meteorological Scociety's Mill Prize, the World Meteorological Organization's Norbert Gerbier-MUMM International Award, and the European Geosciences Union's Oeschger Medal.

Professor Jones was, next to Mann, the key figure in the Climategate emails, in his role as Mann's closest ally at the Climatic Research Unit. But the two men weren't always that amicable. On May 6th 1999 Professor Jones wrote to Michael E Mann noting that "you seem quite pissed off with us all in CRU", and complaining that Mann had gone behind their backs "slanging us all off to Science". (This is presumably a mis-typing of the British vernacular "slagging us off" - ie, badmouthing someone.) Jones then adds[1]:

1) Keith [Briffa] didn't mention in his *Science* piece but both of us think that you're on very dodgy ground with this long-term decline in temperatures on the thousand-year timescale. What the real world has done over the last 6,000 years and what it

---

[1] http://junkscience.com/2011/11/28/climategate-2-0-jones-briffa-say-mann-hokey-stick-on-dodgy-ground/

ought to have done given our understanding of Milankovic forcing[2] are two very different things. I don't think the world was much warmer 6,000 years ago - in a global sense compared to the average of the last one 1,000 years, but this is my opinion and I may change it given more evidence.

2) The errors don't include all the possible factors. Even though the tree-ring chronologies used have robust rbar statistics for the whole thousand years (ie they lose nothing because core numbers stay high throughout), they have lost low frequency because of standardization. We've all tried with RCS/very stiff splines/hardly any detrending to keep this to a minimum, but until we know it is minimal it is still worth mentioning. **It is better we (I mean all of us here) put the caveats in ourselves than let others put them in for us.**

But in Mannworld "caveats" were subordinate to what he called "the cause". Once you've abolished the concept of natural variability, is it really so difficult to then abolish the concept of "uncertainty"? Under the hockey stick regime, certainty was the order of the day - even if, behind the scenes, some of Mann's Hockey Team were extremely uncertain of what he was doing, and what they were going along with. Post-Climategate, a chastened Jones was asked by the BBC why scientists keep insisting that "the debate on climate change is over"[3]:

I don't believe the vast majority of climate scientists think this. This is not my view. There is still much that needs to be undertaken to reduce uncertainties.

---

[2] Milankovitch forcing is the impact on climate of variations in the tilt of the Earth's axis and shape of the orbit, which change the amount of sunlight that reaches us down here. "Forcing" is climate-speak for any physical process that affects the climate.

[3] http://news.bbc.co.uk/2/hi/8511670.stm

43

"I am sick to death of Mann."

PROFESSOR KEITH BRIFFA, PHD

Emeritus Professor and former Deputy Director of the Climatic Research Unit at the University of East Anglia. Lead author of Chapter Six (Paleoclimatology) of Working Group I of the IPCC's Fourth Assessment Report (2007) Former associate editor of *Boreas, Dendrochronologia* and *Holocene.*

Keith Briffa is one of many believers in global warming who got mixed up with Michael E Mann in the wake of his meteoric rise and came to regret it. In the report by NOAA (the US National Oceanic and Atmospheric Administration) that Mann falsely claims "exonerates" him[1], Professor Briffa is quoted as warning a fellow scientist not to let "Mike" "push you (us) beyond where we know is right"[2].

Briffa knew whereof he spoke: pushing people beyond where he knows is right is what Michael Mann has done all his life. On June 17th 2002 Briffa emailed Dr Edward Cook at the Tree-Ring Laboratory of the Lamont-Doherty Earth Observatory in response to a recently published letter by Mann[3]:

I have just read this letter - and **I think it is crap**. I am sick to death of Mann stating his reconstruction represents the tropical area just because it contains a few (poorly temperature representative) tropical series. He is just as capable of regressing these data again[sic] any other "target" series, such as the **increasing trend of self-opinionated verbiage he has produced**

---

[1] http://www.oig.doc.gov/OIGPublications/2011.02.18-IG-to-Inhofe.pdf
[2] http://di2.nu/foia/foia2011/mail/4871.txt
[3] http://www.di2.nu/foia/1024334440.txt

over the last few years, and... (better say no more)
Keith

That statement's as contemptuous of his colleague as anything by any big-time denier: as Professor Briffa sees it, the real hockey stick is the rise in Mann's "self-opinionated verbiage". Dr Cook replied:

Of course, I agree with you. **We both know the probable flaws in Mike's recon**, particularly as it relates to the tropical stuff. Your response is also why I chose not to read the published version of his letter. It would be too aggravating. The only way to deal with this whole issue is to show in a detailed study that **his estimates are clearly deficient** in multi-centennial power, something that you actually did in your Perspectives piece, even if it was not clearly stated because of editorial cuts. **It is puzzling to me that a guy as bright as Mike would be so unwilling to evaluate his own work a bit more objectively.**
Ed

As "sick to death of Mann" as he was in 2002, Professor Briffa would grow a lot sicker of him in the years ahead, before, weary of getting pushed around by Mann "beyond where we know is right", he began pushing back. His recent papers, for example, have "rediscovered" the Medieval Warm Period that the hockey stick supposedly abolished.

Nevertheless, when you read the Climategate emails, Briffa and his CRU colleagues in East Anglia sound like battered wives - reeling from the latest slap but unable to bring themselves to walk out.

44

"Mike is defending something that increasingly cannot be defended."

PROFESSOR EDWARD R COOK, PHD

Ewing Lamont Research Professor and Director of the Tree-Ring Research Laboratory at Columbia University's Lamont-Doherty Earth Observatory. Fellow of the American Geophysical Union.

The least contentious part of Mann's thousand-year reconstruction is the latter half-millennium: Long before he was born, it was received wisdom that there was a Little Ice Age followed by a return to warmer temperatures. But the early centuries were a more controversial business, and, in private at least, even his closest colleagues were not happy with it. On April 3rd 2002 Professor Cook wrote to Professor Tim Osborn in East Anglia re problems with the pre-1400 part of Mann's work[1]:

Hi Tim,

I will be sure not to bring this up to Mike. As you know, **he thinks that CRU is out to get him** in some sense. So, a very carefully worded and described bit by you and Keith will be important. I am afraid that Mike is defending something that increasingly cannot be defended. **He is investing too much personal stuff in this and not letting the science move ahead.** I am afraid that he is losing out in the process. That is too bad.

Cheers,

Ed

---

[1] http://di2.nu/foia/foia2011/mail/4369.txt

A year later - September 3rd 2003 - Professor Cook wrote to Keith Briffa proposing a new paper[2]:

Hi Keith,

> After the meeting in Norway, where I presented the Esper stuff as described in the extended abstract I sent you, and hearing Bradley's follow-up talk on how everybody but him has fucked up in

reconstructing past NH temperatures over the past 1000 years (this is a bit of an overstatement on my part I must admit, but his air of papal infallibility is really quite nauseating at times), I have come up with an idea that I want you to be involved in. Consider the tentative title:

Northern Hemisphere Temperatures Over The Past Millennium: Where Are The Greatest Uncertainties?

Authors: Cook, Briffa, Esper, Osborn, D'Arrigo, Bradley(?), Jones (??), Mann (infinite?) - I am afraid the [sic] **Mike and Phil are too personally invested in things now (i.e. the 2003 GRL paper that is probably the worst paper Phil has ever been involved in** - Bradley hates it as well), but I am willing to offer to include them if they can contribute without just defending their past work - this is the key to having anyone involved. Be honest. Lay it all out on the table and don't start by assuming that ANY reconstruction is better than any other.

Needless to say, nothing came of that idea.

---

[2] http://www.assassinationscience.com/climategate/1/FOIA/mail/1062592331.txt

45

"At the very least MBH is a very sloppy piece of work."

PROFESSOR TOM WIGLEY, PHD

DORA Fellow in Ecology and Environmental Science at the University of Adelaide. Fellow of the American Association for the Advancement of Science. Former Director of the Climatic Research Unit at the University of East Anglia, and Senior Scientist at the US National Center for Atmospheric Research. IPCC contributing author.

Professor Wigley was hired by Hubert Lamb, founder of the Climatic Research Unit, to be his successor. One would like to think he had some misgivings at the way the CRU were co-opted by Mann to trash Dr Lamb's legacy. He certainly had concerns about treemometers and other proxy data. In 1996, long before anyone had heard of Mann or his hockey stick, Professor Wigley wrote to colleagues (including hockey-stick co-authors-to-be Raymond Bradley and Malcolm Hughes) to raise certain issues[1]:

How useful are paleodata? I support the continued collection of such data, but I am disturbed by how some people in the paleo community try to oversell their product.

He then identified a number of proxy data issues, including the reliability of tree rings, ice cores, sedimentary records, seasonal specificity and signal-to-noise. For example:

---

[1] http://www.wsj.com/articles/
SB10001424052748704779704574553652849094482

(a) Sedimentary records - dating. Are 14C-dated records of any value at all..?

(b) Seasonal specificity - how useful is a proxy record that tells us about a single season (or only part of the year)..?

(e) Frequency dependence of explained variance---the classic example here is tree rings, where it is exceedingly difficult to get out a credible low frequency (50+ year time scale) message.

Professor Wigley could not have foreseen that the paleo "product" would be so "oversold" that it would swallow climate science whole. When McIntyre & McKitrick itemized specific problems with Mann's work of the kind he had raised more generally back in 1996, Wigley was sympathetic - if only in private. On October 21st 2004 he emailed his own successor as head of the CRU, Phil Jones[2]:

Phil,

I have just read the M&M stuff critcizing MBH. A lot of it seems valid to me.

At the very least MBH is a very sloppy piece of work - an opinion I have held for some time.

Presumably what you have done with Keith is better? Or is it?

I get asked about this a lot. Can you give me a brief heads up? **Mike is too deep into this to be helpful.**

Tom

---

[2] http://assassinationscience.com/climategate/1/FOIA/mail/1098472400.txt

46

"Is this true? If so, it constitutes a devastating criticism."

DR JONATHAN OVERPECK, PHD

Director of the Environmental Studies Laboratory at the University of Arizona's Department of Geosciences. Formerly with the University of Colorado in a similar capacity, and with Columbia University and the NASA Goddard Institute for Space Studies.

Tom Wigley was not the only colleague of Mann alarmed by McIntyre & McKitrick's critique of the hockey stick. On January 4th 2005 Dr Overpeck emailed Keith Briffa[1]:

The primary criticism of McIntyre & McKitrick, which has gotten a lot of play on the Internet, is that Mann et al transformed each tree ring prior to calculating PCs by subtracting the 1902-1980 mean, rather than using the length of the full time series (e.g., 1400-1980), as is generally done. M&M claim that **when they used that procedure with a red noise spectrum, it always resulted in a "hockey stick"**. Is this true? If so, it constitutes a devastating criticism of the approach...

It is, indeed, a "devastating criticism". But the concern expressed in private by Dr Overpeck is in striking contrast to his public statements. For example, three weeks after the above email - January 24th 2005 - he gave an interview to Michelle Nijhuis of The High Country News[2]:

Overpeck says paleoclimatologists around the world are working

---

[1] http://www.di2.nu/foia/1104893567.txt
[2] https://www.hcn.org/issues/290/15219

to "create a new icon," one based on more tree rings and other proxies. Still, he expects the principal findings of the hockey stick to endure. "The real truth won't look exactly like the hockey stick, but the hockey stick got us so close," he says. "It brought us so much further towards reality than any other study."

Later that year Dr Overpeck gave the prestigious Bjerknes Lecture at the American Geophysical Union's fall meeting. He concluded his presentation with a jocular throwaway[3]:

You didn't really believe what I said, did you?

Actually, it's an interesting question. Even among the most loyal members of the Hockey Team, there were huge misgivings in private, yet ever more bluster in public. If this were simply one graph, one paper, then "devastating criticism" would be bad news for Mann, but no one else. As Dr Kevin Vranes wrote on November 18th 2005[4]:

The HS debate is about the credibility of Drs Mann/Bradley/Hughes (but mostly Dr Mann...)

But Mann had bet otherwise. It's the cli-sci version of the old debt joke: If you owe the bank a thousand dollars, you have a problem; if you owe the bank a million dollars, they have a problem. If you owe your credibility to one damaged paper in a scientific journal, you have a problem. If you owe your credibility to your paper's enthusiastic support from Sir John Houghton, Al Gore, the IPCC, western governments and the rest of the transnational climate-change establishment, then they have a problem.

And so they decided instead that the stick had to be defended.

---

[3] http://www.agu.org/webcast/FM2005/bjerknes/launch.html
[4] http://cstpr.colorado.edu/prometheus/archives/climate_change/000638ipcc_hockey_stick_ma.html

47

"I say to Dr Mann... your job is not to prevent your critics from checking your work."

DR KEVIN VRANES, PHD
PhD in ocean and climate physics from Columbia University.

By 2005, Mann's reaction to routine queries was beginning to strike even supporters of the AGW hypothesis as ...odd. On February 18th that year, four days after a Wall Street Journal *article on the hockey stick by Antonio Regalado[1], Dr Vranes considered the matter at the Science & Technology website of the University of Colorado at Boulder[2]:*

The WSJ is still asking – and trying to answer – the basic questions: hockey stick or no hockey stick? But the background premise of the article, stated explicitly and implicitly throughout, is that it was the hockey stick that led to Kyoto and other climate policy. Is it?

Dr Vranes thought "the notion that Kyoto is based on the Mann curve is utter nonsense" - although Stephen McIntyre and citizens of other western nations where the stick played a big part in Kyoto-promoting might beg to differ. However, Vranes conceded that, if policy makers are indeed relying "solely on the Mann curve to prove definitively the existence of anthropogenic warming, then we're in deeper trouble than

---

[1] http://www.wsj.com/articles/SB110834031507653590
[2] http://cstpr.colorado.edu/prometheus/archives/climate_change/000355open_season_on_hocke.html

115

anybody realizes":

But maybe we are in that much trouble. The WSJ highlights what Regalado and McIntyre says is Mann's resistance or outright refusal to provide to inquiring minds his data, all details of his statistical analysis, and his code. The WSJ's anecdotal treatment of the subject goes toward **confirming what I've been hearing for years in climatology circles about not just Mann**, but others collecting original climate data.

Dr Vranes agrees that there are problems with "peer review":

For that matter, why does Table 1 in Mann et al (1999) list many chronologies in the Southern Hemisphere while the rest of the paper promotes a Northern Hemisphere reconstruction? Legit or not, it's a confusing aspect of the paper that **should never have made it past peer review...**

So this is what I say to Dr Mann..: **give up your data, methods and code freely** and with a smile on your face. That is real peer review. A 12-year-old hacker prodigy in her grandparents' basement should have as much opportunity to check your work as a "semi-retired Toronto minerals consultant." Those without three letters after their name can be every bit as intellectually qualified, and will likely have the time for careful review that typical academic reviewers find lacking.

Specious analysis of your work will be borne out by your colleagues, and will enter the debate with every other original work. Your job is not to prevent your critics from checking your work and potentially distorting it; your job is to continue to publish insightful, detailed analyses of the data and let the community decide. **You can be part of the debate without seeming to hinder access to it.**

48

"I am not forced to assume good faith of criminals and the people who don't follow the rules of scientific integrity."

DR LUBOŠ MOTL, PHD

Theoretical physicist and string theorist who, while still an undergraduate at a Czech university with no specialists in the subject, "scooped" Rutgers string expert Professor Tom Banks with a paper on matrix string theory. Author of *L'Équation Bogdanov: Le secret de l'origine de l'Univers?*, and of peer-reviewed papers published in *The Journal of High Energy Physics*, *Advances in Theoretical and Mathematical Physics*, and other journals. Former assistant professor at Harvard University.

Not everyone was as restrained as Dr Vranes. But, in a glimpse of the Hockey Team's reach, over at Wikipedia (the "authoritative" Internet encyclopedia), William M Connolley, a UK Green Party activist, appointed himself Guardian of the Stick when it came to vacuuming criticism and chastising dissidents. In February 2005, in a backstage discussion re how to characterize the hockey stick, Dr Motl was blunt[1]:

This article needs attention. **The discredited theories of "hockey stick" created by the "hockey team"** should be rewritten as a historical discussion of the myths that were believed at various points.

Mr Connolley responded:

---

[1] http://en.wikipedia.org/?title=Talk:Temperature_record_of_the_past_1000_ years/Archive_1#Hockey_Stick_disinformation

Thank you for making your biases so obvious.

Dr Motl replied:

You may call it "biases", but the more important thing is that it is reality... What the "hockey team" has done is very serious... I am not forced to assume good faith of criminals and the people who don't follow the rules of scientific integrity.

Nor would he. Even before Climategate, Dr Motl had delivered a brutal assessment of Mann's 2008 version of his hockey stick[2]:

It seems that the paper is **not only a case of sub-prime science but an example of scientific fraud.**

Dr Motl noted that for his 2008 stick Mann had used 55 data sets that showed an upward sweep in the late 20th century - but rejected another 64 data sets that showed a downward curve in the late 20th century:

Wow, it's just amazing.

The numbers 55 and 64 are pretty large. Don't tell me that you will get these two qualitatively different curves by averaging "random" subsets of the datasets... The "convenient" datasets were clearly chosen by hand while the "inconvenient" ones were manually thrown away.

If this is not fraud, what is?

After Climategate, Mann threatened to sue a Minnesota website over a satirical "hide the decline" music video. Dr Motl responded by linking to a Czech version and reminded the litigious hockey-sticker[3]:

We have the freedom of speech in Czechia, especially when it comes to nasty gangsters of Mann's caliber.

---

[2] http://motls.blogspot.com/2008/09/jeff-id-cherry-picking-in-new-hockey.html
[3] http://motls.blogspot.com/2010/04/robbert-dijkgraaf-climategate-unrelated.html

49

"Is the PCA approach robust? Are the results statistically significant? It seems to me that in the case of MBH the answer in each is no."

DR JOHN MITCHELL, OBE, FRS, PHD

Chief Scientist at the United Kingdom Met Office. Chair of the Working Group on Climate Modelling of the World Meteorological Organization's Joint Scientific Committee on Climate Variability. Officer of the Most Excellent Order of the British Empire and Fellow of the Royal Society. Recipient of the Hans Oeschger Medal from the European Geosciences Union and the Norbert Gerbier-MUMM Prize from the World Meteorological Organization.

Dr Mitchell is said to be the most cited scientist in the world on the subject of global warming. In June 2006, he emailed Jonathan Overpeck, Eystein Jansen, Keith Briffa and Tim Osborn regarding questions that "need to be addressed" about the hockey stick[1]:

I am in Geneva at the WMO EC meeting, so I have not had a lot of time to look at the SOD[2] comments. I cannot get to Bergen before Tuesday. I had a quick look at the comments on the hockey stick and include below the questions I think need to be addressed which I hope will help the discussions. I do tbelieve [sic] we need a clear answer to the skeptics.

---

[1] http://www.assassinationscience.com/climategate/1/FOIA/mail/1150923423.txt
[2] The Second Order Draft of the IPCC's Fourth Assessment Report, published the following year

These were the questions Professor Mitchell wanted addressed:

1. There needs to be a clear statement of why the instrumental and proxy data are shown on the same graph. **The issue of why we don't show the proxy data for the last few decades (they don't show continued warming) but assume that they are valid for early warm periods needs to be explained.**

2. There are number of methodological issues which need a clear response. There are two aspects to this. First, in relation to the TAR and MBA [sic - presumably MBH] which seems to be the obsession of certain reviewers. Secondly (and this I believe this is the main priority for us) in relation to conclusions we make in the chapter. We should make it clear where our comments apply to only MBH (if that is appropriate), and where they apply to the overall findings of the chapter. Our response should consider all the issues for both MBH and the overall chapter conclusions

    a. The role of bristlecone pine data
        Is it reliable?
        Is it necessary to include this data to arrive at the conclusion that recent warmth is unprecedented?

    b. Is the PCA approach robust? Are the results statistically significant? It seems to me that in the case of MBH the answer in each is no. It is not clear how robust and significant the more recent approaches are...

If only Dr Mitchell and his colleagues had thought to share some of these "uncertainties" about the hockey stick with the public. But, as one CRU scientist would later concede, when it came to Mann, they were "not especially honest".

50

"Did Mann et al get it wrong? Yes, Mann et al got it wrong."

PROFESSOR SIMON TETT, PHD

Chair of Earth System Dynamics and Modelling at the University of Edinburgh's School of Geosciences. Head of the Global Change Research Institute. Formerly with the Met Office's Hadley Centre, where he worked on mechanisms of climate variability. Recipient of the Norber-Gerbier Prize from the World Meteorological Organization and the LG Groves Prize for Meteorology. Contributor to the IPCC and Margary lecturer to the Royal Meteorological Society. Principal Investigator for the National Centre for Atmospheric Science.

The most disturbing aspect of Climategate was the revelation that the Big Climate establishment largely shared the "deniers'" view of Mann's appalling science - but they kept it to themselves. On October 18th 2004, Dr David Warrilow, Head of Science Policy on Climate Change at Britain's Department of the Environment, Food and Rural Affairs, emailed Professor Tett, then with the Met Office, to raise his concerns about McIntyre & McKitrick's critique of the hockey stick[1]:

It is therefore important to know whether a) Mann et al got it wrong and b) M&M are right and c) how unusual is the last 50 years in the longer term context. **I suspect the truth is in between somewhere.**

That afternoon Professor Tett emailed back:

I think there are issues in Mann et al's approach - recall the Esper et al paper which produced a reconstruction with lots more low

---

[1] http://di2.nu/foia/foia2011/mail/0518.txt

121

frequency variability than others... Mann's reconstruction had the least variability of any of the reconstructions...

In answer to your specific questions.

a) Did Mann et al get it wrong? Yes Mann et al got it wrong. How wrong is still under debate...

b) Are M&M right? M&M may be right. However I think it unlikely that the Medieval warm period is as warm as today... Their criticisms seem to be extremely technical.

c) How unusual is the last 50 years? I think it still likely to be the warmest period on record (see b) BUT the rate of warming may not be highly unusual.

I agree that one of the important claims in the TAR looks like not being correct. This result could be spun to cast doubt on worries about anthropogenic climate change as the evidence that the 20th century is unusual becomes less clear cut...

Simon

Dr Tett has always been consistent. Way back in 2001, while checking a paper for revisions, he wrote of Mann's then new hockey stick[2]:

No justification for regional reconstructions rather than what Mann et al did (I don't think we can say **we didn't do Mann et al because we think it is crap!**)

If only he and Dr Warrilow had seen fit to share their expert assessment with the uncredentialed plebs 15 years ago. But then "the result could be spun to cast doubt on worries about anthropogenic climate change". By "spun", Dr Tett appears to mean "using the actual evidence to reach an objective conclusion".

---

[2] http://di2.nu/foia/foia2011/mail/0562.txt

VI
Mannsplaining
THE CLIME SYNDICATE

I simply can't believe that there is a kind of mafia that is trying to inhibit critical papers from being published.[1]
DR MOJIB LATIF, PHD
INTERVIEW WITH THE WALL STREET JOURNAL
(NOVEMBER 23RD 2009)

---

[1] http://www.wsj.com/articles/SB125883405294859215

IF MANN AND the Hockey Team's behavior was bad (in a scientific sense) before McIntyre & McKitrick came along, it got worse (in a far more basic sense) after the two Canadians began asking questions, as the leak of the Climategate emails in November 2009 made clear.

Dr Latif was one of many scientists stunned by the glimpse behind the climate curtain - and he's no denier. As he once told National Public Radio, "If my name was not Mojib Latif, my name would be Global Warming."[2] Nonetheless, he was shocked by what the Climategate emails disclosed about some of the leading figures in climate science. On November 23rd *The Wall Street Journal* reported:

> *Mojib Latif, a climate researcher at Germany's Leibniz Institute of Marine Sciences, said he found it hard to believe that climate scientists were trying to squelch dissent.*[3]

Whether or not Dr Latif could believe it, it was certainly happening. It had been known for years that Mann took the view that his graphs were like, say, the Coca-Cola or Kentucky Fried Chicken formula: Your job is to swallow it, not figure out how it's made.

This is in itself discreditable, and very different from other scientific areas. For example, Richard Smith, editor of *The British Medical Journal* from 1991 to 2004:

> *It is a condition of submitting a study to the BMJ that if we ask to see the original data, you have to produce it. And if you can't, then I'm afraid the assumption is that probably this was*

---

[2] http://www.npr.org/templates/story/story.php?storyId=120668812&ft=1&f=1007
[3] http://www.wsj.com/articles/SB125883405294859215

invented.[4]

Nature, once the most prestigious scientific journal on the planet, is evidently less picky. And Mann was not any old scientist but a paleoclimatologist - which is, at least as he practices it, essentially an exercise in data processing. It's not about finding a tree or a borehole and measuring it, but about the statistical treatment of those trees and boreholes. The gulf between the observations and the results is so vast that it can only be judged if you have access to both the data and Mann's secret formula for whisking it together.

Which is exactly what the Hockey Team attempted to obstruct. As Professor Jonathan Jones wrote of Mann's closest ally:

> *You can't spend long digging around the Hockey Stick without stumbling across other areas of climate science pathology. The next one that really struck me was the famous Phil Jones quote: 'Why should I make the data available to you, when your aim is to try and find something wrong with it.' To any practising scientist that's a huge red flag. Sure we all feel a bit like that on occasion, but to actually say something like that in an email is practically equivalent to getting up on a public platform and saying 'I'm a pathological scientist, and I'm proud.'[5]*

Jonathan Jones charitably assumed Phil Jones, Mann's close colleague, was just having a bad day. Au contraire, it was standard operating procedure. If you can get away with something so *unscientific*, why would you leave it at that? The Climategate conspiracies advanced smoothly from the unscientific to the

---

[4] http://climateaudit.org/2006/04/14/failure-of-oversight-and-peer-review/
[5] http://www.bishop-hill.net/blog/2011/12/2/tim-barnett-on-the-hockey-stick.html

unethical to the unlawful. Phil Jones to Michael Mann on February 3rd 2005:

> *The two MMs [McIntyre & McKitrick] have been after the CRU station data for years. If they ever hear there is a Freedom of Information Act now in the UK, I think I'll delete the file rather than send to anyone.*[6]

And, indeed, the CRU subsequently announced that they had "inadvertently deleted" the requested data.

The Settled Scientists also acknowledged that the skeptics were right on another point. At exactly the moment Mann's hockey stick proclaimed the hottest year *evah!!!!* global warming ...stopped. Jones again:

> *The scientific community would come down on me in no uncertain terms if I said the world had cooled from 1998. Okay it has but it is only seven years of data and it isn't statistically significant.*[7]

Yet perhaps the most important revelation was not the collusion, the bullying, the politicization and the evidence-planting, but the fact that, even if you wanted to do honest "climate research" at the Climatic Research Unit, the data and the models are now so diseased by the above that they're all but useless. Phil Jones and Michael Mann are two of the most influential figures in the "climate change" establishment. What these documents reveal is the greatest scientific scandal of our times - and a tragedy. It's not just their graphs but their battle lines that are drawn all wrong.

---

[6] http://www.wsj.com/articles/
SB10001424052748704779704574553652849094482
[7] http://www.assassinationscience.com/climategate/1/FOIA/mail/1120593115.txt

51

"Hit on the head with a hockey stick... And now we pay the price for these guys grabbing so much attention."

PROFESSOR JOSEPH M PROSPERO, PHD

Professor Emeritus at the University of Miami's Division of Marine and Atmospheric Chemistry and the Rosenstiel School of Marine and Atmospheric Science. Author of peer-reviewed papers published in *Atmospheric Chemistry and Physics*, *The Quarterly Journal of the Royal Meteorological Society*, *The Journal of North African Studies* and many more.

On November 17th 2009, the University of East Anglia discovered that the email accounts of its Climatic Research Unit had been breached. Two days later, over a thousand emails and two thousand other documents were uploaded to the Internet - and "Climategate" (as the Telegraph*'s James Delingpole dubbed it) was underway. Professor Prospero, emailing Susan Solomon[1] at NOAA, reflected the view of many scientists who'd watched the hockey-stick promoters with dismay[2]:*

---

[1] Dr Solomon is a pioneering ozone-hole researcher and recipient of the National Medal of Science, named by *Time* by 2008 as one of the 100 most influential people in the world. It is somewhat mystifying why Professor Prospero would think her open to his line of argument: at the IPCC, she threatened Stephen McIntyre with being banned as a reviewer for requesting the data of certain Hockey Team members.

[2] http://wattsupwiththat.com/2012/08/22/first-look-hit-on-the-head-with-a-hockey-stick-some-selected-emails-from-the-recent-noaa-foia-release-2-years-later/

127

Subject: hit on the head with a hockey stick

The mess as [sic] UEA is a disaster for the climate community. The paleodata always got a lot more attention from the general public than it deserved. And now we pay the price for these guys grabbing so much attention in the past and, especially, now...

But that aside, I think the climate community is in general doing a lousy job of getting information out to the public... Everything is left to the media to explain, and they often do it badly. Usually it is simplified and exaggerated in such a way as to leave the community open to question - e.g., the hockey stick.

As things stand, the climate community is being clobbered... The climate community is handling this issue with the same degree of skill as Kerry handled the gunboat fiasco.

Professor Prospero is correct that, initially, the "climate community" was unsure how to react. There was a more-in-sorrow-than-in-anger tone in the first reactions from fellow scientists. Shortly after the Climategate emails were leaked, Dr Petr Chylek sent "An Open Letter to the Climate Community" that began[3]:

I am sure that most of you are aware of the incident that took place recently at the University of East Anglia's Climatic Research Unit (CRU). The identity of the whistle-blower or hacker is still not known...

For me, science is the search for truth, the never-ending path towards finding out how things are arranged in this world so that they can work as they do. That search is never finished.

It seems that the climate research community has betrayed that mighty goal...

---

[3] http://rankexploits.com/musings/2009/petr-chylek/

52

"There was a perceived need to 'prove' that the current global average temperature is higher than it was at any other time... It became more important than scientific integrity."

DR PETR CHYLEK, PHD

Researcher for Space and Remote Sensing Sciences at Los Alamos National Laboratory. Fellow of the American Geophysical Union, of the Optical Society of America, and of the Los Alamos National Laboratory. Former professor at Dalhousie University, the University of Oklahoma, Purdue University and SUNY Albany.

Dr Chylek's post-Climategate "Open Letter to the Climate Community" addressed directly the Mann-Jones cabal's damage to science[1]:

They have substituted the search for truth with an attempt at proving one point of view. It seems that some of the most prominent leaders of the climate research community, like prophets of Old Israel, believed that they could see the future of humankind and that the only remaining task was to convince or force all others to accept and follow...

Climate research made significant advancements during the last few decades... This includes the construction of the HadCRUT and NASA GISS datasets documenting the rise of

---

[1] http://rankexploits.com/musings/2009/petr-chylek/

globally averaged temperature during the last century. I do not believe that this work can be affected in any way by the recent email revelations. Thus, the first of the three pillars supporting the hypothesis of manmade global warming seems to be solid.

However, the two other pillars are much more controversial. To blame the current warming on humans, there was a perceived need to "prove" that the current global average temperature is higher than it was at any other time in recent history (the last few thousand years). This task is one of the main topics of the released CRU emails. Some people were so eager to prove this point that it became more important than scientific integrity.

The next step was to show that this "unprecedented high current temperature" has to be a result of the increasing atmospheric concentration of carbon dioxide from the burning of fossil fuels. The fact that the Atmosphere Ocean General Circulation Models are not able to explain the post-1970 temperature increase by natural forcing was interpreted as proof that it was caused by humans. It is more logical to admit that the models are not yet good enough to capture natural climate variability... Thus, two of the three pillars of the global warming and carbon dioxide paradigm are open to reinvestigation.

The damage has been done. The public trust in climate science has been eroded... So what comes next? Let us stop making unjustified claims and exaggerated projections about the future even if the editors of some eminent journals are just waiting to publish them. Let us admit that our understanding of the climate is less perfect than we have tried to make the public believe. Let us drastically modify or temporarily discontinue the IPCC... Only open discussion and intense searching of all possibilities will let us regain the public's trust and move forward.

53

"The final stage of corruption - cover-up - had taken hold."

PROFESSOR JEROME RAVETZ, PHD

Associate Fellow of the Institute for Science, Innovation and Society at the University of Oxford. Co-creator of the NUSAP notational system for uncertain information, and developer of the theory of post-normal science. Former member of the Genetic Manipulation Advisory Group. Former Visiting Scientist at the European Commission Joint Research Centre and Director of the Council for Science and Society. Honorary Senior Research Fellow of the Department of Science and Technology Studies at University College, London, Senior Fellow of the Green Center for Science and Society at the University of Texas, Dallas, visiting professor at Fudan University in Shanghai.

When "Climategate" broke, Professor Ravetz, a man of the left, compared the climate community's deceptions to Tony Blair's famously "sexed-up" dossier justifying war against Saddam's Iraq[1]:

Politics will doubtless survive, for it is not a fiduciary institution; but for science the dangers are real. Climategate is particularly significant because it cannot be blamed on the well-known malign influences from outside science, be they greedy corporations or an unscrupulous State. This scandal, and the resulting crisis, was created by people within science.

As Professor Ravetz understood, were Climategate to result in a "serious discrediting" of global warming claims, it would be "the community of science itself" that was damaged. The problem, as he saw it, was the

---

[1] http://wattsupwiththat.com/2010/02/09/climategate-plausibility-and-the-blogosphere-in-the-post-normal-age/

embrace of "evangelical science":

They propounded, as a proven fact, Anthropogenic Carbon-based Global Warming. **There is little room for uncertainty in this thesis; it effectively needs hockey-stick behaviour in all indicators** of global temperature, so that it is all due to industrialisation.

But the hockey stick itself had run into what Professor Ravetz called "increasingly severe problems":

It relied totally on a small set of deeply uncertain tree-ring data for the medieval period, to refute the historical evidence of a warming then; but it needed to discard that sort of data for recent decades, as they showed a sudden cooling from the 1960s onwards!

The cause had now become another crusading "'War', like those on ...Drugs and 'Terror'":

This new War, on Carbon, was equally simplistic, and equally prone to corruption and failure. Global warming science became the core element of this major worldwide campaign to save the planet. Any weakening of the scientific case would have amounted to a betrayal of the good cause.... All critics, even those who were full members of the scientific peer community, had to be derided and dismissed. As we learned from the CRU e-mails, they were not considered to be entitled to the normal courtesies of scientific sharing and debate... and as one witty blogger has put it, "peer review" was replaced by "pal review"...

Details of shoddy science and dirty tricks abound. By the end, the committed inner core were confessing to each other that global temperatures were falling, but it was far too late to change course. The final stage of corruption, cover-up, had taken hold.

54

"These researchers are guilty of brazen fraud."

PROFESSOR ZBIGNIEW JAWOROWSKI, PHD (1927-2011)

Chairman of the UN Scientific Committee on the Effects of Atomic Radiation, and of the Scientific Council of the Central Laboratory for Radiological Protection in Warsaw. Principal investigator for four research projects of the International Atomic Energy Agency, and three of the US Environmental Protection Agency. Author of peer-reviewed papers published by *Nature* and other journals.

Other scientists were blunter than Chylek or even Ravetz. In December 2009 Professor Jaworowski gave an interview about Climategate to Mariusz Bober of the Polish daily Our Journal[1]:

QUESTION: This means that the scientists who are responsible for research in this field, lied to frighten people about a coming apocalypse? Why?

JAWOROWSKI: Indeed, these researchers are guilty of brazen fraud, bringing us into a trap, which has dire consequences. For many years they have been incredibly confident, ignoring any criticism of their arguments. But they had the overwhelming support of the United Nations, and specifically the IPCC, the United Nations group charged with examining the impact of human activities on climate change, which takes the lead in all this confusion...

QUESTION: You are not afraid of revenge from the "warming"

---

[1] http://www.21stcenturysciencetech.com/Articles_2010/Jaworowski_interview.pdf

lobby?

JAWOROWSKI: Now I am 82 years old, and the financial consequences of the views which I preach are not of importance to me. But among researchers who share my views, there are not many younger scientists, especially those who have families dependent on them, who can afford to support such views.

Professor Jaworowski chose to end on an optimistic note:

JAWOROWSKI: This illustrates how credulous the public and politicians have been for decades. They were falsely made to believe that they were well informed, with 90 per cemt certainty and full scientific consensus! Climategate might become a catharsis, a bitter medicine, that will free science and the public from the gloomy climatic phantom, save the world from global economic disaster, and allow us to enjoy the golden gift of nature: our Modern Warm Period. Let it last long.

It would be easy for the somewhat insular climate community to dismiss Jaworowski as a fringe foreigner, far from the big Anglo-American climate action. But, on December 10th 2009, the Massachusetts Institute of Technology chaired what it billed as "The Great Climategate Debate" between five of its professors.[2] As Professor Michael Kelly commented in his notes to the Oxburgh inquiry[3]:

Three of the five MIT scientists who commented in the week before Copenhagen on the leaked emails... thought that they saw **prima facie evidence of unprofessional activity.**

Among them was the prominent and respected professor Ronald Prinn...

---

[2] http://video.mit.edu/watch/the-great-climategate-debate-9529/
[3] https://www.whatdotheyknow.com/request/35907/response/94112/attach/4/David%20Hand%20s%20attachments%20from%20emails%20supplied.pdf

55

"I was disturbed.
The discussions between
Michael Mann and Phil Jones
...simply disturbed me."

PROFESSOR RONALD G PRINN, SCD

Tepco Professor of Atmospheric Science in the Department of Earth, Atmospheric and Planetary Sciences at the Massachusetts Institute of Technology, and also Director of MIT's Center for Global Change Science and Co-Director of its Joint Program on the Science and Policy of Global Change. Fellow of the American Geophysical Union and recipient of its Macelwane Medal. Fellow of the American Association for the Advancement of Science, and its former chairman for Atmospheric and Hydrospheric Sciences. Former chairman of the US National Research Committee on Earth Sciences and the US Global Tropospheric Chemistry Program, and member of its Space Science Board and Committee for the International Geosphere-Biosphere Program. Former member of the NASA Earth System Sciences Committee and the Space Science and Applications Advisory Committee. IPCC Lead Author.

On December 10th 2009 Professor Prinn was one of five faculty to participate in MIT's "Great Climategate Debate"[1]:

The first question I've asked myself is: Are some of these emails unprofessional..? I've particularly looked at the set of emails that revolved around what was called "the hockey stick" ...and I was disturbed. I was disturbed. The discussions between Michael

---

[1] http://video.mit.edu/watch/the-great-climategate-debate-9529/

Mann and Phil Jones about the work of Stephen McIntyre and McKitrick in particular - whether you believe that McIntyre and McKitrick were right or wrong - it simply disturbed me ...looking at those emails to see the personal nature of the discussion between these folks at the University of East Anglia and Penn State. So **are some of the emails unprofessional? My answer is yes, they are...**

Is public perception of climate science affected? My answer is yes, it is.

As for the hockey stick:

There's a significant case to be made for the temperature being highest in recent times and the century-scale rate of rise of temperature being highest in the last hundred years. That's the "blade". In other words the blade I think has survived the scrutiny... But, as I've already pointed out or intimated, **it's unclear whether the "handle" is straight or broken.**

The Q&A that followed the professors' remarks had some memorable moments. The second questioner, a member of the MIT faculty, felt "the ethical situation" had been given short shrift, and that "the professional societies" needed to get involved. With respect to Mann, Jones et al, "their papers should be retracted". Professor Stephen Ansolabehere cooed blandly:

Everybody here who's a faculty member at MIT, use this as a teachable moment on ethics, on data recording, on everything about your scientific method. It's a great example for your students.

But oddly enough that never happened...

56

"There is no point in any scientific group endorsing this. We are not crooks. And yet if we endorse this we are becoming that."

PROFESSOR RICHARD LINDZEN, PHD

Alfred P Sloan Professor of Meteorology at the Massachusetts Institute of Technology and Distinguished Visiting Scientist at the California Institute of Technology's Jet Propulsion Laboratory. Fellow of the American Geophysical Union and recipient of its Macelwane Medal. Fellow of the American Meteorological Society and recipient of its Meisinger and Charney awards. Fellow of the American Academy of Arts and Sciences, and of the American Association for the Advancement of Sciences. Member of the National Academy of Sciences, the European Geophysical Society and the Norwegian Academy of Science and Letters, and first recipient of the Wallin Foundation's Leo Prize. IPCC lead author.

Like Professor Prinn, Professor Lindzen was one of five faculty members on the panel of MIT's "Great Climategate Debate"[1]:

What we're here to talk about are these emails and computer code, a total of over 3,000 documents that someone for some reason revealed... The likelihood is it's a whistle-blower who couldn't take it anymore. Now that is ...speculation, but the documents themselves are not speculation. **They are unambiguously dealing with things that are unethical and in**

---

[1] http://video.mit.edu/watch/the-great-climategate-debate-9529/

many cases illegal. There is no point in any scientific group endorsing this. We are not crooks. And yet if we endorse this we are becoming that.

We have scientists manipulating raw temperature data... The refusal to allow outsiders access to data, the willingness to destroy data rather than release it, the avoidance of Freedom of Information requests... The discussion on preventing publication was cute...

There is another issue though. Since I think **very few people can actually read these documents and not conclude that there were bad things going on**, the question is what will it do to popular support for science..? There is a diminishing popular support for this issue. That is common. Very often there are distinct differences in the way ordinary people see things and the way "the educated elite" do. Somebody was mentioning this is not mass hysteria, this is elite hysteria. But, you know, ordinary people vote, and most of us are funded by their taxes. And so the notion that science 1) is subject to cheating and distortion; and 2) if Kerry[2] is right, that this is supported and endorsed by the professional societies, it's going to be devastating for popular support of science. I think we should be very cautious about this.

The first question demanded to know of Richard Lindzen what would be found if people went through "all of your emails and letters over the past 30 years". Professor Lindzen seemed indifferent to the prospect:

There would be things that you know might be personal, but **there is nothing in any email I have ever written that compares to what is in these.** At all. I would not object to any of mine being searched.

---

[2] Kerry Emanuel, Professor of Meteorology at MIT

57

"That's no way to do science."

PROFESSOR JAMES LOVELOCK, CH, CBE, FRS, PHD

Scientist, inventor and originator of the Gaia hypothesis. Companion of Honour, Commander of the Most Excellent Order of the British Empire, and Fellow of the Royal Society. Recipient of three NASA Certificates of Recognition for his various inventions, including the electron capture detector and the microwave oven. Recipient of the highest award of the Geological Society, the Wollaston Medal (whose previous recipients include Charles Darwin), the Discovery Lifetime Award from the Royal Geographical Society, the Dr A H Heineken Prize for the Environment, the Norbert Gerbier Prize from the World Meteorological Society, the first Amsterdam Prize for the Environment from the Royal Netherlands Academy of Arts and Sciences, the Tswett Medal for Chromatography, the Silver Medal from the Plymouth Marine Laboratory, and the American Chemical Society's Award for Chromatography. Former President of the Marine Biological Association.

On March 29th 2010 the Gaia man himself, James Lovelock, gave a wide-ranging interview to The Guardian, *beginning with his reaction to Climategate[1]:*

I was utterly disgusted. My second thought was that it was inevitable. It was bound to happen. Science, not so very long ago, pre-1960s, was largely vocational. Back when I was young, I didn't want to do anything else other than be a scientist. They're not like that nowadays. They don't give a damn... They say: "Science is a good career. You can get a job for life doing government work." That's no way to do science...

---

[1] http://www.theguardian.com/environment/blog/2010/mar/29/james-lovelock

That's no way to do science...

Fudging the data in any way whatsoever is quite literally a sin against the holy ghost of science. I'm not religious, but I put it that way because I feel so strongly. It's the one thing you do not ever do. You've got to have standards...

I would only have been too pleased if someone had asked me for my data. **If you really believed in your data, you wouldn't mind someone looking at it.** You should be able to respond that if you don't believe me go out and do the measurements yourself.

You don't hide data.

Yet Mann did - for years. On climate skeptics, Professor Lovelock had this to say:

What I like about sceptics is that in good science you need critics that make you think: "Crumbs, have I made a mistake here?" If you don't have that continuously, you really are up the creek...

The great climate science centres around the world are more than well aware how weak their science is. If you talk to them privately they're scared stiff of the fact that they don't really know what the clouds and the aerosols are doing... So why on earth are the politicians spending a fortune of our money when we can least afford it on doing things to prevent events 50 years from now? They've employed scientists to tell them what they want to hear. The Germans and the Danes are making a fortune out of renewable energy. I'm puzzled why politicians are not a bit more pragmatic about all this.

We do need scepticism about the predictions about what will happen to the climate in 50 years, or whatever. It's almost naive, scientifically speaking, to think we can give relatively accurate predictions for future climate. There are so many unknowns that it's wrong to do it.

58

"What I don't like about this is that someone took out some climate data to make the record look 'better.' That's a no-no."

DR WILLIAM A SPRIGG, PHD

Research Professor at the Department of Atmospheric Sciences, the Institute of Atmospheric Physics, and the Department of Soil, Water and Environmental Sciences at the University of Arizona. Consultant to the World Meteorological Organization. Director of the Sino-US Centers for Soil and Water Conservation and Environmental Protection. Former co-Principal Investigator for the NASA REASoN project.

A few weeks after the Climategate emails were released, Dr Sprigg spoke at the 13th Energy & Environment Expo in Phoenix[1]:

Focusing closely on the Climategate scandal, in which leaked emails revealed IPCC gatekeepers hid, manipulated, and destroyed scientific data that contradicted claims of substantial human-induced global warming, Sprigg said the scandal has harmed the movement's scientific credibility.

Sprigg highlighted as particularly embarrassing an email from University of East Anglia Climatic Research Unit climatologist Phil Jones instructing Penn State University

---

[1] http://news.heartland.org/newspaper-article/2010/02/03/former-ipcc-leader-says-alternative-group-needed

141

climatologist Michael Mann and two others not to tell people the United Kingdom has a Freedom of Information Act. **Sprigg called for full and open sharing of data** for research and education.

Dr Sprigg also commented on "Mike's Nature *trick" to "hide the decline":*

"What I don't like about this is that someone took out some climate data to make the record look 'better.' That's a no-no," said Sprigg.

During the question and answer period, Sprigg said IPCC should undergo substantial reform in the wake of Climategate, Glaciergate, Amazongate, and other recent scandals.

"There will be some reforms," he said. "There will be changes in the peer-review process. There are calls for [IPCC chair Rajendra] Pachauri to resign..."

Sprigg's observations are particularly noteworthy because he held such an important role with IPCC and he is not one of the skeptics who have strongly challenged IPCC and its claims of human activity creating a global warming crisis.

During his presentation, Sprigg said the lack of warming in the past ten years does not mean global warming has stopped or is no longer a concern.

"Don't get excited if temperatures go down in the next year or two," said Sprigg.

As Dr Sprigg demonstrated, there is no contradiction between believing in anthropogenic global warming, and being revolted by the conduct of Mann, Jones and others. In fact, honest proponents of the CO_2 hypothesis have most to lose from the damage done by the Hockey Team.

59

"Scientists like Mike Mann, Phil Jones and others should no longer participate in the peer-review process."

PROFESSOR HANS VON STORCH, PHD

Professor at the University of Hamburg's Meteorological Institute, and Director of the Institute for Coastal Research at the Helmholtz Research Centre. Recipient of the International Meetings on Statistical Climatology achievement award. Member of the advisory boards of *The Journal of Climate* and *Annals of Geophysics*. Former editor-in-chief of *Climate Research*.

Professor von Storch was one of the first climate scientists to be critical in public and on the record about Mann's hockey stick, going so far as to describe it as "quatsch" ("nonsense" or "rubbish") in a story in Der Spiegel *headlined "Die Kurve ist Quatsch" - or, to retain the alliteration, "The curve is crap"[1]:*

Methodologically it is wrong. One could also say: nonsense.

In November 2009, a few days after the Climategate revelations, Professor von Storch wrote (in English) of Mann & Co's emails[2]:

There are a number of problematic statements, which will be discussed in the media and the blogosphere. I found the style of

---

[1] http://www.spiegel.de/spiegel/print/d-32362275.html
[2] http://rankexploits.com/musings/2009/von-storch-cru-reaction/

143

communication revealing, speaking about other people and their ideas, joining forces to "kill" papers, exchanges of "improving" presentations without explaining.

Also mails from/to Eduardo Zorita and myself are included; also we have been subject of frequent mentioning, usually not in a flattering manner. Interesting exchanges, and evidences, are contained about efforts to destroy *Climate Research*; that we in the heydays of the hockeystick debate shared our ECHO-G data with our adversaries; and that Mike Mann was successful to exclude me from a review-type meeting on historical reconstructions in Wengen (demonstrating again **his problematic but powerful role of acting as a gatekeeper.**)

I would assume that more interesting issues will be found in the files, and that a useful debate about the degree of politicization of climate science will emerge. A conclusion could be that **the principle, according to which data must be made public,** so that also adversaries may check the analysis, **must be really enforced.** Another conclusion could be that scientists like Mike Mann, Phil Jones and others should no longer participate in the peer-review process or in assessment activities like IPCC.

This would have been about the very minimum one might have expected after the disclosures of paranoia and cronyism among those who purported to speak for "thousands" of scientists from the collected member states of the United Nations. Yet, after the initial outrage, Big Climate dug in, adding - to the hidden data and corruption of peer review - yet another failing: an inability to self-correct.

60

"It is the greatest and most successful pseudoscientific fraud I have seen in my long life as a physicist."

PROFESSOR HAROLD LEWIS, PHD (1923-2011)

Emeritus Professor of Physics at the University of California, Santa Barbara. Member of the US Defense Science Board, and chairman of the 1977-79 Risk Assessment Review for the US Nuclear Regulatory Commission. Recipient of the Science Writing Award for his book *Technological Risk* (Norton, New York, 1990).

On October 6th 2010, Professor Lewis, one of the American Physical Society's most distinguished members, wrote to its president, Curtis Callan Jr[1]:

Dear Curt:

When I first joined the American Physical Society sixty-seven years ago it was much smaller, much gentler, and as yet uncorrupted by the money flood (a threat against which Dwight Eisenhower warned a half-century ago).

Indeed, the choice of physics as a profession was then a guarantor of a life of poverty and abstinence... The prospect of worldly gain drove few physicists...

How different it is now... For reasons that will soon become clear my former pride at being an APS Fellow all these years has been turned into shame, and I am forced, with no pleasure at all, to offer you my resignation from the Society.

---

[1] http://wattsupwiththat.com/2010/10/16/hal-lewis-my-resignation-from-the-american-physical-society/

It is of course, the global warming scam, with the (literally) trillions of dollars driving it, that has corrupted so many scientists, and has carried APS before it like a rogue wave. It is the greatest and most successful pseudoscientific fraud I have seen in my long life as a physicist. Anyone who has the faintest doubt that this is so should force himself to read the Climategate documents, which lay it bare. (Montford's book [*The Hockey Stick Illusion*] organizes the facts very well.) **I don't believe that any real physicist, nay scientist, can read that stuff without revulsion. I would almost make that revulsion a definition of the word scientist...**

The Climategate scandal broke into the news, and the machinations of the principal alarmists were revealed to the world. It was a fraud on a scale I have never seen, and I lack the words to describe its enormity. Effect on the APS position: none. None at all. This is not science; other forces are at work... There are indeed trillions of dollars involved, to say nothing of the fame and glory (and frequent trips to exotic islands) that go with being a member of the club. Your own Physics Department (of which you are chairman) would lose millions a year if the global warming bubble burst. **When Penn State absolved Mike Mann of wrongdoing, and the University of East Anglia did the same for Phil Jones, they cannot have been unaware of the financial penalty for doing otherwise...** Since I am no philosopher, I'm not going to explore at just which point enlightened self-interest crosses the line into corruption, but a careful reading of the Climategate releases makes it clear that this is not an academic question.

I want no part of it, so please accept my resignation. APS no longer represents me, but I hope we are still friends.

Hal

VII

The Mann that got away

CASE CLOSED?

The impression Mann gives is that all he cares about is saving his own reputation.[1]

PROFESSOR REINER GRUNDMANN, PHD

"MANN ANGRY AT WSJ ARTICLE" (DIE KLIMAZWIEBEL, 2010)

---

[1] http://klimazwiebel.blogspot.com/2010/02/mann-angry-at-wsj-article.html

MANN HAS PLAYED fast and loose with details all his professional life, from his original "innocent" errors on the hockey stick to his "innocent" promotion of himself as a Nobel Prize winner. But, when you're calling in effect for the entire reorientation of the global economy, even "innocent" mistakes have consequences. By 2006 McIntyre & McKitrick had inflicted sufficient damage on the hockey stick for the United States Congress and the National Academy of Sciences both to appoint expert panels to investigate the matter. Four years later, another handful of committees would look into the Climategate leaks at the University of East Anglia. Mann would later claim in his court pleadings that he had been "exonerated" by at least eight different bodies on both sides of the Atlantic. Indeed, his "amended complaint" (amended after having to withdraw the original over his false claim to be a "Nobel Prize recipient") has an entire section called "The exoneration of Dr Mann".

Most of the bodies that he claims "exonerated" him (including, so he says, the British House of Commons) in fact never investigated him. But a lazy enviro-press was generally content to take him at his own estimation, and those official reports that did address aspects of his science were generally written with a circumlocutory evasiveness that does not reflect well on their authors. Yet a close reading of the actual documents, as opposed to the fawning press coverage, is devastating to both the credibility and the integrity of Mann's science.

The National Research Council, for example, was prepared to stand by the hockey stick only post-1600 - that's to say, the Little Ice Age and the world's emergence therefrom ...which was the conventional wisdom long before Mann was born. So his principal contribution to science - the repeal of the Medieval Warm Period - was itself repealed.

The NRC also slapped Mann down on withholding data:

The committee recognizes that access to research data is a complicated, discipline-dependent issue, and that access to computer models and methods is especially challenging because intellectual property rights must be considered. Our view is that all research benefits from full and open access to published datasets and that a clear explanation of analytical methods is mandatory. Peers should have access to the information needed to reproduce published results, so that increased confidence in the outcome of the study can be generated inside and outside the scientific community.[2]

Even while he was claiming to have been "exonerated" by the NRC, Mann ignored its findings. He and his chums continued to obstruct access to their computer codes and raw data. As for his actual "science", the NRC tap-danced around like Michael Flatley in the Dublin premiere of *Treedance*. This is a fine example of their style:

Reconstructions that have poor validation statistics (i.e., low CE) will have correspondingly wide uncertainty bounds, and so can be seen to be unreliable in an objective way. Moreover, a CE statistic close to zero or negative suggests that the reconstruction is no better than the mean, and so its skill for time averages shorter than the validation period will be low. Some recent results reported in Table 1S of Wahl & Ammann indicate that their reconstruction, which uses the same procedure and full set of proxies used by Mann et al... gives CE values ranging from 0.103 to –0.215, depending on how far back in time the reconstruction is carried.

---

[2] http://dels.nas.edu/Report/Surface-Temperature-Reconstructions-Last/11676?bname=

Professor Ross McKitrick "unpeeled the obfuscations" and helpfully translated:

> ~ *Reconstructions can be assessed using a variety of tests, including RE, r2 and the coefficient of efficiency (CE) scores;*
>
> ~ *If the CE score is near zero or negative your model is junk;*
>
> ~ *Wahl & Ammann include a table in which they use Mann's data and code and compute the test scores that he didn't report; and*
>
> ~ *The CE scores range from near zero to negative, which tells us that Mann's results were junk.* [3]

Nevertheless, Mann got quite a long way simply by claiming that everyone who ever investigated him gave him a clean bill of health and knowing that the environmental media would never check a thing. In his legal pleadings Mann claims to have been "exonerated" by Lord Oxburgh's committee, but in his book *The Hockey Stick and the Climate Wars* he says his work "did not fall within the remit of the committee". So which is it? Is Mann lying to the court? Or is he lying to his book customers? In fact, his only "exoneration" came in the Penn State inquiry set up by the university's president, Graham Spanier - a man now under criminal indictment and facing 20 years in the slammer for obstruction of justice and child endangerment in the Sandusky matter.

The average eco-activist interviewing Mann is happy to drool like a *Tiger Beat* interviewer, albeit a slightly out-of-touch one still besotted over last decade's teen idol. Nonetheless, taken as a whole, the investigations do not give Mann's science "a clean bill of health", but make plain just how toxic and malodorous it is.

---

[3] ed Moran: *Climate Change: The Facts* (Stockade, 2015) page 208

61

"Mann et al used a type of principal component analysis that tends to bias the shape of the reconstructions."

DR GERALD R NORTH, PHD ET AL

Gerald North is Distinguished Professor of Meteorology and Oceanography at Texas A&M University. Franco Biondi is Associate Professor of Physical Geography at the University of Nevada, Reno. Peter Bloomfield is Professor of Statistics at North Carolina State University, Raleigh. John Christy is director of the Earth System Science Center at the University of Alabama in Huntsville. Kurt Cuffey is Professor of Geography at the University of California, Berkeley. Robert Dickinson is a professor at Georgia Institute of Technology's School of Earth and Atmospheric Sciences. Ellen Druffel is Professor of Earth System Science at the University of California, Irvine. Douglas Nychka is a senior scientist at NCAR (the National Center for Atmospheric Research). Bette Otto-Bliesner is a scientist in NCAR's Climate and Global Dynamics Division. Neil Roberts is the head of the University of Plymouth's School of Geography. Karl Turekian is the Sterling Professor of Geology and Geophysics at Yale University. John Wallace is Director of the Joint Institute for the Study of the Atmosphere and Ocean at the University of Washington, Seattle.

The first investigation into Mann's stick was published by the National Research Council of the National Academies in June 2006. In its report on Surface Temperature Reconstructions for the Last 2,000 Years, *Professor North and his colleagues concluded[1]:*

---

[1] http://dels.nas.edu/Report/Surface-Temperature-Reconstructions-Last/11676?bname=

~It can be said with a high level of confidence that global mean surface temperature was higher during the last few decades of the 20th century than during any comparable period during the preceding four centuries. This statement is justified by the consistency of the evidence from a wide variety of geographically diverse proxies.

~Less confidence can be placed in large-scale surface temperature reconstructions for the period from AD 900 to 1600...

~Very little confidence can be assigned to statements concerning the hemispheric mean or global mean surface temperature prior to about AD 900 because of sparse data coverage and because the uncertainties associated with proxy data and the methods used to analyze and combine them are larger than during more recent time periods.

So "less confidence" for the years 900-1600 and "very little confidence" for pre-900 AD. So the only part of the hockey stick to which the NRC was prepared to give "a high level of confidence" was that late 20th century temperatures were the highest of the preceding four centuries - ie, since the Little Ice Age. That's not a breakthrough finding by Michael Mann: It was the conventional wisdom long before Mann got his PhD - indeed, long before he was born. So for the NRC to give a clean bill of health to the hockey stick for the years 1600-1998 is equivalent to declaring that the hockey stick tells us nothing.

Along the way, however, the NRC makes some very telling criticisms of Mann. Page 113:

Mann et al used a type of principal component analysis that tends to bias the shape of the reconstructions.

62

"We had much the same misgivings about his work."

DR PETER BLOOMFIELD, PHD

Professor of Statistics at North Carolina State University. Fellow of the Royal Statistical Society, Fellow of the American Statistical Association, and Fellow of the Institute of Mathematical Statistics. Member of the Hydraulic Fracturing Research Advisory Panel to the US Environmental Protection Agency. Former Chairman of the Department of Statistics at Princeton University, Visiting Fellow at the Climatic Research Unit, University of East Anglia, and Lecturer at Imperial College of Science and Technology.

The statistician on the NRC hockey-stick investigation, Professor Bloomfield testified under oath before Congress in July 2006[1]:

JOE BARTON (CHAIRMAN OF THE HOUSE COMMITTEE ON ENERGY AND COMMERCE): We know that Dr Wegman has said that Dr Mann's methodology is incorrect. Do you agree with that? I mean, it doesn't mean Dr Mann's conclusions are wrong, but we can stipulate now that we have - and if you want to ask your statistician expert from North Carolina that Dr Mann's methodology cannot be documented and cannot be verified by independent review.

GERALD NORTH (NRC PANEL CHAIR): Do you mind if he speaks?

BARTON: Yes, if he would like to come to the microphone.

PETER BLOOMFIELD: Thank you. Yes, Peter Bloomfield. Our

---

[1] http://www.gpo.gov/fdsys/pkg/CHRG-109hhrg31362/html/CHRG-109hhrg31362.htm

committee reviewed the methodology used by Dr Mann and his coworkers and **we felt that some of the choices they made were inappropriate.** We had much the same misgivings about his work that was documented at much greater length by Dr Wegman.

ED WHITFIELD (CHAIRMAN OF THE SUB-COMMITTEE ON OVERSIGHT AND INVESTIGATION): If I may interrupt just one minute. We didn't swear you in so I want you to swear now that the testimony you gave was the truth.

[*Witness sworn*]

WHITFIELD: Thank you.

Four years later, David Hand, President of the Royal Statistical Society, would observe that the hockey stick had used "inappropriate methods". Mann responded[2]:

> I would note that our '98 article was reviewed by the US National Academy of Sciences, the highest scientific authority in the United States, and given a clean bill of health... In fact, the statistician on the panel, Peter Bloomfield, a member of the Royal Statistical Society, came to the opposite conclusion of Prof Hand.

Er, no, he didn't. He used exactly the same word: "inappropriate". Professor Richard Smith, no denier and an eminent University of North Carolina statistician, writing on both the North and Wegman reports for the American Statistical Association newsletter, was even blunter[3]:

> At the core of the controversy is **an incorrect use by Mann** et al of principal components.

---

[2] http://www.telegraph.co.uk/news/earth/environment/climatechange/7589897/Hockey-stick-graph-was-exaggerated.html

[3] http://lv-twk.oekosys.tu-berlin.de/project/lv-twk/images/pdfs/ENVR_9_1.pdf

63

"It is very surprising that research in an area that depends so heavily on statistical methods has not been carried out in close collaboration with professional statisticians."

PROFESSOR THE LORD OXBURGH OF LIVERPOOL, KBE, FRS

ET AL

Ron Oxburgh is a geologist, geophysicist, member of the House of Lords Select Committee on Science and Technology, deputy chairman of Singapore's Science and Engineering Research Council, member of Hong Kong's University Grants Committee, and formerly chief scientific advisor to the United Kingdom's Ministry of Defence and Head of the Department of Earth Sciences at the University of Cambridge. Huw Davies is head of the Dynamical Meteorology Group at the Swiss Federal Institute of Technology in Zürich. Kerry Emanuel is Cecil & Ida Green Professor of Atmospheric Sciences at the Massachusetts Institute of Technology. Lisa Graumlich is Dean of the University of Washington's College of the Environment. David Hand is a former President of the Royal Statistical Society. Herbert Huppert is Professor of Theoretical Geophysics and Michael Kelly is Professor of Solid State Electronics and Nanoscale Science, both at the University of Cambridge.

After the Climategate revelations, there were several "investigations" of the CRU. Lord Oxburgh's, published in April 2010, was widely regarded as perfunctory and "beyond parody", as Labour Member of Parliament Graham Stringer described it. Among its conclusions[1]:

1. We saw no evidence of any deliberate scientific malpractice in any of the work of the Climatic Research Unit and had it been there we believe that it is likely that we would have detected it. Rather we found a small group of dedicated if slightly disorganised researchers who were ill-prepared for being the focus of public attention. As with many small research groups their internal procedures were rather informal.

2. We cannot help remarking that it is very surprising that research in an area that depends so heavily on statistical methods has not been carried out in close collaboration with professional statisticians. Indeed **there would be mutual benefit if there were closer collaboration and interaction between CRU and a much wider scientific group outside the relatively small international circle of temperature specialists.**

This was a recommendation that had been made and ignored for years (see Professors Smith and Zidek earlier). Graham Stringer, a Labour member of the House of Commons Science & Technology Committee and an analytical chemist by profession, was horrified by the report. On the point about the "climate community"'s isolation from professional statisticians, he remarked[2]:

This is the equivalent of claiming medical competence whilst operating on a patient without an anaesthetist.

---

[1] https://www.uea.ac.uk/documents/3154295/7847337/SAP.pdf/a6f591fc-fc6e-4a70-9648-8b943d84782b

[2] http://www.thegwpf.com/graham-stringer-climate-jiggery-pokery/#sthash.Pp4sVyXf.dpuf

64

"That is turning centuries of science on its head."

PROFESSOR MICHAEL KELLY, FRS, FRENG, PHD

Prince Philip Professor of Technology at the University of Cambridge and Professorial Fellow at Trinity Hall. Former Chief Scientific Advisor to the UK Department for Communities and Local Government. Fellow of the Royal Society, the Royal Academy of Engineering, the Royal Society of New Zealand, the Institute of Physics, the Institution of Engineering and Technology, and Senior Member of the US Institute of Electronic and Electrical Engineering. Recipient of prizes from the Institute of Physics, the Royal Academy of Engineering and the Royal Society. Former Executive Director of the Cambridge-MIT Institute.

In his notes for the Oxburgh investigation, Professor Kelly remarked[1]:

I take real exception to having simulation runs described as experiments (without at least the qualification of "computer" experiments). It does a disservice to centuries of real experimentation and allows simulations output to be considered as real data. This last is a very serious matter, as **it can lead to the idea that real "real data" might be wrong simply because it disagrees with the models!** That is turning centuries of science on its head.

That "idea" would manifest itself very strongly, as Mann & Co devoted their energies to figuring how to recalibrate reality to fit their models.
      Professor Kelly also said:

Up to and throughout this exercise, I have remained puzzled how

---

[1] https://www.whatdotheyknow.com/request/35907/response/94112/attach/4/
David%20Hand%20s%20attachments%20from%20emails%20supplied.pdf

the real humility of the scientists in this area, as evident in their papers, including all these here, and the talks I have heard them give, is morphed into statements of confidence at the 95 per cent level for public consumption through the IPCC process. This does not happen in other subjects of equal importance to humanity, e.g. energy futures or environmental degradation or resource depletion. I can only think it is the "authority" appropriated by the IPCC itself that is the root cause.

Michael Kelly is perhaps being a little naïve here. There is no "IPCC" - other than a few administrators in Switzerland, and Rajendra Pachauri jetting back and forth between cricket matches in India and climate conferences of nubile young activists around the globe. In practice, the IPCC is the small group of scientists who control its content. So the work of "humble" scientist Michael Mann got "morphed" into 95 per cent confidence by not-so-humble IPCC Lead Author Michael Mann.

In his notes Professor Kelly posed a good question to Keith Briffa that could equally be asked of Mann and Jones:

Given that the outputs of your work are being used to promote **the largest revolution mankind has ever contemplated**, do you have any sense of the extent to which the quality control and rigour of approach must be of the highest standards in clear expectation of deep scrutiny?

The answer would seem to be no. In February 2012, Professor Kelly wrote to The Times *in London:*

The interpretation of the observational science has been consistently over-egged to produce alarm. All real-world data over the past 20 years has shown the climate models to be exaggerating the likely impacts - if the models cannot account for the near term, why should I trust them in the long term?

65
"Exaggerated... Inappropriate..."

PROFESSOR DAVID HAND, OBE, FBA, PHD
Professor of Statistics at Imperial College, London and former
President of the Royal Statistical Society. Recipient of the Guy
Medal from the RSS, Fellow of the British Academy, and Officer of
the Most Excellent Order of the British Empire for services to
research and innovation. Co-author of *Principles Of Data Mining* and
author of *The Improbability Principle*.

At the press conference to release the findings of Lord Oxburgh's panel,
Professor Hand chose to single out the work of Michael Mann. As New
Scientist *reported[1]:*

David Hand, president of the UK Royal Statistical Society and a
member of Oxburgh's panel, said the work of climate scientists is
a "particularly challenging statistics exercise because the data are
incredibly messy..."

He said the strongest example he had found of imperfect
statistics in the work of the CRU and collaborators elsewhere was
the iconic "hockey stick" graph, produced by Michael Mann of
Pennsylvania State University...

Hand pointed out that the statistical tool Mann used to
integrate temperature data from a number of difference sources –
including tree-ring data and actual thermometer readings –
produced an "exaggerated" rise in temperatures over the 20th
century, relative to pre-industrial temperatures.

Professor Hand said he was "impressed" by Stephen McIntyre's statistical

---

[1] http://www.newscientist.com/article/dn18776-climategate-scientists-chastised-over-statistics.html#.VUkt7pO4K_E

work and told New Scientist *that an accurate graph would look "more like a field-hockey stick than an ice-hockey stick."*

The Daily Telegraph *also reported his comments[2]:*

Professor David Hand said that the research – led by US scientist Michael Mann – would have shown less dramatic results if more reliable techniques had been used to analyse the data...

Prof Hand singled out a 1998 paper by Prof Mann of Pennsylvania State University, a constant target for climate change sceptics, as an example of this...

"The particular technique they used exaggerated the size of the blade at the end of the hockey stick. Had they used an appropriate technique the size of the blade of the hockey stick would have been smaller," he said. "The change in temperature is not as great over the 20th century compared to the past as suggested by the Mann paper..."

The graph used data from hundreds of studies of past temperatures using tree rings, lake sediment, and glacier ice cores and then merged these with more reliable recent temperature records.

Prof Hand said many of the reproductions of the graph do not make clear when these different sets of data are used.

"It is only misleading in the sense they merged two different things," he said.

Prof Hand praised the blogger Steve McIntyre of Climate Audit for uncovering the fact that inappropriate methods were used which could produce misleading results.

"The Mann 1998 hockey stick paper used a particular technique that exaggerated the hockey stick effect," he said.

---

[2] http://www.telegraph.co.uk/news/earth/environment/climatechange/7589897/Hockey-stick-graph-was-exaggerated.html

66

"Given its subsequent iconic significance... the figure supplied for the WMO Report was misleading."

SIR MUIR RUSSELL, KCB, DL, FRSE ET AL

Muir Russell is a Fellow of the Royal Society of Edinburgh, chairman of the Judicial Appointments Board for Scotland, and formerly Vice-Chancellor of the University of Glasgow and first Permanent Secretary to the Scottish Executive. Professor Geoffrey Boulton, OBE, FRS, FRSE is Regius Professor Emeritus of Geology at the University of Edinburgh. Professor Peter Clarke, FInstP, CPhys, FIET, CEng is Professor of Physics at the University of Edinburgh. David Eyton is Group Head of Research & Technology at BP. Professor James Norton, FRSA, FBCS, FIET is a board member of the British Parliament's Science & Technology Committee, a council member of the Parliamentary IT Commission, and a member of the Electronic Communications Expert Advisory Panel of the Irish Commission for Communications Regulation.

Sir Muir was appointed by the University of East Anglia to head the "independent review" into the CRU emails. Published in July 2010, his report was widely regarded as a joke, but it nevertheless had some harsh words for those involved, particularly with respect to the graph Mann co-authored for the World Meteorological Organization[1]:

FINDING: In relation to "hide the decline" we find that, given its subsequent iconic significance (not least the use of a similar figure in the TAR), the figure supplied for the WMO Report was misleading in not describing that one of the series was truncated

---

[1] http://www.cce-review.org/pdf/FINAL%20REPORT.pdf

post 1960 for the figure, and in not being clear on the fact that proxy and instrumental data were spliced together. We do not find that it is misleading to curtail reconstructions at some point per se, or to splice data, but we believe that both of these procedures should have been made plain – ideally in the figure but certainly clearly described in either the caption or the text.

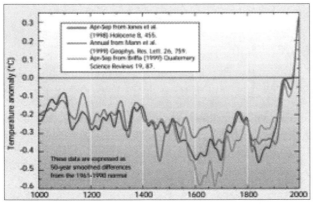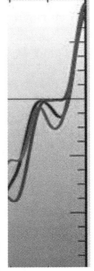

The decline they hid: The WMO tangle of spaghetti strands looks fine on the cover, but if you close in on the right-hand side you see that one of the strands is cut off - because, if it continued, it would head downwards and there'd be no hockey stick. Dr Judith Curry of Georgia Tech[2]:

There is no question that the diagrams and accompanying text in the IPCC TAR, AR4 and WMO 1999 are misleading. I was misled... It did not occur to me that recent paleo data was not consistent with the historical record... It is obvious that there has been **deletion of adverse data**... **Not only is this misleading, but it is dishonest.**

---

[2] http://judithcurry.com/2011/02/22/hiding-the-decline/

67

"An overly simplified and artistic depiction."

ATTORNEYS FOR DR MICHAEL E MANN, PHD

John B Williams is a Fellow of the American College of Trial Lawyers and an attorney with Williams Lopatto whose previous clients include the notorious fossil-fuel-funded Mobil Oil Corporation and Big Tobacco pitchman Joe Camel. Catherine Rosato Reilly and Peter J Fontaine are attorneys with Cozen O'Connor, Mr Fontaine being a founder of the Climate Science Legal Defense Fund.

On September 3rd 2014, acting for Michael Mann in his pleadings to the District of Columbia Court of Appeals, his lawyers forcefully addressed what Muir Russell's report had called a "misleading" graph[1]:

In their brief, the CEI Defendants suggest that the University of East Anglia's investigation actually found that the hockey stick graph was "misleading" because it did not identify that certain data was "truncated" and that other proxy and instrumental temperature data had been spliced together... This allegation is yet another example of Defendants' attempts to obfuscate the evidence in this case. The "misleading" comment made in this report had **absolutely nothing to do with Dr Mann, or with any graph prepared by him**. Rather, the report's comment was directed at an overly simplified and artistic depiction of the hockey stick that was reproduced on the frontispiece of the World Meteorological Organization's Statement on the Status of the Global Climate in 1999. Dr Mann did not create this

---

[1] http://www.steynonline.com/documents/6556.pdf

depiction, and the attempt to suggest that this report suggested an effort by Dr Mann to mislead is disingenuous.

Gotcha. That 1999 graph from the WMO 50th anniversary report is "absolutely nothing to do with Dr Mann". So, if it's "misleading" (as Sir Muir's panel found) or "overly simplified and artistic" (as Mann describes it), don't blame Dr Mann because "Dr Mann did not create this depiction". It's like going to Rolex and complaining that the Rollix you bought from that market stall has stopped ticking.

Yet, at the same time he was denying having anything to do with the WMO graph[2], Dr Mann's own curriculum vitae was boasting that he was a proud co-author of it[3]:

Jones, P.D., Briffa, K.R., Osborn, T.J., Mann, M.E., Bradley, R.S., Hughes, M.K., Cover Figure for World Meteorological Organization (WMO) 50th Year Anniversary Publication: *Temperature changes over the last Millennium,* 2000.

So the graph that has "absolutely nothing to do with Dr Mann" is listed on Dr Mann's own CV as one of his published works. And, when Mann's lawyers state baldly that "Dr Mann did not create this depiction", he is, by his own admission, one of said depiction's creators.

Irving Caesar, lyricist of "Tea For Two" and "Swanee", had a legendary Broadway flop with a show called My Dear Public. *The reviews were scathing, and singled Caesar out particularly, as he was the show's producer, lyricist, co-author and co-composer. The following morning he bumped into Oscar Hammerstein and said, "So they didn't like it. But why pick on me?" That's Mann's attitude to the 1999 hockey stick he co-authored: So it's misleading and over-simplified. But why pick on me?*

---

[2] http://climateaudit.org/2014/09/10/another-porky-from-mann-williams-and-fontaine/
[3] http://www.steynonline.com/pics/943.jpg

68

"'Our' reaction on the errors found in Mike Mann's work were not especially honest."

DR DOUGLAS MARAUN, PHD

Head of the Working Group of Statistical Climatology and Extreme Events at the GEOMAR Helmholtz Centre for Ocean Research. Former Senior Research Associate at the University of East Anglia's Climatic Research Unit.

And yet for all the "exonerations" of Mann perhaps the most straightforward judgment on his work came from a colleague. On October 24th 2007, two years before the Climategate leaks, Dr Maraun sent an email to fellow CRU staff with an interesting admission[1]:

I'd like to invite all of you to todays [sic] discussion seminar, 4pm in the coffee room:

"Climate science and the media"

After the publication of the latest IPCC, the media wrote a vast number of articles about possible and likely impacts, many of them greatly exaggerated. The issue seemed to dominate news for a long time and every company had to consider global warming in its advertisement.

However, much of this sympathy turned out to be either whitewashing or political correctness. Furthermore, recently and maybe especially after the "inconvenient truth" case and the

---

[1] http://junkscience.com/2011/11/22/climategate-2-0-alarmist-introspection-admits-dishonesty-on-hockey-stick/

Nobel peace prize going to Al Gore, many irritated and sceptical comments about so-called "climatism" appeared also in respectable newspapers.

Hence the coffee chat, which proposed to address seven topics. This was Number Two:

How should we deal with flaws inside the climate community? I think, that "our" reaction on the errors found in Mike Mann's work were not especially honest.

It is not known what conclusions the seminar plus coffee reached on "the errors found in Mike Mann's work".

One of the most startling of the Climategate emails was one sent on May 29th 2008 from Phil Jones to Michael Mann[2]:

Mike,

Can you delete any emails you may have had with Keith re AR4? Keith will do likewise… Can you also email Gene and get him to do the same? I don't have his new email address. We will be getting Caspar to do likewise.

Caspar is "Caspar Ammann" and Gene is "Eugene Wahl", authors of one of those "independent" studies that, according to Mann, confirms his hockey stick. If Mann was surprised at being asked to delete emails to get around Freedom of Information laws, he didn't indicate it in his response to Jones:

Hi Phil,

…I'll contact Gene about this ASAP. His new email is: generwahl@xxx

talk to you later,

mike

---

[2] http://junksciencearchive.com/FOIA/mail/1212063122.txt

69

"Q. Did you ever receive a request by either Michael Mann or any others to delete any emails? A. I did receive that email... I did delete the emails."

DR EUGENE WAHL, PHD

Physical Scientist with the Paleoclimatology Program at the US National Oceanic and Atmospheric Administration's National Climatic Data Center. Member of the American Association for the Advancement of Science, the American Geophysical Union and the Ecological Society of America.

Mann's official position on the email from Jones is that he forwarded it, as requested, but that he did not delete his own data, nor did he urge Wahl to delete his. When Todd Zinser, the Inspector-General of the US Commerce Department (which includes NOAA), came to investigate Climategate, he asked Dr Wahl about the matter[1]:

TODD ZINSER: Did you ever receive a request by either Michael Mann or any others to delete any emails?

EUGENE WAHL: I did receive that email. That's the last one on your list here. I did receive that...

ZINSER: ...and it was Michael Mann I guess ...that you received

---

[1] http://climateaudit.org/2011/03/08/wahl-transcript-excerpt/

the email from?

WAHL: Correct...

ZINSER: And what were the actions that you took?

WAHL: Well, to the best of my recollection, I did delete the emails...

ZINSER: So, did you find the request unusual ...that you were being requested to delete such emails?

WAHL: Well, I had never received one like it. In that sense, it was unusual...

ZINSER: I guess if the exchange of comments and your review was appropriate, I guess what I'm just trying to understand why you'd be asked to delete the emails after the fact, at the time that they're - it appears that the CRU is receiving FOIA requests

WAHL: Yeah. I had no knowledge of anything like that. But that's what they were..

"I did delete the emails": So mission accomplished. As the Inspector-General's final report explained[2]:

> The Director of the CRU requested a researcher from Pennsylvania State University [Mann] to ask an individual, who is now a NOAA scientist, to delete certain emails related to his participation in the IPCC AR4.
>
> This scientist explained to us that he believes he deleted the referenced emails at that time.

As the Inspector-General noted, Wahl was not yet an employee of NOAA - or acting on Mann's email would have been a serious breach of data retention rules.

---

[2] http://www.oig.doc.gov/OIGPublications/2011.02.18-IG-to-Inhofe.pdf

70

"He was not entirely truthful in a court case."

PROFESSOR RICHARD TOL, PHD

Professor of Economics at the University of Sussex and Professor of the Economics of Climate Change at the Free University, Amsterdam. Member of the Academia Europaea. Former Michael Otto Professor of Sustainability and Global Change, Director of the Center for Marine and Atmospheric Sciences and board member of the University of Hamburg's Center for Marine and Climate Research. Board member of the International Max Planck Research Schools on Earth System Modeling and Maritime Affairs, and of the European Forum on Integrated Environmental Assessment. IPCC author. Editor *of Energy Economics*, associate editor of *Environmental and Resource Economics*, editorial board member of *Environmental Science and Policy* and *Integrated Assessment*.

Whether or not he has been "exonerated" by the NRC, Lord Oxburgh, Sir Muir Russell, the NSF or any other body, anyone who's heard Mann interviewed on radio or introduced on stage knows that he has been acclaimed by the most eminent body of all. In 2012, when Michael Mann launched his lawsuit against the editor of this book and National Review, *he filed with the court a Statement of Claim accusing the defendants of the hitherto unknown crime of "defamation of a Nobel prize recipient"[1]. It was news to other Nobel Laureates that Dr Mann was among their number. It was also news to Professor Geir Lundestad, the director of the Nobel Institute in Oslo[2]:*

---

[1] http://legaltimes.typepad.com/files/michael-mann-complaint.pdf
[2] http://www.nationalreview.com/corner/331738/michael-manns-false-nobel-claim-charles-c-w-cooke

No, no. **He has never won the Nobel prize.**

Mann's claim to be a "Nobel prize recipient" - and thus in the same pantheon as Banting, Einstein and the Curies - rests on the fact that in 2007 the IPCC shared with Al Gore the Nobel Peace Prize and thus, as one of thousands of contributors to IPCC reports over the previous 17 years, Mann himself is now a Nobel Laureate. Similarly, in 2012 the European Union was awarded the Nobel Peace Prize and, by the same logic, as citizens of the EU, Brigitte Bardot, Bono and Antonio Banderas are all also "Nobel prize recipients".

After both the Nobel Institute and the IPCC told him to knock it off, Mann was obliged to file an amended complaint[3], withdrawing his self-conferred Nobel. Professor Tol is Mann's fellow IPC author and a citizen of the Netherlands and thus a two-time "Nobel prize recipient". Tweeter Roddy Campbell asked him about the "clarification" that appeared on Mann's Facebook page[4]. Professor Tol tweeted back[5]:

Maybe it is because he was not entirely truthful in a court case.

Indeed. In a comment at Dr Judith Curry's website, Professor Tol put it bluntly[6]:

Who does most damage to the climate movement? Michael Mann, Phil Jones, Jim Hansen, Peter Gleick, Al Gore, Rajendra Pachauri (not necessarily in that order).

So Mann is not necessarily Number One but he's certainly Top Six.

---

[3] http://www.steynonline.com/documents/6110.pdf
[4] https://www.facebook.com/photo.php?fbid=441602745895933&set=a.221233134599563.54502.221222081267335&type=1
[5] https://twitter.com/RichardTol/status/264643090848026625
[6] http://judithcurry.com/2012/02/24/why-target-heartland/#comment-175134

VIII

Mannspreading

SPAWN OF THE STICK

Based on the literature we have reviewed, there is no overarching consensus on MBH98/99. As analyzed in our social network, there is a tightly knit group of individuals who passionately believe in their thesis. However, our perception is that this group has a self-reinforcing feedback mechanism and, moreover, the work has been sufficiently politicized that they can hardly reassess their public positions without losing credibility.[1]

DR EDWARD J WEGMAN, PHD ET AL

AD HOC COMMITTEE REPORT ON

THE "HOCKEY STICK" GLOBAL CLIMATE RECONSTRUCTION (2006)

---

[1] https://climateaudit.files.wordpress.com/2007/11/07142006_wegman_report.pdf

CRITICS OF the hockey stick are often told that you can whine all you like but it's been "independently replicated". For example, climate blogger David Appell:

Mann et al's 'hockey stick' work is now established science - it's been replicated by many different groups, some using completely independent mathematical techniques (www. ncdc.noaa.gov/paleo/pubs/mann2008/mann2008.html).[2]

Er, well, that first link is to Mann himself. So, aside from Mann replicating Mann, what else have you got?

'A reconstruction of regional and global temperature for the past 11,300 years,' Marcott et al.

As we shall see in a few pages, that's all shaft and no blade. So no stick there. As Dr Craig Loehle says[3]:

A cluster of papers with overlapping authors and heavily overlapping data is not any sort of independent test.

Dr Barry Cooke of the Canadian government's Northern Forestry Centre[4]:

To the extent that multi-proxy reconstructions are built on the same proxy data, they are statistically non-independent (i.e. correlated). It's not the non-independence that make the model worthless. It's the uncertainty.

Nevertheless, go beyond Mann and a small group of associates and a

---

[2] http://davidappell.blogspot.com/2014/05/conrad-black-sees-michael-mann-winning.html
[3] http://wattsupwiththat.com/2012/04/17/scientists-rebuttal-of-michael-manns-denierand-other-unsavory-labels-in-his-book/
[4] http://www.ecowho.com/foia.php?file=1153172761.txt

hockey stick gets harder to find. Here's what Mann's stick looks like:

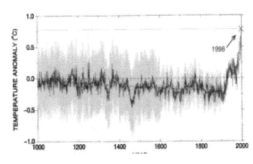

Keep your eye on the left end around zero, and the right end up at 0.8. That's what a hockey-stick replication needs to show - the Medieval non-Warm Period flatlined on the ground floor, and the late 20th century heading up through the roof.

Spot the Hockey Stick: Round One. How about these[5]?

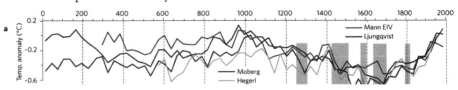

From the peak just left of the year 1000, that's in descending order Ljungqvist et al, "Mann EIV", Moberg et al, and Hegerl et al. That peak is the restored MWP, which instead of being 0.8° colder than now is instead about the same. So, instead of "replicating" Mann's findings, these guys put late 20th-century warming back within the range of natural variability. No hockey stick there.

Spot the Hockey Stick: Round Two[6]:

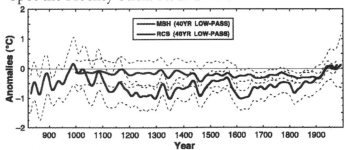

[5] http://skepticinkcom.c.presscdn.com/prussian/files/2014/03/pages2k.jpg
[6] http://www.sciencemag.org/content/295/5563/2250.full

That's Northern Hemisphere reconstructions (same turf as Mann) by Jan Esper and Fritz Schweingruber of the Swiss Federal Research Institute, and Edward Cook of the Lamont-Doherty Earth Observatory. At the year 1300 the top line is Mann, and the lower line is Esper, who has an MWP and a chilly Little Ice Age - and no stick.

Spot the Hockey Stick: Round Three[7]. The top line is from Håkan Grudd in 2008 and the one below it from Professor Grudd in 2002, as used in a talk by Professor Vincent Courtillot, who said. "Recent global warming is often labeled as 'abnormal' or 'without precedent'. It actually had equivalents in 750, 1000, 1400 and 1750."

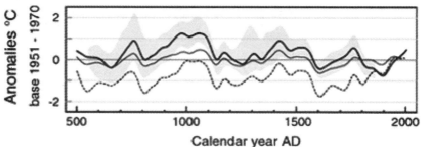

Spot the Hockey Stick: Round Four[8]. Craig Loehle:

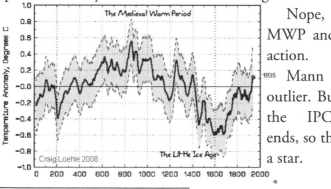

Nope, there's the MWP and LIA back in action.

Mann was always an outlier. But his graph fit the IPCC's political ends, so the stick became a star.

[7] https://www.youtube.com/watch?v=IG_7zK8ODGA
[8] http://joannenova.com.au/2009/12/fraudulent-hockey-sticks-and-hidden-data/

174

71

"Competent scientists do not doubt the hockey stick because it does not have enough publications... They doubt it because it has been shown to be based on incorrect math and inadequate data."

DR DONALD RAPP, PHD

Former research professor at the University of Southern California's Viterbi School of Engineering and former Professor of Physics and Environmental Engineering at the University of Texas. Former Senior Research Scientist at the Jet Propulsion Laboratory in Pasadena and Senior Staff Scientist at the Lockheed Palo Alto Research Laboratory. Contributor to *The Encyclopedia of Snow, Ice And Glaciers*.

Mann's cheerleaders among the climate activists continue to insist that his hockey stick has been replicated in dozens of "independent" studies. On page 136 of his book Assessing Climate Change: Temperature, Solar Radiation and Heat Balance, *Dr Rapp considered their claims[1]:*

To support their position, they mention: "nearly a dozen model-based and proxy-based reconstructions... by different groups all suggest that late 20th century warmth is anomalous in a long-

---

[1] Rapp: *Assessing Climate Change* (Springer-Praxis, 2010)

term (multi-century to millennial) context". However, the other publications typically utilized PCA with the mean chosen only for the calibration period, leading inevitably to some form of hockey stick if some of the proxies had an upward trend in the 20th century. It is not the number of papers that counts here.

In other words, if you use Mann's methods, it leads to Mann's madness. Aside from any statistical bias, they're mostly reprocessing the same very limited proxy data. As Professor North's report for the National Academy of Sciences concluded[2]:

> Because the data are so limited, different large-scale reconstructions are sometimes based on the same datasets and thus **cannot be considered as completely independent.**

Dr Rapp continued:

> As Bob Foster emphasized, truth in science is not a matter of voting. The issue here is whether the reconstruction is correct, independently of whether the reconstruction was done in two, 20 or 200 papers... Competent scientists do not doubt the hockey stick because it does not have enough publications to back it up. They doubt it because it has been shown to be based on incorrect math and inadequate data.

The above-mentioned Bob Foster is the late Australian geologist, who in a paper for Energy & Environment *put it very bluntly[3]:*

> This infamous 'hockey-stick' graph is anathema to palaeo-climatologists like me.

---

[2] http://dels.nas.edu/Report/Surface-Temperature-Reconstructions-Last/11676?bname=

[3] http://wattsupwiththat.com/2009/03/22/natural-drivers-of-weather-and-climate/

72

"A can of worms."

PROFESSOR ULRICH CUBASCH, PHD

Chair of the Interactions of Earth's Climate System at the Meteorological Institute at Berlin Free University. Former Dean of the Geoscience Faculty. Former Senior Scientist and Head of the Model and Data Group at the Max Planck Institute for Meteorology. Lead author for the IPCC on the First, Third, Fourth and Fifth Assessments. Review editor of *Climate Research*.

What happens if you're genuinely independent - that is, you're not a member of the tight-knit Hockey Team - and you try to replicate Mann's stick? In 2005 Professor Cubasch gave it a go[1]:

In my view, the present debate about Michael Mann's diagram is actually an expression of a healthy scientific discussion. **Whoever questions the curve does not have to be a climate skeptic.** My team of researchers is also working on the curve. I had set one of my PhD students the task to replicate Mann's work. Quite soon, she came to the conclusion that she cannot reproduce his diagram. We strove to look deeply into it – and promptly found a can of worms. After all, that's how science works.

The real problem in this case, in my view, is that **Michael Mann does not disclose his data.** It is also problematic that the discussion has become politically explosive. As climate skeptics notice that there are uncertainties in the results, they immediately see that as proof that climate research produces only nonsense.

It might be fairer to say that skeptics are bemused by the way that

---

[1] http://climateaudit.org/2005/03/04/cubasch-on-mbh/ - translation from the original German by Benny Peiser

significant and often unquantifiable "uncertainties" in the raw material get magically transformed in the final distillation to confident assertions about the warmest year of the millennium.

Notwithstanding that he found the hockey stick to be "a can of worms", Professor Cubasch deplored the way technical criticisms of Mann's work had been used to tar the broader climate establishment:

I consider it inadmissible to turn a completely specialist science debate into a fundamental criticism of climate research and the IPCC. After all, Mann's study appeared in *Nature*, a renowned peer-reviewed specialist journal. In such cases, the IPCC team has to rely on peer review. To check each publication used in the IPCC report would take far too long.

Thus the accumulation of authority: The IPCC would never have accepted it if Nature *hadn't accepted it, and* Nature *would never have accepted it if the science hadn't been sound - right?*

Meanwhile, everywhere but the hockey-stick science, that old inconvenient Medieval Warm Period kept turning up. Here's how Professor Brad Linsley of the Lamont-Doherty Earth Observatory summarized his own recent paper[2] to The New York Times[3]*:*

Things are more interconnected, I think, than we thought. We can't think of these as just European events or Northern Hemisphere events. We're in the middle of the warm pool in the western Pacific on the Equator or south of the Equator and still we're seeing these century-scale events - the Medieval Warm Period and the Little Ice Age... I think these events are global and we would expect other events to be, as well.

---

[2] http://www.sciencemag.org/content/342/6158/617
[3] http://dotearth.blogs.nytimes.com/2013/10/31/10000-year-study-finds-oceans-warming-fast-but-from-a-cool-baseline/

73

"Records with strong trends will be selected and that will effectively force a hockey stick result. Then Stephen McIntyre criticism is valid."

PROFESSOR DAVID KAROLY, PHD

Professor of Atmospheric Science at the University of Melbourne's School of Earth Sciences and ARC Centre of Excellence for Climate System Science. Member of Australia's Climate Change Authority. Former Professor of Meteorology at the University of Oklahoma and Director of Monash University's Cooperative Research Centre for Southern Hemisphere Meteorology. IPCC lead author and reviewer.

A typical hockey stick of recent years was the paper on which Professor Karoly worked with Dr Joëlle Gergis and others. In May of 2012, it got rave reviews[1]:

'1000 years of climate data confirms Australia's warming,' said the press release from University of Melbourne. It was picked up by *The Guardian*: 'Australasia has hottest 60 years in a millennium, scientists find'; *The Age* and *The Australian* led with 'Warming since 1950 "unprecedented"'. The story was on ABC 24 and ABC news where Gergis proclaimed: 'There are no other warm periods in the last 1,000 years that match the warming experienced in Australasia since 1950.' It was all over the

---

[1] http://joannenova.com.au/2012/10/gergis-hockey-stick-withdrawn-this-is-what-95-certainty-looks-like-in-climate-science/

ABC including ABC Radio National, and they were '95 per cent certain'! On ABC AM, 'the last five decades years [sic] in Australia have been the warmest.'

But then Stephen McIntyre got to work, and within three weeks the paper was in big trouble. Professor Karoly did not respond with the juvenile sneers of Mann. As he wrote to co-author Raphael Neukom[2]:

Thanks for the info on the correlations for the SR reconstructions during the 1911-90 period for detrended and full data. I think that it is much better to use the detrended data for the selection of proxies, as you can then say that you have identified the proxies that are responding to the temperature variations on interannual time scales, ie temp-sensitive proxies, without any influence from the trend over the 20th century. This is very important to be able to rebut the criticism ...that **you only selected proxies that show a large increase over the 20th century ie a hockey stick.**

The same argument applies for the Australasian proxy selection. If the selection is done on the proxies without detrending ie the full proxy records over the 20th century, then records with strong trends will be selected and that will effectively force a hockey stick result. Then Stephen Mcintyre criticism is valid. I think that it is really important to use detrended proxy data for the selection, and then choose proxies that exceed a threshold for correlations over the calibration period for either interannual variability or decadal variability for detrended data... **The criticism that the selection process forces a hockey stick result will be valid** if the trend is not excluded in the proxy selection step.

---

[2] http://climateaudit.org/2012/10/30/karoly-and-gergis-vs-journal-of-climate/

74

"Due to errors discovered in this paper during the publication process, it was withdrawn by the authors."

THE JOURNAL OF CLIMATE ON JOËLLE GERGIS ET AL

The Journal of Climate is a scientific journal published by the American Meteorological Society.

After Professor Karoly and Dr Gergis brought the problem to the attention of The Journal of Climate, *they received the following email:*

After consulting with the Chief Editor, I have decided to rescind acceptance of the paper- you'll receive an official email from *J Climate* to this effect as soon as we figure out how it should be properly done...

Also, since it appears that you will have to redo the entire analysis (and which may result in different conclusions), I will also be requesting that you withdraw the paper from consideration. Again, you'll hear officially from *J Climate* in due course. I invite you to resubmit once the necessary analyses and changes to the manuscript have been made.

Unsure what to do next, Professor Karoly consulted the master:

Following some email discussions with Mike Mann and helpful discussions with you both last week, there appear to be several different approaches that we can take with revising the Australasian temp recon paper. I am going to go through some of them briefly, and then raise some suggestions for further data analysis that might be needed.

1. Amend the manuscript so that it states the actual way that the proxy selection was done, based on correls that included trends and were significant at the 5% level. The calibration was also done using the full data variations, including trends, over the calibration period. **As Mike Mann says below** and in the attached papers, this is a common approach. **Don't seriously address the proxy selection for detrended data...**

Dr Gergis in turn wrote back to The Journal of Climate *with an appeal to, er, authority:*

People have argued that **detrending proxy records when reconstructing temperature is in fact undesirable** (see two papers attached provided **courtesy of Professor Michael Mann**).

Despite their best efforts, the Gergis paper was dead. As Joanne Nova wrote[1]:

In May it was all over the newspapers, in June it was shown to be badly flawed. By October, it quietly gets withdrawn.

Yes, indeed[2]:

Due to errors discovered in this paper during the publication process, it was withdrawn by the authors prior to being published in final form.

---

[1] http://joannenova.com.au/2012/10/gergis-hockey-stick-withdrawn-this-is-what-95-certainty-looks-like-in-climate-science/
[2] http://retractionwatch.com/2012/10/18/updates-journal-of-climate-adds-info-about-withdrawn-hot-temps-paper-chemistry-journal-corrects-retraction-notice/

75

"The hockey stick does not represent global climate and thus should not be used in any argument."

DR GEORGE DENTON, PHD

Professor at the University of Maine's Climate Change Institute and School of Earth and Climate Sciences. Author of peer-reviewed papers in *Nature, Science, Quaternary Geochronology, Quaternary Science Reviews, Geology, Nature Geoscience, Polar Research* and *Proceedings of the National Academy of Sciences.*

What about if you're not a member of the Hockey Team and you go looking for a hockey stick in the Southern Hemisphere? In 2012, in a project for the Cooperative Institute for Climate Applications and Research of Columbia University's Earth Institute, Dr Denton wrote[1]:

The classic hockey stick diagram lies at the core of placing ongoing global warming into the context of the natural climate changes of the last millennium. Mountain glaciers in the Southern Alps and southern Andes were very sensitive trackers of atmospheric temperature. Therefore, they can be used to determine if the hockey-stick pattern is present in the middle latitudes of the Southern Hemisphere. The answer is no. **In fact, the pattern is quite different from that of a hockey stick.** During the Middle Ages, southern glaciers were more extensive than they were at the time of the northern Little Ice Age. During the Little Ice Age, southern glaciers slowly receded and lost

[1] http://cicar.ei.columbia.edu/sitefiles/file/CICAR_Shadow_Award_0912_
Listing&Report2012_Web.pdf

volume while northern glaciers expanded. However, this southern volume loss accelerated after AD 1865, in concert with recession of northern glaciers at the end of the Little Ice Age. Thus north-south glacier behavior was dissimilar during the Middle Ages and Little Ice Age, but similar after AD 1865, a time of rising atmospheric CO_2. These results are consistent with global glacier recession during the last century and a half, a time of rising atmospheric CO_2. But they indicate that the hockey stick does not represent global climate and thus should not be used in any argument comparing the current warming with that of the Middle Ages or placing the ongoing warming in the context of natural global climate variation.

The Middle Ages? Ha! The hockey stick's only getting warmed up. As Professor Marcel Leroux wrote in 2005[2]:

> This 'warming' may well have been without precedent during the last 1,000 years, but this seems not to be long enough for the IPCC! The period in question had to be extended: from the original 600 years (1998) through 1,000 (1999), and finally to two millennia, according to Jones and Mann (2004), who pushed the starting point back by 1,800 years, and even beyond, though, obviously, the same conclusions were reached. And the conclusions will always be the same, as long as the thermal curve used relies upon the trick of mixing incompatible data: **one can blithely go back in time as far as one cares to, knowing that the curve will terminate every time with the 'reconstituted' temperatures!**

But that's no reason not to shoot for the greatest hockey stick of all...

---

[2] Leroux: *Global Warming: Myth or Reality? The Erring Ways of Climatology* (Springer-Praxis, 2005)

76

"The paper should be withdrawn immediately."

PROFESSOR PAUL MATTHEWS, PHD

Associate Professor and Reader in Applied Mathematics in the Faculty of Science at the University of Nottingham. Author of peer-reviewed papers published by *Physical Review*, *Mathematical Medicine and Biology*, and *The Proceedings of the Royal Society of Edinburgh*.

The life-span of replica hockey sticks is inversely proportional to the millennia they claim to delineate. In 2013 Dr Shaun Marcott and his co-authors came up with the ultimate hockey stick. No messing around with one millennium or two, this was a hockey stick for the entire Holocene[1] - ie, 11,300 years. It was published by Science, *Mann himself hailed it as "an important paper", and it was cooed over by Andrew Revkin of* The New York Times[2]:

> The work reveals a fresh, and very long, climate 'hockey stick.'

The lead author himself made it clear he was a chip off the old stick[3]:

> 'What's striking,' said lead author Shaun Marcott of Oregon State University in an interview, 'is that the records we use are completely independent, and produce the same result.'

---

[1] http://www.sciencemag.org/content/339/6124/1198.abstract
[2] http://dotearth.blogs.nytimes.com/2013/03/07/scientists-find-an-abrupt-warm-jog-after-a-very-long-cooling/
[3] http://www.climatecentral.org/news/climate-to-warm-beyond-levels-seen-for-at-least-11300-years-15701

And then Professor Matthews took a look at it[4]:

This paper includes several graphs that show slow temperature variation over the last 10,000 years followed by a rapid rise over the 20th century. This aspect of the paper has unsurprisingly been seized upon enthusiastically by climate activists and journalists. However it is clear that this result is spurious. Note the following points:

1. The proxy data in the accompanying Excel file show **no dramatic increase in the 20th century.** This can easily be checked simply by plotting the supplied data.

2. Figures S5 and S6 show no recent upturn at all.

3. The PhD thesis of the first author uses the same data sets and plots similar graphs, but with no trace of any sharp increase. This earlier contradictory work is not cited in the paper.

4. The supplementary material provides no explanation for how the graphs were constructed. Carrying out an averaging of the proxy data yields a graph similar to that in the thesis, quite different from that in the paper. Why was no detailed explanation of the procedure reported? Will the authors supply the code that was used?

Any one of these issues would raise serious questions about the validity of this work. Taken together they leave no doubt that **the results presented are spurious and misleading.** The paper should be withdrawn immediately. **The fact that such an obviously flawed paper was published raises serious questions about the authors, the quality of the refereeing process and the handling of the paper by the editors of *Science*.**

---

[4] http://bishophill.squarespace.com/blog/2013/3/15/marcott-in-freefall.html?currentPage=2#comment19838456

77

"The 20th-century portion of our paleotemperature stack is not statistically robust. "

DR SHAUN MARCOTT, PHD ET AL

Shaun Marcott is Assistant Professor at the University of Wisconsin-Madison. Jeremy Shakun is Assistant Professor of the Department of Earth and Environmental Sciences at Boston College. Peter Clark and Alan Mix are professors at Oregon State University's College of Earth, Ocean and Atmospheric Sciences.

Mann had no time for criticisms of the Marcott paper by the likes of Professor Matthews. As he gloated on Twitter[1]:

Watching the pro #climatechange #denial smear artists spinning desperately in wake of new article... Dagger in heart?

Poor old Mann. Most hockey-stick reconstructions turn out to have no long, straight handle. This time round, it emerged that Mann's "dagger" had no blade. As Dr Marcott et al explained to the Mann-boys of Real Climate[2]:

Our global paleotemperature reconstruction includes a so-called "uptick" in temperatures during the 20th-century. However, in the paper we make the point that this particular feature is of

---

[1] https://twitter.com/MichaelEMann/status/310381414157799425
[2] http://www.realclimate.org/index.php/archives/2013/03/response-by-marcott-et-al/

shorter duration than the inherent smoothing in our statistical averaging procedure, and that it is based on only a few available paleo-reconstructions of the type we used. Thus, the 20th century portion of our paleotemperature stack is not statistically robust, **cannot be considered representative of global temperature changes**, and therefore is not the basis of any of our conclusions.

What was that? The 20th century portion is "not statistically robust"? So, as Professor Roger Pielke Jr summarized it, it's a hockey stick with no blade[3]. Just a long, long shaft. He went to the trouble of removing the non-robust section from the graphic:

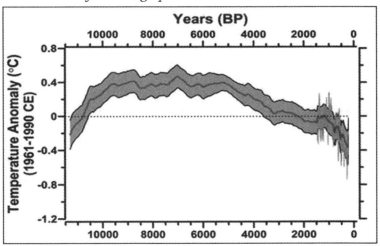

You can't get the climate puck in the back of the net with that.

  So the world's first 11,000-year hockey stick lasted all of a fortnight.

  Oh, well, back to the old drawing board...

---

[3] http://rogerpielkejr.blogspot.com/2013/03/fixing-marcott-mess-in-climate-science.html

78

"*The new hockey stick is no such thing... Does the public misrepresentation amount to scientific misconduct?*"

DR ROGER PIELKE JR, PHD

Professor of Environmental Sciences and Fellow of the Cooperative Institute for Research in Environmental Sciences at the University of Colorado, Boulder. Co-editor of *Prediction: Science, Decision Making and the Future of Nature*. Former Director of the Center for Science and Technology Policy Research at Boulder, visiting scholar at Oxford University's James Martin Institute for Science and Civilization, and staff scientist at the National Center for Atmospheric Research.

As noted on the previous page, Dr Pielke pointed out the obvious - Marcott et al's pan-Holocene if-you-only-buy-one-hockey-stick-this-interglacial-make-it-this-one Ultimate Xtreme Hockey Stick was, in fact, all shaft and no blade[1]:

What that means is that **this paper actually has nothing to do with a "hockey stick"** as it does not have the ability to reproduce 20th century temperatures in a manner that is "statistically robust." The new "hockey stick" is no such thing as Marcott et al has no blade... The temperature reconstruction does not allow any conclusions to be made about the period after 1900.

---

[1] http://rogerpielkejr.blogspot.com/2013/03/fixing-marcott-mess-in-climate-science.html

Thus, like Mann's original, the new stick can tell us nothing about the relationship of present temperatures to the past. But that's not the impression you'd have got from the National Science Foundation press release[2]:

> With data from 73 ice and sediment core monitoring sites around the world, scientists have reconstructed Earth's temperature history back to the end of the last Ice Age.
>
> The analysis reveals that the planet today is warmer than it's been during 70 to 80 per cent of the last 11,300 years... "We already knew that on a global scale, Earth is warmer today than it was over much of the past 2,000 years," Marcott says. "Now we know that it is warmer than most of the past 11,300 years..."
>
> "This research shows that we've experienced almost the same range of temperature change since the beginning of the industrial revolution," says [the NSF's Candace] Major, "as over the previous 11,000 years of Earth history..."
>
> "What is most troubling," [co-author Peter] Clark says, "is that this warming will be significantly greater than at any time during the past 11,300 years."

Why would they say such things? As Dr Pielke commented:

Surely there is great value in such an analysis of pre-20th century temperatures... But one point that any observer should be able to clearly conclude is that the public representation of the paper was grossly in error...

Does the public misrepresentation amount to scientific misconduct? I'm not sure, but it is far too close to that line for comfort.

---

[2] http://www.nsf.gov/news/news_summ.jsp?cntn_id=127133

79

"Excuse me while I puke."

DR RAYMOND S BRADLEY, PHD

Distinguished Professor in the Department of Geosciences and Research Director of the Climate System Research Center at the University of Massachusetts Amherst. Michael E Mann's co-author on the original two hockey sticks. Co-editor of *Climate Since AD 1500* (Routledge, London, 1992) and co-author of *Climate Change And Society* (Stanley Thornes, Cheltenham, 2001).

What is Mann looking for in a proxy reconstruction? That's easy: Undeviating loyalty. As a result, even his closest friends and colleagues are not always comfortable with the Mann style. Dr Bradley was there with him at the beginning - the "B" in MBH98, the older, distinguished scientist who co-authored Mann's original hockey stick. In April 1999 the CRU's Keith Briffa and Tim Osborn were preparing a submission to Science *that had the impertinence to mention "uncertainties in tree-ring data". Mann inserted himself into the review process and declared Briffa and Osborn's mild difference of opinion "unacceptable". Dr Bradley emailed the editor to distance himself:*

I would like to diasassociate myself from Mike Mann's view... As for thinking that it is "Better that nothing appear, than something unnacceptable [sic] to us" ...as though we are the gatekeepers of all that is acceptable in the world of paleoclimatology seems amazingly arrogant. Science moves forward whether we agree with individiual [sic] articles or not.

Sincerely, Raymond S Bradley

---

[1] http://junkscience.com/2011/11/28/climategate-2-0-mann-bid-to-be-science-gatekeeper-is-amazingly-arrogant/

And yet "gatekeeper of all that is acceptable" is exactly how Mann saw himself even then, way back in 1999. As the years went by, his determination to exclude any dissenting views from the peer-reviewed literature would grow ever more fierce. But in this instance his pressure paid off, and the "unacceptable" was rendered "acceptable" - to him[2]:

Dear all,

Thanks for working so hard to insure a final product that was acceptable to all...

I appreciate having had the opportunity to respond to the original draft. I think this opportunity is very important in such cases (ie, where a particular author/groups work is the focus of a commentary by someone else), and hope that this would be considered standard procedure in the future in such instances.

I think we have some honest disagreements amonst us about some of the underlying issues, but these were fairly treated in the piece and that's what is important (The choice of wording in the final version was much better too. Wording matters!).

Thanks all for the hard work and a job well done. I like to think that may [sic] feedback helped here - so I take some pride here as well.

best regards,

mike

Upon receipt of Mann's email, Professor Bradley sent Keith Briffa a one-line reaction under the subject header "vomit":

Excuse me while I puke...

Ray

---

[2] http://di2.nu/foia/foia2011/mail/1364.txt

80

"A very misleading message about how resolved this part of the scientific research was."

PROFESSOR KURT M CUFFEY, PHD

Professor of Geography and Martin Distinguished Chair in Ocean, Earth and Climate Science at the University of California, Berkeley. Recipient of the American Geophysical Union's Macelwane Medal, whose citation notes his pioneering use of borehole thermometry to obtain a temperature calibration of the oxygen isotope record in ice cores. Co-author of *The Physics of Glaciers*. Author of peer-reviewed papers in *Nature*, *Science* and other journals.

Professor Cuffey was a member of one the many expert panels Mann claims has "exonerated" him - in this case, the NRC investigation. After the report's release, he spoke to the journal Science[1]:

Panel members were less sanguine, however, about whether the original work should have loomed so large in the executive summary of the IPCC's 2001 report. "The IPCC used it as a visual prominently in the report," says Kurt Cuffey, a panel member and geographer at the University of California, Berkeley. "I think that sent a very misleading message about how resolved this part of the scientific research was."

"No individual paper tells the whole story," agrees North. "It's very dangerous to pull one fresh paper out from the literature."

---

[1] http://www.nature.com/nature/journal/v441/n7097/full/4411032a.html

Nature *also reported on Professor Cuffey's remarks at the press conference*[2]:

> The committee has "less confidence" in Mann's conclusion that recent temperatures have set a record for the entire millennium. "The committee concluded that **Mann and his colleagues underestimated the uncertainty**" in the earlier part of the record, said Cuffey, for which records are of lower quality and fewer in number. "In fact, these uncertainties aren't fully quantified," he said...

In the years since, have those uncertainties been resolved in Mann's favor? No. Most papers find greater natural variability - as Professor Cuffey well knows. He's the man who demonstrated that temperature changes were much greater than previously assumed and that the transition from glacial to Holocene conditions was accompanied by a 15°C increase in Greenland - without any assistance from you or your SUV. The press conference continued:

> The committee has "even less confidence" in Mann et al's 1999 conclusion that "the 1990s are likely the warmest decade, and 1998 the warmest year, in at least a millennium." "That's plausible," said Cuffey. "**We don't know if it's true or not.**" A year or a decade is just too short an interval for comparison to the older paleotemperature record, he said.

And, until some new technological advance is made, that is still the case. Mann and his acolytes can produce as many hockey sticks as they want, going back through all of time, and the fact remains:

> We don't know if it's true or not.

---

[2] http://www.sciencemag.org/content/312/5782/1854

IX

Mann boobs

ONE-STICK PONY

They show that one of the most important and widely known results of climate analysis, the 'hockey stick' diagram of Mann et al, was based on a mistake.[1]

REFEREE FOR GEOPHYSICAL RESEARCH LETTERS
REVIEW OF "HOCKEY STICKS, PRINCIPAL COMPONENTS, AND
SPURIOUS SIGNIFICANCE" (2005)

---

[1] http://www.uoguelph.ca/~rmckitri/research/Climate_H.pdf

IN THE YEARS since Mann's very first stick, he's produced ...more sticks. Hockey sticks aren't just for temperature anymore, you can use them for hurricanes and Gulf Streams and reconstructing fake Nobel Prize claims, 1998-2008. In 2015, the respected science writer Matt Ridley wrote:

> In March this year Dr Mann published a paper claiming the Gulf Stream was slowing down[2]. This garnered headlines all across the world. Astonishingly, his evidence that the Gulf Stream is slowing down came not from the Gulf Stream, but from 'proxies' which included - yes - bristlecone pine trees in Arizona, upside-down lake sediments in Scandinavia and larch trees in Siberia.[3]

Indeed. The actual observed real-world measurements of the currents over the last two decades data show the Gulf Stream *isn't* slowing down - according to a 2014 paper[4] by oceanographer Thomas Rosby, winner of the AGU's Maurice Ewing Medal, and inventor of the SOFAR (sound-fixing and ranging) float which in 1973 provided the first dense-resolution animation of the deep ocean flow. But obviously that can't begin to compete with Mann and a rub of his magic bristlecone.

Mann's Gulf Stream paper didn't make much of a splash. Not much of his science has since those first hockey sticks at the turn of the century. If you do to his hockey stick what he did to Mia Tiljander's Finnish sediments and flip it, you have a pretty good graph of his career: at the front, a short sharp upward "blade" showing his meteoric rise - and then the long, slow shaft.

When someone criticizes Mann's science, the first response is

---

[2] http://www.nature.com/nclimate/journal/v5/n5/full/nclimate2554.html
[3] http://quadrant.org.au/magazine/2015/06/climate-wars-done-science/
[4] http://onlinelibrary.wiley.com/wol1/doi/10.1002/2013GL058636/full

generally that the criticism is invalid because the critic is "not a scientist". If it turns out he *is* a scientist, then it's still dismissable because he's not a climate scientist - even though as the late physicist Hal Lewis observed apropos this line, you can't do climate science without physics, but you can certainly do physics without climate science. And, if it transpires that he is indeed a climate scientist, he's not the right kind of climate scientist - which is to say he may know a lot about ocean currents or cloud formation, but he's not a big-picture planet-wide millennial-reconstructionist climate scientist like Mann.

Climate science has changed over the years. A couple of generations back, it was a branch of physical geography. Today it's computer modeling. When Mann got into the game, paleo-climatology was a backwater, sneered at by the modelers. Mann's genius was to move in and turn paleoclimatology into computer modeling for all space and all time: Instead of wasting months up to your neck in Scandinavian sediments, why not just take everything ever, toss it in the Mann woodchipper and see what comes out?

In a sense, he invented his art, and therefore, on his defenders' terms, no one is qualified to criticize Mann. It would be as absurd as a painter or sculptor criticizing Damien Hirst's prize-winning dead sheep preserved in formaldehyde. What does Rembrandt know of formaldehyde? Where are Titian's credentials on ovine preservation?

There are peer-reviewed studies by over 750 scientists from over 450 research institutions in over 40 countries that have found a Medieval Warm Period of between 0.1° and 3.2°C warmer than today in every corner of the globe[5] - from Alaska to South Africa, Morocco to New Zealand, Bolivia to China, Egypt to New

---

[5] http://joannenova.com.au/2009/12/fraudulent-hockey-sticks-and-hidden-data/

Guinea... Everywhere they look for it, they find it. But when it's all processed into Mike's worldwide paleoproxypalooza, it vanishes every time - and don't you dare question it, because Mike's whole is always greater than the sum of everybody else's parts.

Fun things happen to all that boringly local data along the way. In their original 2003 paper[6], McIntyre & McKitrick found that Mann had reassigned an instrumental precipitation record from Paris to New England - an error for which McIntyre channeled *My Fair Lady*: "The rain in Maine falls mainly in the Seine." McIntyre subsequently discovered that what Mann declares as a South Carolina gridcell in MBH98 appears to be from Toulouse, and what Mann credits as a Bombay set appears to be from Philadelphia. Close enough! When you're bestriding the planet like a colossus, who cares about assigning the right data to the right continent?

The Parisian "rain in Maine" went uncorrected all the way up to Mann's 2007 paper. A year or so later, McIntyre noticed that Mann had reassigned a Spanish data set to Tanzania: The rain in Spain falls mainly on the (East African) plain. This time Mann was forced to correct the error and recalculate, although in breach of Penn State's code of conduct he did not credit McIntyre as the source of the correction. Mann's usual line when forced to admit he bungled something is that his various errors never make any difference to his big picture. So it's worth noting that correcting just that one itsy-bitsy dataset and moving it back from East Africa to the Iberian peninsula raised his estimated temperature by half-a-degree Celsius for the entire 18th century[7].

It makes one wonder what the graph might look like if he corrected *all* his boobs.

---

[6] https://climateaudit.files.wordpress.com/2005/09/mcintyre.mckitrick.2003.pdf
[7] http://climateaudit.org/2008/11/09/the-rain-in-spain/

81

"Mike is misleading...
Mike does not properly distinguish...
Mike is in error...
Mike misses the point... "

DR ROGER PIELKE SR, PHD

Emeritus Professor at Colorado State University's Department of Atmospheric Science and Senior Research Scientist at the Cooperative Institute for Research in Environmental Sciences at Colorado University, Boulder. Fellow of the American Meteorological Society and former chairman of its Committee on Weather Forecasting and Analysis. Fellow of the American Geophysical Union. Pioneered development of the Regional Atmospheric Modeling System. Former research scientist at NOAA's Experimental Meteorology Lab. Former Editor-in-Chief of *The US National Science Report*, Chief Editor of *Monthly Weather Review* and Co-Chief Editor of *The Journal of Atmospheric Sciences*.

Mann is nothing if not boundlessly confident. But a 2012 interview with Scientific American *gave a glimpse of how hermetically sealed from reality is his science[1]. Dr Pielke responded at his website[2]:*

Mike is misleading in his defense of multi-decadal climate models predictions as a robust scientific tool to forecast changes in climate statistics decades from now...

---

[1] http://www.scientificamerican.com/podcast/episode/michael-mann-defends-climate-comput-12-01-10/
[2] https://pielkeclimatesci.wordpress.com/2012/01/26/comment-on-the-scientific-american-interview-by-david-biello-titled-michael-mann-defends-climate-computer-models/

Mike does not properly distinguish between the types of modeling. When airplanes or cars are built, the engineers are testing their models using real world airplanes and cars, as well as with wind tunnel evaluations. They can ground-truth their models.

With respect to atmospheric modeling, numerical modeling prediction of the weather for the coming days is ground-truthing, as the forecasts can be compared with real-world observations just a few days later.

With multi-decadal climate predictions, they can only realistically be tested from past climate conditions, unless we wait for the coming decades to pass. Even in the hindcast mode, however, the global climate models (whether downscaled to regions or not) have failed to predict changes in the statistics of regional climate...

Mike is in error. With the Higgs Boson, its existence (the theory) is being tested against real world data. With the prediction of climate change, even with coarse metrics such as the magnitude of global warming as diagnosed by changes in the heat content of the climate system, these global average forecasts on the verge of failing (e.g. see)! With respect to the prediction of multi-decadal changes in regional climate statistics, which are needed by the impact community, these models have failed so far to show any skill...

Mike misses the point that this knowledge of physics does not then result in skillful global and regional predictions of changes in climate statistics. The climate system is much more than just changes in the atmospheric concentration of $CO2$ and a few other greenhouse gases. Mike is misunderstanding "the way models are used". He is confusing tested and verified model predictions with unverified model results.

82

"Just bad science."

DR DAVID S CHAPMAN, PHD, DR MARSHALL G BARTLETT, PHD AND DR ROBERT N HARRIS, PHD

David S Chapman is Distinguished Professor Emeritus and Robert N Harris is Adjunct Associate Professor in the Department of Geology and Geophysics at the University of Utah. Marshall G Bartlett, formerly of the University of Utah, is Chairman of the Science Department at the Hockaday School in Texas.

In 2003 Geophysical Research Letters unveiled Mann and Gavin Schmidt's paper "Ground vs. surface air temperature trends: Implications for borehole surface temperature reconstructions". In April the following year they published Drs Chapman, Bartlett and Harris' comment on Mann and Schmidt's work. For a peer-reviewed scientific journal, Chapman, Bartlett and Harris' language was unusually forceful[1]:

Borehole temperatures respond to an integrated, continuous time series of temperature at the Earth's surface [Harris and Chapman, 1998]. Furthermore, the process of heat conduction smoothes out high frequency temperature fluctuations so subsurface temperature profiles contain information on average surface temperatures over decade to century time scales, depending on the depth of a particular anomaly. It is these characteristics, direct measurement of temperature, sensitivity to a continuous rather than a discontinuous or seasonal time series, and low-pass filtering that make borehole temperature analysis such a useful

---

[1] https://ir.library.oregonstate.edu/xmlui/bitstream/handle/1957/18797/ Chapman_et_al_Geophys_Res_Lett_2004.pdf?sequence=1

complement of climate change studies. When Mann and Schmidt [2003] break their model output time series into warm season and cold season series their results may be of interest to seasonal investigations but have **little relevance** to, and are **misleading** in, the comparison of GST [ground surface temperature] and SAT [surface air temperature] tracking...

A second misleading analysis made by Mann and Schmidt [2003] concerns inappropriate use of end-points in reaching a numerical conclusion. In their paper, Mann and Schmidt focus on the model period 1971–1998 in which significant warming takes place. They state, "During a period of coincident surface warming and cold-season snow cover decrease in the model (1971–1998) mean [GST] increases are 0.2°C less than those in SAT, a consequence of greater exposure of the ground surface to winter cold air outbreaks. Interpretations of past SAT trends from borehole-based [GST] reconstructions may therefore be substantially biased by seasonal influences and snow cover changes." [Mann and Schmidt, 2003, paragraph 1] The 0.2°C difference in this period is misleading. It is based on using end points in computing changes in an oscillating time series, and is just bad science. For example, had they chosen the time period 1975–1996 the equally erroneous end-point analysis would have lead to an opposite conclusion that GST changes are 0.14°C more than the SAT changes...

The third misleading conclusion reached by Mann and Schmidt [2003] is that "[snow cover] and pre-conditioning [of the ground] by prior warm-season SAT exhibits a sizable and, in places, dominant influence" on cold season GST, (r = 0.7) thereby apparently degrading tracking between SAT and GST. [Mann and Schmidt, 2003, paragraph 1].

83

"The data used in Mann et al (2008) does not allow reliable temperature prediction."

PROFESSOR LASSE HOLMSTRÖM, PHD

Professor in the University of Oulu's Department of Mathematical Sciences. Author of peer-reviewed papers published in *The Journal of Applied Statistics*, *The Annals of Applied Statistics*, *The Journal of Geophysical Research*, *The Holocene*, *The Journal of Statistical Computation and Simulation*, and other journals.

In 2011, in a discussion of the McShane & Wyner paper[1], Professor Holmström wrote in The Annals of Applied Statistics[2]:

This [McShane & Wyner] is an impressive paper. The authors present a thorough examination of the ability of various climate proxies to predict temperature. The prediction method is one much used in climate science literature and assumes a linear relationship between the proxies and the temperature. The idea is to use instrumental temperature data together with the corresponding proxy records to estimate a regression model to which historical proxy values are then input in order to produce a backcast of past temperature variation. The authors demonstrate convincingly that the data used in Mann et al (2008) does not allow reliable temperature prediction using this approach and that purely random artificial proxy records, in fact, perform

---

[1] See page 49
[2] https://archive.org/stream/arxiv-1104.4185/1104.4185_djvu.txt

equally well or even better.

That was a reference to Mann's 2008 paper called "Proxy-based reconstructions of hemispheric and global surface temperature variations over the past two millennia"[3] - yet another re-tilling of familiar soil.

The following year he decided to try something different - a so-called "hurricane hockey stick"[4], written with Jonathan Woodruff of the University of Massachusetts, Jeffrey Donnelly of Woods Hole and Zhihua Zhang, also of Penn State. As usual, however, Mann couldn't resist overselling the product - to the irritation of a genuine hurricane man, Dr Christopher Landsea[5]:

> What is curious, too, is the press release[6] issued at Penn State that concluded: "It seems that the paleodata support the contention that greenhouse warming may increase the frequency of Atlantic tropical storms," said Mann. "It may not be just that the storms are stronger, but that there are there may be more of them as well."
>
> **Why would such a strong statement be included in a press release that isn't even discussed in the paper?** Would the paper's co-authors agree with this very public pronouncement about the implications of the work?

That would seem unlikely given that in Nature *in 2007 Woodruff and Donnelly's review of 5,000 years of hurricane activity[7] had found no evidence of any greenhouse-gas connection. Was this another example of Mann "pushing" his colleagues "beyond where we know is right"?*

---

[3] http://www.pnas.org/content/early/2008/09/02/0805721105.full.pdf+html
[4] http://www.nature.com/nature/journal/v460/n7257/full/nature08219.html
[5] http://www.sott.net/article/191397-Chris-Landsea-Response-to-Michael-Mann-Hurricane-Hockey-Stick
[6] http://www.eurekalert.org/pub_releases/2009-08/ps-hoi081009.php
[7] http://www.nature.com/nature/journal/v447/n7143/full/nature05834.html

84

"The paper comes to very erroneous conclusions because of using improper data and illogical techniques."

DR CHRISTOPHER LANDSEA, PHD

Science and Operations Officer at the US National Hurricane Center. Recipient of the Banner I Miller Award from the American Meteorological Society for "best contribution to the science of hurricane and tropical weather forecasting", and of the NOAA Administrator's Award for establishing NOAA's first US Weather Research Program testbed. Former chair of the AMS Committee on Tropical Meteorology and Tropical Cyclone. Member of the American Geophysical Union and the American Meteorological Society.

Dr Landsea's problems with Mann's "hurricane hockey stick" went beyond the press release[1]:

Dear Michael and tropical storm folks,

I have some additional concerns about this new paper... The two gravest issues are the paper's use of the Atlantic basin tropical storm frequency data without consideration of new studies and the merger of the paleo-tempestology record to the historical storm data...

The first issue was that Mann had disregarded research showing that, thanks to improvements in observations, whereas three-to-four tropical storms a year were "missed" in the late 19th century, by the 1960s it was

---

[1] http://www.sott.net/article/191397-Chris-Landsea-Response-to-Michael-Mann-Hurricane-Hockey-Stick

only one per year. Likewise, recent research indicated that two-thirds of the supposed "increase" in storms were what Dr Landsea called "shorties", of less than two days' duration:

Taking out these "shorties" (very likely due just to our vastly improved observational capabilities) from the record and adding in the estimated number of "missed" medium to long-lived tropical storms **causes the long-term trend to completely disappear...** This isn't a small quibble: it's the difference between a massive trend with doubling in the last 100 years, versus no trend with only multidecadal variability remaining. This new peer-reviewed research should not have been ignored completely.

And yet again Mann was mixing observational apples and paleo bananas:

The merging of the paleo record with the historical all-basin tropical storm counts is very problematic. Instead of trying to upscale the paleo-tempestology data... to all basin tropical cyclone activity.., an apples-to-apples comparison directly of paleo landfall data to historical (1851 to today) hurricane-only landfall data should have been performed. Not surprisingly, **the historical landfall record for those five sites shows no trend.** How could this be considered a homogenous comparison: landfall of (primarily) major hurricanes at five locations versus all basin tropical storm and hurricane numbers whose trend is mainly due to very short-lived, weak tropical storms that we simply couldn't observe decades ago..?

The bottom line is that the paper comes to very erroneous conclusions because of using improper data and illogical techniques. In my opinion, **this work is, unfortunately, a step backwards** in helping climate researchers understand how hurricanes have changed over the last several centuries.

85

"Normally, this would be considered as a scientific forgery."

PROFESSOR ATTE KORHOLA, PHD

Professor of Environmental Change at the University of Helsinki's Department of Environmental Sciences. Member of the Environment Panel of the European Academies Science Advisory Council. Board member of *The Journal of Paleolimnology*. Visiting Professor at University College, London and Queen's University, Kingston.

When Mann claims his hockey stick has been replicated, what he usually means is that his errors have been replicated, in papers by fellow Hockey Teamsters down through the years. If you're the fellow who went out and collected the original data, this can be frustrating. As Professor Korhola wrote in 2009 in the Finnish web journal CO_2-rapporti[1]:

When later generations learn about climate science, they will classify the beginning of the 21st century as **an embarrassing chapter in the history of science.** They will wonder at our time, and use it as a warning of how the core values and criteria of science were allowed little by little to be forgotten as the actual research topic - climate change - turned into a political and social playground.

Professor Korhola is nominally on the same side as Mann. But the cause of his ire was the misuse of Finnish data. Mann had flipped Mia Tiljander's Finnish sediments on their head in his 2008 paper. That is, he used somebody else's research upside down, and thereby switched the

---

[1] http://www.co2-raportti.fi/index.php?page=blogi&news_id=1370; English translation here: http://climateaudit.org/2009/10/02/atte-korhola-scientific-and-social-playground/

Medieval Warm Period and Little Ice Age. Needless to say, he huffily refused to admit his error, and dismissed "the claim that 'upside-down' data were used" as "bizarre"[2]. So no one did anything, and the same mistake was repeated in yet another peer-reviewed paper the following year by other Hockey Teamsters. Professor Korhola didn't mince words:

Another example is a study recently published in the prestigious journal *Science*[3]. It is concluded in the article that the average temperatures in the Arctic region are much higher now than at any time in the past two thousand years. The result may well be true, but the way the researchers ended up with this conclusion raises questions. **Proxies have been included selectively, they have been digested, manipulated, filtered, and combined - for example, data collected from Finland in the past by my own colleagues has even been turned upside down such that the warm periods become cold and vice versa.** Normally, this would be considered as a scientific forgery, which has **serious consequences.**

But in Mannworld a scientific forgery quickly becomes "settled science". As Robert Way privately conceded to Mann's allies at Skeptical Science[4]:

Mann's response of 'Bizarre' was pretty lazy if you ask me. The original Tiljander series people even said **Mann and Kaufmann used it wrong.** That being said Mc[Intyre] is a conspiracy wackjob...

As for Mann et al 2008, Way advised:

Stay away from Mann's 2008 paper... it has actually been invalidated.

---

[2] http://www.pnas.org/content/106/6/E11.full
[3] http://www.sciencemag.org/content/325/5945/1236.short
[4] http://climateaudit.org/2013/11/20/behind-the-sks-curtain/

86

"The graph was flipped upside-down ...and now I doubt if it can be a mistake anymore."

PROFESSOR MATTI SAARNISTO, PHD

Professor of Geology and former Research Director of the Geological Survey of Finland. Former Secretary General of the Finnish Academy of Science and Letters. Member of the Estonian Academy of Sciences.

Professor Saarnisto talked about Mann's recurring abuse of other people's data on the Finnish TV show "A-talk" in 2010[1]:

SARI HUOVINEN: Matti, your own research result has been distorted in public. Tell us what was done.

MATTI SAARNISTO: Well, indeed... One of the people who have been in the public eye, Professor Mann from Pennsylvania State University, he has published several articles about the climate history of the past thousand years. The last time it was the history of the last two thousand years... In that article, my group's research material from Korttajärvi, near Jyväskylä, was used in such a way that the Medieval Warm Period was shown as a mirror image.

HUOVINEN: That is, the graph was flipped?

SAARNISTO: The graph was flipped upside-down... It was in *Science...*

---

[1] http://climateaudit.org/2010/02/06/say-my-name-%E2%80%93-february-rerun/

HUOVINEN: Why was that done, how do you interpret that?

SAARNISTO: That is something I've tried to sort out… In this email I received yesterday from one of the authors of the article, my good friend Professor Ray Bradley …says there was a large group of researchers who had been handling an extremely large amount of research material, and **at some point it happened that this graph was turned upside-down.**

HUOVINEN: So it was not done on purpose? It was a mistake?

SAARNISTO: Well, when Bradley says so to me, I don't doubt for a moment… But then this happened yet another time in *Science* …a little before Christmas. Again this Korttajärvi material, which was a part of Mia Tiljander's PhD thesis. Mia Tiljander is a known person worldwide, and …the article where the material appeared was published in 2003. Mia Tiljander was the first author, I was the second, and good younger colleagues of mine, Timo Saarinen and Antti Ojala, came after…

HUOVINEN: Yes…

SAARNISTO: It has been turned upside-down twice in *Science*, and now I doubt if it can be a mistake anymore… This group, which has been seen in a negative light by the public, I know them… They have been somehow skeptical about this Medieval Warm Period and have tried to hide it to some extent. **I have always thought that this was purely a case of scientific critique, but now in the last few days I have come somewhat to a conclusion that there is some purposefulness in this…** But how it is possible that this type of material is repeatedly published in these top science journals? It is because of the peer review process central to science. **There is a small circle going round and around, relatively few people are reviewing each other's papers**, and that is in my opinion the worrying aspect.

210

87

"The regional temperatures during the MWP exceeded those in the recent warm period."

PROFESSOR YUXIN HE, PHD ET AL

Yuxin He is Assistant Professor of the Department of Earth Sciences at Zhejiang University. WeiGuo Liu, Zheng Wang, HuanYe Wang and ZhiSheng An are with the Institude of Earth Environment at the Chinese Academy of Sciences, Xi'an. Cheng Zhao is at the UK National Oceanography Centre in Southampton. Yi Liu, XianYan Qin and QiHou Hu are with the Insitute of Polar Environment at the University of Science and Technology of China. ZhongHui Liu is at the University of Hong Kong's Department of Earth Sciences.

In 2009, for the purposes of a new paper[1], Mann appeared to rediscover the Medieval Warm Period - or, as he called it, the Medieval Climate Anomaly - for the purpose of demonstrating that it was a purely local phenomenon. Dr Sebastian Lüning explains[2]:

The idea behind the paper was to show that the warmth in some areas was offset by cold in other parts of the world. To show this the authors searched out places that were colder than normal 1,000 years ago.

The problem was the Atlantic region, which had an excellent amount of data to support the medieval warmth. Here the temperatures stood at least at today's levels. Therefore Michael Mann searched around for other

---

[1] http://www.sciencemag.org/content/326/5957/1256.full
[2] http://notrickszone.com/2013/04/15/back-to-the-penalty-box-chinese-paleo-climatolgists-slap-down-high-sticking-michael-mann/#sthash.tMSZaa7K.dpbs

regions where far less data was available and found the Central Eurasian region would do just fine. The scarcity of available data left lots of room for interpretation. This is how the authors plotted a huge region of cold over a large swath of Central Eurasia during the Medieval Warm Period, which supposedly offset the inconvenient Atlantic warmth.

These results struck a group of scientists rather closer to the scene as "curious". As they wrote in The Chinese Science Bulletin[3]*:*

A recent analysis suggests that the MWP warmth matches or exceeds the current level in some regions, but not globally [Mann et al 2009]. Curiously, they also reported "anomalous coolness" during the MWP in central Eurasia including the northern Tibetan Plateau, a region with limited high-quality paleoclimatic reconstructions available.

Yuxin He and his colleagues took a look at what Dr Lüning calls "Mann's liberally interpreted data and his postulated Central Eurasian cold zone" - and found that yet again he'd got things upside down:

Our records show that the regional temperatures during the MWP exceeded those in the recent warm period.

As Professor He et al note:

The substantially warmer condition on the northern Tibetan Plateau, together with the relatively warmer conditions on Greenland, the persistent positive North Atlantic Oscillation mode, negative Southern Oscillation Index and the prevailing La Niña-like conditions in the tropical Pacific, suggest **anomalous climatic conditions during the MWP, beyond the climate variability captured by the recent warm period.**

Mann is running out of places to find a Medieval non-Warm Period.

---

[3] http://link.springer.com/article/10.1007%2Fs11434-012-5619-8#page-1

"We have discovered that the geographic orientation of the CCSM field used by Mann et al (2005), Mann et al (2007a), and Mann et al (2007b) was incorrect."

DR JASON E SMERDON, PHD ET AL

Jason E Smerdon, PhD and Alexey Kaplan, PhD are Lamont Associate Research Professors at Columbia University's Lamont-Doherty Earth Observatory. Daniel E Amrhein is a PhD candidate at the Massachusetts Institute of Technology/Woods Hole Oceanographic Institution Joint Program in Physical Oceanography.

Mann has never learned the lessons from his first bungled papers. These days other scientists are bulk-discounting them. In 2010 Dr Smerdon et al published a paper in The Journal of Climate *with the intriguing title "Erroneous model field representations in multiple pseudoproxy studies: corrections and implications". Now who does that sound like? As Dr Smerdon and his colleagues explained[1]:*

We have discovered that the geographic orientation of the CCSM field used by Mann et al. (2005, hereinafter M05), Mann et al. (2007a, hereinafter M07), and Mann et al. (2007b) was incorrect.

Whether you slice the globe north/south or east/west, you wind up with only two hemispheres. Not a lot to remember. Yet Mann managed to

---

[1] http://www.ldeo.columbia.edu/~jsmerdon/papers/2010b_jclim_smerdonetal.pdf

mix up the Eastern and Western Hemispheres, not in one paper but three. In a slightly more sophisticated error, he "smoothed" one hemisphere but not the other:

> We also have discovered that the ECHO-g field used in M07 was corrupted by a hemispheric-scale smoothing in the Western Hemisphere.

As Dr Eduardo Zorita explained at his website[2]:

> The new paper by Smerdon et al has identified basic and surprising errors in the testing of the RegEM method by the Mann group... In one case, when interpolating the climate model data onto a different grid, the data were rotated around the Earth 180 degrees, so that model data that should be located on the Greenwich Meridian were erroneously placed at 180 degrees longitude; in another case the data in the Western Hemisphere were spatially smoothed, while the data in the Eastern Hemisphere were not. These errors bear some consequences: the location of the pseudo-proxies did not match the location of real proxies anymore; the spatial covariance of the temperature data was not correct; when the authors though they were testing the skill of the method to reconstruct the temperature in the ENSO region by proxies located in North America, they were actually testing the reconstruction of temperature ...by proxies located somewhere else.
>
> Stuff happens and errors like these can creep in every study by any group... It is, however, surprising that **these errors went undetected for several years**, affecting two key manuscripts that used the same data sets.

---

[2] http://klimazwiebel.blogspot.com/2010/07/mistake-with-consequences.html

89

"Several aspects of their tree-ring growth simulations are erroneous."

DR KEVIN J ANCHUKAITIS, PHD ET AL

Kevin J Anchukaitis is Assistant Scientist at Woods Hole Oceanographic Institution and Adjunct Associate Research Scientist. For the "et al" crowd, see below.

In 2012, Mann published, with Jose D Fuentes and Scott Rutherford, a paper in Nature Geoscience[1]. *This time* nobody *liked it[2]:*

To the Editor...

Several aspects of their tree-ring growth simulations are erroneous. First, **they use an algorithm that has not been tested for its ability to reflect actual observations**, even though established growth models, such as the Vaganov–Shashkin model are available. They rely on a minimum growth temperature threshold of 10°C that is **incompatible with real-world observations**. This condition is rarely met in regions near the limit of tree growth, where ring formation demonstrably occurs well below this temperature: there is abundant empirical evidence that the temperature limit for tree-ring formation is around 5°C. Mann and colleagues **arbitrarily and without justification** require 26 days with temperatures above their unrealistic threshold for ring formation. Their resulting growing season becomes unusually short, at 50–60 days rather than the more commonly observed 70–137 days. Furthermore, they use a

---

[1] http://www.nature.com/ngeo/journal/v5/n3/full/ngeo1394.html
[2] https://www.st-andrews.ac.uk/~rjsw/all%20pdfs/Anchukaitisetal2012.pdf

quadratic function to describe growth that has **no basis in observation or theory**, and they ignore any daylength and moisture constraints on growth...

Etc. But it's the sign-off that catches the eye:

Kevin J Anchukaitis[1,2], Petra Breitenmoser[3], Keith R Briffa[4], Agata Buchwal[5,6], Ulf Büntgen[3,5], Edward R Cook[1], Rosanne D D'Arrigo[1], Jan Esper[7], Michael N Evans[8], David Frank[3,5], Håkan Grudd[9], Björn E Gunnarson[9], Malcolm K Hughes[10], Alexander V Kirdyanov[11], Christian Körner[12], Paul J Krusic[9], Brian Luckman[13], Thomas M Melvin[4], Matthew W Salzer[10], Alexander V Shashkin[11], Claudia Timmreck[14], Eugene A Vaganov[11,15] and Rob J S Wilson [1,16]

1 Lamont Doherty Earth Observatory of Columbia University; 2 Department of Geology and Geophysics, Woods Hole Oceanographic Institution; 3 Oeschger Centre for Climate Change Research, University of Bern; 4 Climatic Research Unit, School of Environmental Sciences, University of East Anglia; 5 Swiss Federal Research Institute WSL; 6 Institute of Geoecology and Geoinformation, Adam Mickiewicz University; 7 Department of Geography, Johannes Gutenberg University; 8 Department of Geology and Earth System Science Interdisciplinary Center, University of Maryland; 9 Bert Bolin Centre for Climate Research, Department of Physical Geography and Quaternary Geology, Stockholm University; 10 Laboratory of Tree-Ring Research, University of Arizona; 11 V N Sukachev Institute of Forest SB RAS; 12 Institute of Botany, University of Basel; 13 Department of Geography, University of Western Ontario; 14 Max-Planck-Institut für Meteorologie; 15 Institute of Forest and Siberian Federal University; 16 School of Geography and Geosciences, University of St Andrews.

Is that unanimous? Or would Mann like a recount?

Oh, wait. Rosanne D'Arrigo isn't done with that Mann et al 2012 paper. As Tweeted by Nature *correspondent Alexandra Witze, here's Professor D'Arrigo with one for the road[3]:*

D'Arrigo: @MichaelEMann paper is "**highly questionable.**" Questions entire science of tree ring dating. **Misleads public.**

---

[3] https://twitter.com/alexwitze/status/213231148019613698

90

*"A crock of sh*t."*

DR ROB WILSON, PHD

Senior Lecturer in the Department of Geography and Sustainable Development at the University of St Andrews. Associate Research Scientist at Columbia University's Tree-Ring Laboratory. Former tree-ring technician at the Institute of Antarctic and Southern Ocean Studies in Tasmania and in his own laboratory in Germany, undertaking historical dating in the Bavarian Forest Region. Author of peer-reviewed papers published by *The Holocene*, *The International Journal of Climatology*, *Scientific Reports*, *Dendrochronologia* and other journals.

In October 2013 Professor Wilson gave a lecture at the University of St Andrews. Among the audience was the author of The Hockey Stick Illusion, *A W Montford[1]:*

As readers here know, Rob is no kind of a sceptic (a point he repeated over lunch), but on the northern hemisphere paleo studies his position is not a million miles away from mine...

Because of the prominence of Michael Mann's work in the area, some of the lecture was devoted to the Hockey Stick, to the 2008 paper (the "upside down Tiljander" study to the initiated) and to Mann's most recent area of focus, the influence of volcanoes on tree ring growth. Students learned that **the Hockey Stick included a whole lot of inappropriate proxies** and heard something of the issues with its verification statistics. The wallpapering of the Third Assessment with Mann's magnum opus and John Houghton's **claims about unprecedented**

---

[1] http://bishophill.squarespace.com/blog/2013/10/21/wilson-on-millennial-temperature-reconstructions.html

warmth based on this single study were described as "ridiculous". "Ultimately a flawed study" was the conclusion, with **a gory list of problems** set out: inappropriate data, infilling of gaps, use of poorly replicated chronologies, flawed PC analysis, data and code withheld until prised from the grasp of the principals...

We also heard about Mann's parvum opus, *The Hockey Stick and the Climate Wars*, which Rob, like so many others, had given up on in fairly short order...

That was the gentle beginning. When we got onto Mann et al 2008, we learned about the silliness of the screening process, and students were invited to try screening a set of random generated timeseries in the way Mann had gone about this study... The real fireworks came when Mann's latest papers, which hypothesise that tree-ring proxies have large numbers of missing rings after major volcanic eruptions, were described as "a crock of xxxx".

In the comments section below Mr Montford's post, Professor Wilson confirmed that he had, indeed, characterized Mann's work as such:

I want to clarify that my 2 hour lecture was, I hope, a critical look at all of the northern hemispheric reconstructions of past temperature to date. It was not focussed entirely on Michael Mann's work. I described each of the major studies and tried to highlight both their strengths and weaknesses...

The "crock of xxxx" statement was focussed entirely on recent work by Michael Mann w.r.t. hypothesised missing rings in tree-ring records. Although a rather flippant statement, **I stand by it and Mann is well aware of my criticisms** (privately and through the peer reviewed literature) of his recent work.

Rob

X

Mann o' war

CAPTAIN CLIMATE BATTLES THE DENIERS

Aspen Island Theatre Company:
To assist with costs of the creative development of a new
theatre work, Kill Climate Deniers - *$18,793[1]*
AWARD OF TAXPAYER FUNDING FROM
AUSTRALIAN CAPITAL TERRITORY ARTS FUND (2015)

---

[1] http://www.arts.act.gov.au/__data/assets/pdf_file/0009/643374/2015-Project-funding-successful-applicants.pdf

PROFESSOR Mike Hulme's review of Mann's book *The Hockey Stick and the Climate Wars: Dispatches from the Front Lines,* begins as follows:

> *The climate wars of which this book speaks have been persistent and, not infrequently, dramatic and brutal. Vast human and capital resources have been invested by both sides in pursuing front-line assaults and covert guerrilla tactics against the enemy. Few prisoners have been taken but many casualties inflicted, including innocent bystanders. Yet decisive victory for either side has been elusive. Recent efforts at mediation by peacemakers such as Jerry Ravetz and Hans von Storch have made little headway...*
>
> *I could continue in this trope for several sentences more... The attraction of the war metaphor in many types of communication and journalism is that it is so rich in vocabulary and imagery.[2]*

Indeed. As Professor Hulme notes, Mann's prose style marches to a martial beat: "assault", "battle of the bulge", "battle-scars", "climate wars", "denial offensive", "dispatches", "drumbeat", "fight", "fighting back", "front line", "ground attack", "line of fire", "trenches", "war trophy"...

This is a strange tack for a man of science. But then Mann has always seen this as total war: Promoting his book on C-SPAN[3], he said the argument over climate change has been "likened at times to a fight between a boy scout and a terrorist - and you know, we are the boy scouts". So you're either with us or you're with the

---

[2] http://www.nature.com/nclimate/journal/v2/n4/full/nclimate1459.html?WT. ec_id=NCLIMATE-201204

[3] "http://www.c-span.org/video/?305972-1/book-discussion-hockey-stick-climate-wars

terrorists.

His first means of control was the venerable scientific tradition of "peer review". To most of us, "peer review" sounds so reassuringly respectable that a drowsy numbness descends midway through the phrase. In the days after Climategate, Mann buddy Ed Begley Jr was keen to talk it up. Mr Begley was the star of the 1980s medical drama "St Elsewhere" but has latterly been better known as an "activist" in environmental matters. He's been in a competition with Bill Nye ("the Science Guy") to see who can have the lowest "carbon footprint". Pistols at dawn would seem the quickest way of resolving that one, but presumably you couldn't get a reality series out of it. Interviewed by Stuart Varney on Fox News[4], Ed was relaxed about the mountain of documents leaked from the CRU on how to "hide the decline" and other interesting matters.

Nothing to see here, folks. Nothing to worry about. "We'll go down the path and see what happens in peer-reviewed studies," said Ed airily. "Those are the key words here, Stuart. 'Peer-reviewed studies.'"

Hang on. Could you say that again more slowly so we can write it down? Not to worry. Ed said it every twelve seconds, as if it were the magic charm that could make all the bad publicity go away. "'Peer-reviewed studies' is the key words. And if it comes out in peer-reviewed studies... Go to *Science* magazine, folks. Go to *Nature*," babbled Ed. "Read peer-reviewed studies. That's all you need to do. Don't get it from you or me."

Look for the peer-reviewed label! And then just believe whatever it is they tell you!

The trouble with outsourcing your marbles to the peer-reviewed set is that, if you take away one single thing from

---

[4] https://www.youtube.com/watch?v=77PDVqC84VA

Climategate, it's that the global warm-mongers have wholly corrupted the "peer-review" process.

"Coaching reviewers, stacking panels, and litmus testing for associate editors are wrong," insisted Dr David Rutledge, former editor of *Transactions on Microwave Theory and Techniques*, adding with remarkable restraint that, in his day "these things were not done"[5]. The more frantically Mann & Co talked up "peer review" as the only legitimate basis for criticism, the more assiduously they turned the process into what scientist James Lewis called the Chicago machine politics of international science[6], pressuring publishers, firing editors, blacklisting scientists, as their echo chamber shriveled, and they yelled louder and louder that they and only they represent the "peer-reviewed" "consensus."

"Quis custodiet ipsos custodes?" wondered Juvenal: Who watches the watchmen? But the beauty of the climate-change circus is that you never need to ask "Who peer-reviews the peer-reviewers?" Mann peer-reviewed Jones, and Jones peer-reviewed Mann, and anyone who questioned their views got exiled to the unwarmed wastes of Siberia. The "consensus" warm-mongers could have declared it only counts as "peer-reviewed" if it's published in *Peer-Reviewed Studies* published by Mann & Jones Publishing Inc (Peermate of the Month: Michael Mann, reclining naked, draped in dead polar-bear fur, on a melting ice floe), and Ed Begley Jr would still have wandered out glassy-eyed into the streets droning "Peer-reviewed studies. Cannot question. Peer-reviewed studies. The science is settled..."

With the arrival of social media, Mann-style climate control advanced to the next level...

---

[5] http://climateaudit.org/2010/06/15/unthreaded-39/#comment-232577
[6] http://pjmedia.com/blog/climategate-its-the-totalitarianism-stupid/

91

"Framing the science of climate change as a war between two sides hardly does justice to the complexities of scientific enquiry, judgement and assessment."

PROFESSOR MIKE HULME, PHD

Professor of Climate and Culture in the Department of Geography at King's College, London. Founder of the Tyndall Centre for Climate Change Research, and founding editor-in-chief of the journal *Climate Change*. Formerly Professor of Climate Change at the University of East Anglia, and senior researcher at the Climatic Research Unit.

In 2012, Professor Hulme reviewed Mann's self-aggrandizing book, The Hockey Stick and the Climate Wars: Dispatches from the Front Lines, *for the journal where it all began,* Nature - *or at any rate for its sexy spin-off* Nature Climate Change[1]*:*

A two-sided war story makes it easier for us to make sense of the world and our place in it.

But after reading *The Hockey Stick and the Climate Wars* I am left contemplating **the futility of framing the important yet difficult issues surrounding the idea of climate change in this way.** Are climate scientists ...really in a war over climate change? If so, are we sure about which side we are supposed to be on and are we clear about who is the enemy? And is the war winnable..?

---

[1] http://www.nature.com/nclimate/journal/v2/n4/full/nclimate1459.html?WT. ec_id=NCLIMATE-201204

Framing the science of climate change as a war between two sides hardly does justice to the complexities of scientific enquiry, judgement and assessment concerning the physical functioning of the Earth system... But this seems to be how Mann and many other climate scientists approach their work - "the duelling narratives of the two sides". This framing forces Mann into classifying all protagonists into either legitimate or illegitimate camps.

Rejecting this "binary framing", Professor Hulme was bemused by the reduction of complicated, shifting issues into "a set-piece duel" in which everyone had to pick one of two sides and stick with it:

A public continually exposed to the rhetoric of warfare and battle about climate science need to understand the underlying reasons for the public arguments that flare around climate change... These differences will not be altered or reconciled by climate science. The tragedy is that Michael Mann's hockey stick has become a powerful icon for perpetuating the view that they will be.

In May 2014 The Guardian had the temerity to publish a piece that included a quote from Professor Hulme on Mann's hockey stick[2]:

The data was **absolutely scanty.**

So Mann, with the characteristic insecurity of the bully, spent half the day Tweeting about Hulme, starting with a suggestion that he ought to bone up on "actual science[3]". Mike Hulme is a climate prof, a climate researcher, a climate journal editor ...but he's "anti-science" because Michael Mann says so.

---

[2] http://www.theguardian.com/global-development-professionals-network/2014/may/14/climate-change-science-scepticism
[3] https://twitter.com/MichaelEMann/status/466557548359737344

92

"It's a completely rigged peer-review system..."

DR DAVID RUTLEDGE, PHD

Chair of the Division of Engineering and Applied Science at the California Institute of Technology, and Director of its Lee Center for Advanced Networking. Recipient of the National Science Foundation Presidential Investigator Award, the Millennium Medal from the Institute of Electrical and Electronics Engineers, and the Microwave Prize from the Microwave Theory and Techniques Society. Fellow of the Institute of Electrical and Electronics Engineers and the Japan Society for the Promotion of Science. Former editor of *Transactions on Microwave Theory and Techniques.*

The us-and-them mentality was present from the start. Having been a journal editor, Dr Rutledge was one of those who found Climategate unsettling, and in 2010 began referencing it in his lectures[1]:

There is a lot of emails about editors and reviews... I would have to say it's a completely rigged peer review system. **There's discussion about removing editors** - it apparently happened - that simply published a single paper these people don't like. **There's badgering of reviewers** to get the kind of response they want... Again, **it doesn't look good.**

Dr Rutledge's presentation included slides of all too typical Climategate emails. Tom Wigley emailed to Mann[2]:

If you think that [editor James] Saiers is in the greenhouse

---

[1] http://www.climateaudit.info/pdf/video/california2.mpg
[2] http://rutledge.caltech.edu/Caltech%20talk%202010/
CaltechPhysicsColloquium2010.flv

skeptics camp, then, if we can find documentary evidence of this, we could go through official AGU channels to get him ousted.

And Phil Jones to Mann:

I can't see either of these papers being in the next IPCC report. Kevin [Trenberth] and I will keep them out somehow – even if we have to redefine what the peer-reviewed literature is!

And, as Dr Rutledge notes, in the subsequent IPCC report the papers were, indeed, "kept out". As the professor continues[3]:

The editor wants to reject the paper[4], has one negative review, and he's asking the other reviewer to give a negative review, and then the other reviewer seems to acknowledge this...

The way I interpret the bottom email is that there's some kind of litmus test for the editor, and that the editor needs to be removed from the paper... These are completely outside of my experience. I simply could not imagine as an editor telling a reviewer what to say, I couldn't imagine before you present all the reviews to the author telling one reviewer what another reviewer had said or who'd said it.

In a comment at Stephen McIntyre's Climate Audit, Dr Rutledge added[5]:

Coaching reviewers, stacking panels, and litmus testing for associate editors are wrong.

But not in Mannworld.

---

[3] http://rutledge.caltech.edu/Caltech%20talk%202010/
CaltechPhysicsColloquium2010.flv
[4] Briffa to Cook: "I now need a hard and if required extensive case for rejecting..."
http://assassinationscience.com/climategate/1/FOIA/mail/1054748574.txt
[5] http://climateaudit.org/2010/06/15/unthreaded-39/#comment-232577

93

"I became the target of a number of CRU manoeuvres ...over my publication of several papers that questioned the 'hockey stick' graph."

DR SONJA BOEHMER-CHRISTIANSEN, PHD
Emeritus Reader in the University of Hull's Department of Geography. Editor of the journal *Energy & Environment*. Former member of the UN Environment Programme Stakeholder Forum for a Sustainable Future, and Visiting Fellow at the Science and Technology Policy Research Unit of the University of Sussex.

When you have a tight grip on access to the key peer-reviewed journals, the few you don't control start to irritate you even more. In February 2010 Dr Boehmer-Christiansen gave evidence to the Select Committee on Science and Technology of the British House of Commons[1]:

As a member of the Labour Party and deeply politically engaged person, I have not found life as a "climate sceptic" always easy... As editor of a journal [*Energy & Environment*] which remained open to scientists who challenged the orthodoxy, I became the target of a number of CRU manoeuvres. The hacked emails revealed attempts to manipulate peer review to E&E's disadvantage, and showed that libel threats were considered against its editorial team. Dr Jones even tried to put pressure on my university department. The emailers expressed anger over my

---

[1] http://www.publications.parliament.uk/pa/cm200910/cmselect/cmsctech/memo/climatedata/uc2602.htm

publication of several papers that questioned the "hockey stick" graph... The desire to control the peer review process in their favour is expressed several times...

An American response to McIntyre's and McKitrick's influential paper I published in 2005 challenging the "hockey stick" says, "It is indeed time leading scientists at CRU associated with the UK Met Bureau explain how Mr McIntyre is in error or resign."

Mann and the Hockey Team spent a lot of time chewing over revenge scenarios for these few dissident redoubts[2]:

Dear all...

I am encouraged at the prospect of some sort of action being taken.

The *Energy and Environment* piece is an ad hominem attack against the work of several of us, and could be legally actionable, though I don't think it's worth the effort. But more problematic, in my mind, is the *Climate Research* piece which is a real challenge to the integrity of the peer-review processes in our field. I believe that a boycott against publishing, reviewing for, or even citing articles from *Climate Research* is certainly warranted...

A formal statement of 'loss of confidence' in the journal seems like an excellent idea. It may or may not be useful for me to be directly involved in this, given that I am a primary object of attack by these folks. However, I'm happy to help in any way that I can....

best regards, Mike Mann

So the best way to protect "the integrity of the peer-review process" is to take down anyone who crosses you...

---

[2] http://di2.nu/foia/foia2011/mail/4808.txt

228

94

"The Mann 'hockey stick' is nothing more than a mathematical construct... Sufficient evidence exists to disprove it."

PROFESSOR CHRIS DE FREITAS, PHD

Associate Professor at the University of Auckland's School of Environment, and former Deputy Dean of Science, Head of Science and Technology and Pro Vice-Chancellor. Former Vice-President of the Meteorological Society of New Zealand, and founding member of the Australia-New Zealand Climate Forum. Four-time recipient of the Science Communicator Award from the New Zealand Association of Scientists. Former editor of *Climate Research*.

In 2003, Professor de Freitas, then editing Climate Research, *was interviewed by* The New Zealand Herald. *Simon Collins explained that de Freitas had once warned of "the dangers of global warming", but today he "features prominently in environmentalist demonology"[1]:*

Last week American climatologist Michael Mann told a US Senate committee: "Chris de Freitas... frequently publishes op-ed pieces in newspapers in New Zealand attacking the IPCC and attacking Kyoto... So that is a fairly unusual editor..."

Two graphs sum up the argument. The first, in the IPCC's latest report in 2001, was compiled by the same Michael Mann who attacked de Freitas in the Senate last week... But the two Harvard scientists whose article got de Freitas into trouble believe

---

[1] http://www.nzherald.co.nz/nz/news/article.cfm?c_id=1&objectid=3516831

Mann's hockey-stick is an oversimplification, driven by the same kind of "politics" of which they and de Freitas are accused.

The Harvard authors, Sallie Baliunas and Willie Soon, re-checked 240 studies of the same kind of evidence that Mann used, and found signs that it was warmer in most parts of Earth for at least parts of the medieval warm period than it is today... "The Mann 'hockey stick' is nothing more than a mathematical construct vigorously promoted in the IPCC's 2001 report to affirm the notion that temperature changes of the 20th century were unprecedented," de Freitas wrote. "**The validity of this has been soundly challenged**, and sufficient evidence exists to disprove it..."

Mann didn't care for the cut of de Freitas' jib and emailed Mike Hulme and Phil Jones to enquire how plans for payback were going - or, as he put it in the header, "Climate Research and adequate peer review":

Did anything ever come of this?

Clare Goodness was in touch w/ me indicating that she had discussed the matter w/ Von Storch, and that DeFrietas would be relieved of his position. However, I haven't heard anything...

It seems important that either Clare and Von Storch take imminent action on this, or else actions of the sort you had mentioned below should perhaps be strongly considered again. Non-action or slow action here could be extremely damaging...

Thanks very much for all your help w/ this to date, and for anything additional you may be able to do in this regard to move this forward.

best regards, mike

Mike got his way. De Freitas was removed as editor.

230

95

"The whole climate conversation would be better off with the word 'denier' being dropped completely."

DR RICHARD BETTS, PHD

Head of the Climate Impacts strategic area at the Met Office Hadley Centre, and Chair in Climate Impacts at the University of Exeter. Lead Author for the IPCC Fourth and Fifth Assessment Reports. Editor for *The International Journal of Global Warming*, *The Journal of Environmental Investing*, and *Earth System Dynamics*.

With the arrival of social media, Mann's "war" opened up a new front. In 2015, Dr Betts wrote that he didn't mind accusing climate skeptics of being "in denial", but he wasn't happy about the word "denier"[1]:

The reason that "in denial" and "denier" are different is that the former labels the behaviour while the latter labels the person. Most training in education, communications, management, negotiation etc, advises that when dealing with conflict situations, it is important to address difficulties but to focus on what is being done/said and not the person themselves. Labelling the person makes things more emotive and distracts from discussing the real issue....

The situation is even worse for the label "denier", because it been used by some in connection with holocaust denial. So not only is this making the mistake of giving someone a label as a

---

[1] https://andthentheresphysics.wordpress.com/2015/02/07/guest-post-label-the-behaviour-not-the-person/

person, but the label is associated in people's minds with something horrific. They will understandably find it deeply insulting. If labelling the person rather than the behaviour is poor communications practice, then giving them an extremely insulting label (whether intended or not) is clearly even worse...

I think the whole climate conversation would be better off with the word "denier" being dropped completely, and with "being in denial" only being used very judiciously, when it really is appropriate.

Hmm. Very civilized of Dr Betts. But who cries "Denier!" more than any other scientist? From Michael Mann's Facebook page[2]:

Calling Out A **#ClimateChangeDenier**... Here's the reason Climate **Deniers** use abusive name calling as a tactic... **Deniers** gonna deny... liars gonna lie... Koch-funded climate change **denier** group #ATI...

Or Michael Mann on his Twitter feed[3]:

Crypto-**denier** #BjornLomborg... #climatechange **denier** #JudithCurry... #MattRidley in the London Times, 'My Life as A Compensated Climate Change **Denier**' (I tweaked the title...) #ClimateChnage [sic] **denier** #RoySpencer... #AnthonyWatts: climate change **denier** extremist... Murdoch's company of climate change **deniers** at @australian and his other rags... The #ClimateChange **denier** drive-by reviews of #HSCW[4] continue... #ClimateChange #**Denier** @RepPaulRyan's budget... FL Gov #RickScott's DEP hides behind #Koch-approved **denier**... uber-**denier** #JamesDelingpole...Climate Change **Denier** #JohnColeman... climate **denier** #JoeBast... #ClimateChangeDeniers Tom Nelson' &

---

[2] https://www.facebook.com/MichaelMannScientist
[3] https://twitter.com/MichaelEMann
[4] Mann's book, *The Hockey Stick and the Climate Wars*

96

"Is it not better to tweet which criticisms you disagree about ...rather than call him 'denier'?"

DR TAMSIN EDWARDS, PHD

Lecturer in Environmental Sciences at Britain's Open University, and visiting climate scientist at the University of Bristol's School of Geographical Science. Author of peer-reviewed papers published in *Nature, The Proceedings of the National Academy of Sciences of the United States of America, The Journal of Glaciology* and many more.

Following Professor Rob Wilson's comments on Mann's recent work, Mann Tweeted[1]:

Closet #climatechange #denier Rob Wilson, comes out of the closet big time... #BadScience #DisingenuousBehavior

Dr Edwards responded[2]:

@MichaelEMann **You are seriously calling Rob a denier for criticising your work, M?** That's pretty strong to call a prof climate colleague.

Mann answered:

@flimsin Not for criticizing my work, but for apparently

---

[1] He subsequently deleted it, but it's preserved here:
http://wattsupwiththat.com/2013/10/21/paleoscientist-manns-recent-work-was-a-crock-of-xxxx/
[2] https://twitter.com/flimsin/status/392278255476027393

regurgitating #denialist drivel by the likes of McIntyre, etc.

Dr Edwards made a suggestion to Mann[3]:

Is it not better to tweet which criticisms you disagree about, a technical response, rather than call him "denier"?

Good luck with that. The debate continued. Dr Edwards to Mann:

And if it's the tone you don't like, address that rather than call him denier?

Mann sneered:

@flimsin Tamsin, I don't need to be lectured on 'tone' by you, of all people. Uninterested in a profile-raising twitter debate w/ you.

A "profile-raising" debate? That's Captain Climate telling Lukewarmgirl, "Don't tug on my cape, missy!"

Tamsin Edwards @flimsin 6h
"of all people"? I was interested in hearing which points you disagreed with and how you classified "denier".

...& I think it's important to show scientists discussing technical points & sci comm in public forum.

... but if you don't fancy having that conversation and/or see it as me self-promoting I will sign off, cheers.

As Tweeter O Bothe told Mann:

@MichaelEMann Sorry, but the 'denier'-tweet was (at least) inappropriate and the profile-raising one not much better.

---

[3] https://twitter.com/flimsin/status/392278559114264578

97

"The term denier or denialist to describe sceptics is indicative of the closed mind and a term of abuse for the scientific process."

PROFESSOR ANTHONY TREWAVAS, FRS, FRSE, PHD

Professor Emeritus at the University of Edinburgh, leader of the Edinburgh Molecular Signaling Group, and, according to the Institute of Scientific Information, one of the most highly cited authors in the world in the field of animal and plant sciences. Fellow of the Royal Society, the Royal Society of Arts, the Royal Society of Edinburgh, Academia Europea, and corresponding member of the American Society of Plant Biologists.

As Professor Ross McKitrick subsequently wrote of Mann's spat with Dr Edwards and his charcterization of Professor Wilson[1]:

Mann's tweet just reveals openly what has long been his working assumption. To Mann, a "skeptic" is anyone who doesn't accept his work uncritically, and **a "denier" is anyone who actually disagrees with him.**

*Reflecting on the exchange later in the day, Dr Edwards remarked that Mann was "**jumping the shark**"[2]. She made a further perceptive point[3]:*

---

[1] http://bishophill.squarespace.com/blog/2013/10/21/wilson-on-millennial-temperature-reconstructions.html?currentPage=2#comments

[2] http://bishophill.squarespace.com/blog/2013/10/21/wilson-on-millennial-temperature-reconstructions.html

[3] https://twitter.com/flimsin/status/392365554579025920

To me denier is different ballgame, unfounded name-calling, looked like attempt to ostracise a professional.

But that's Mann's modus operandi. In 2013, Professor Trewavas gave evidence to the House of Commons Science & Technology Committee and addressed the descent of science into poisonous name-calling[4]:

The term Denier or Denialist to describe sceptics is indicative of the closed mind and a term of abuse for the scientific process. **It is reminiscent of Galileo's problem with the inquisition in the 16th century** and politicians of all kinds should have slapped the term down.

If Professor Trewavas is correct, then Mann has the most closed mind in the scientific community. Of the 2014 congressional hearings, Mann tweeted that it was "#Science" — i.e., the guy who agrees with him — vs. "#AntiScience"[5] — i.e., Dr Judith Curry. She is by profession a scientist, but because she has the impertinence to dissent from Mann's view she is "#AntiScience". Mann is the climatological equivalent of those firebreathing inarticulate imams on al-Arabiya raging about infidel whores: He can't refute Dr Curry, he can only label her, as he does routinely ("serial climate disinformer"[6]). Her challenge to him[7]:

Since you have publicly accused my Congressional testimony of being 'anti-science,' I expect you to (publicly) document and rebut any statement in my testimony that is factually inaccurate.

The head mullah of Sharia science fell suddenly silent.

---

[4] http://www.publications.parliament.uk/pa/cm201314/cmselect/cmsctech/254/254vw13.htm

[5] https://twitter.com/michaelemann/status/423914894207877120

[6] http://www.theguardian.com/commentisfree/2013/sep/28/ipcc-climate-change-deniers

[7] http://judithcurry.com/2014/01/26/mann-versus-steyn/

98

"Mann's setup for discussing my work is borderline libel... It is unacceptable to portray those who disagree with you scientifically as evil."

DR CRAIG LOEHLE, PHD

Chief Scientist at the National Council for Air and Stream Improvement. Member of the International Society for Ecological Modeling, the Ecological Society of America and the Society of American Foresters. Former research ecologist at Savannah River Laboratory and the Environmental Research Division of the Argonne National Laboratory.

Twitter is an excitable medium, and we are all human and Tweet in haste to repent at leisure. Yet Mann maintains the same tone in his supposedly more considered work. After being consigned in Mann's book to what he calls "the denialosphere", Dr Loehle responded[1]:

My work is categorized as another assault from the denialosphere, with me being part of the "Hydra" that is hatefully out to get Mann. Simply because I published a paper that does a reconstruction and expressed a view that tree rings might have issues (which the Climategate emails show was a hidden view of many in the field) I was engaging in a "fight" against Mann? Really..? So, I am lumped in with politically motivated and evil "deniers" and "denialists". I find these terms and the entire

---

[1] http://wattsupwiththat.com/2012/04/17/scientists-rebuttal-of-michael-manns-denierand-other-unsavory-labels-in-his-book/

context for discussing my work offensive. I am not a "denialist" and my recent paper[2] attributes about 40 per cent of recent warming to human activity...

What I would deny is that tree rings are good thermometers, but this is a scientific view based on my knowledge of trees, not a political view... I have never received money from fossil fuel interests, as Mann states is true of all sceptics... My disagreements with the use of tree rings (by anyone, not just Mann) have nothing to do with a conspiracy, are not organized or directed by anyone, and are not personal. I just think tree rings (especially strip bark) are not valid more than about 100 years back in time...

In his book, Mann also writes:

> By contrast with the hockey stick studies - and every other peer reviewed scientific article on the subject - Loehle claimed that medieval warm period temperatures were warmer than '20th century values.'

"Every" other article? Mann has just declared there is not one paper finding the MWP as warm or warmer than the present. That's evidence of either insanity or a man trapped in his own impenetrable bubble. As Dr Loehle concludes:

> Mann's setup for discussing my work is borderline libel... It is unacceptable to portray those who disagree with you scientifically as evil and politically motivated. Science is full to the brim with disagreements about everything, from which treatment is best for coronary blockage to whether frequentist or Bayesian methods are best. By Mann's logic, we should all be using slanderous language to refer to anyone who disagrees with us. I don't think so.

---

[2] http://arxiv.org/ftp/arxiv/papers/1206/1206.5845.pdf

99

"Mann, Ehrlich and Rahmstorf: What a scurrilous bunch... They're gravediggers of science."

DANIEL S GREENBERG

Founder of *Science & Government Report*, and former news editor of *Science*, the journal of the American Association for the Advancement of Science. Former Visiting Scholar at Johns Hopkins University's Department of History of Science, Medicine and Technology. Former columnist for *The Lancet* and *The New England Journal of Medicine*. Recipient of the Columbia University Medal for Excellence. Creator of the fictional character Dr Grant Swinger, Director of the Center for the Absorption of Federal Funds.

In 2010, Mr Greenberg, one of the most respected science writers, was invited to review a book for one of the most respected journals, Nature[1]. *Unfortunately, the author was one of Mann's many enemies, and Greenberg was insufficiently hostile to it. So Mann, Paul Ehrlich and Stefan Rahmstorf felt obliged to remind* Nature *just who was boss[2]:*

> In our view, Daniel Greenberg's book review of *The Climate Fix* by Roger Pielke Jr (*Nature* 467, 526–527; 2010) does a disservice to your readership by besmirching the integrity of the climate-research community.

Interesting. Care to elaborate? Well, no. Time to move on to the ol' #KochMachine #BigOil guilt-by-association shtick:

> *Nature* should have pointed out to its readers that

---

[1] http://www.nature.com/nature/journal/v467/n7315/full/467526a.html
[2] http://www.nature.com/nature/journal/v467/n7318/full/467920a.html

Greenberg has served as a round-table speaker and written a report (see go.nature.com/otwvz2) for the Marshall Institute (see go.nature.com/4u9ttd).

Oh, my. As Mr Greenberg subsequently wrote to Professor Pielke[3]:

Roger, Re my stirring experience of jousting with Mann, Ehrlich, and Rahmstorf: What a scurrilous bunch. My sympathy to you and anyone else who has to deal with them. They're gravediggers of science... Below, my further exchanges with the low-life trio.

The "further exchanges with the low-life trio" concluded thus:

Dear Professors Mann, Ehrlich, and Rahmstorf,

Your correspondence concerning my review of Roger Pielke's book *Climate Fix* has provided me with a deeper understanding of the widespread public skepticism toward climate science. **In your hands, apple pie and motherhood would come under public suspicion.**

Furthermore, your insinuation of an undisclosed relationship between me and a conservative think tank is preposterous. In 2006, I participated in a panel discussion sponsored by the Marshall Institute - as I have done with numerous other organizations... Nor did I, as you allege, write a report, or anything, for the Marshall Institute. The panel's words were transcribed and published by the Institute. I wrote nothing for them. You guys are the devil's gift to the Tea Party and other climate-change wackos.

Sincerely, Dan Greenberg

As you can deduce from that last line, Mr Greenberg is an unlikely member of the #DenialMachine. But it matters not to Mann. No deviancy will be permitted! One hundred per cent compliance - or else.

---

[3] http://rogerpielkejr.blogspot.com/2010/10/daniel-greenberg-meets-climate.html

100

"I would never have expected anything similar in such a... peaceful community as meteorology. Apparently it has been transformed."

PROFESSOR LENNART BENGTSSON, PHD

Senior Research Fellow at the Environmental Systems Science Centre of the University of Reading. Recipient of the IMO Prize from the World Meteorological Organization and of the René Descartes Prize for Collaborative Research from the Nansen Environmental and Remote Sensing Centre Former Director of the Max Planck Institute for Meteorology and of the European Centre for Medium-Range Weather Forecasts.

In May 2014, Professor Bengtsson, a man whose contributions to science far outweigh Michael Mann's, revealed that he was joining the advisory board of the Global Warming Policy Foundation, a think-tank for rational skepticism founded in London by Nigel Lawson.

Retribution from the "climate community" was swift and merciless. Less than two weeks later the 79-year old Swedish scientist announced[1]:

I have been put under such an enormous group pressure in recent days from all over the world that has become virtually unbearable to me. If this is going to continue I will be unable to conduct my

---

[1] http://klimazwiebel.blogspot.com.au/2014/05/lennart-bengtsson-leaves-advisory-board.html

normal work and will even start to worry about my health and safety. I see therefore no other way out therefore than resigning from GWPF. I had not expecting such an enormous world-wide pressure put at me from a community that I have been close to all my active life. Colleagues are withdrawing their support, other colleagues are withdrawing from joint authorship etc. I see no limit and end to what will happen. It is a situation that reminds me about the time of McCarthy. I would never have expecting [sic] anything similar in such an original peaceful community as meteorology. Apparently it has been transformed in recent years.

Under these situation I will be unable to contribute positively to the work of GWPF and consequently therefore I believe it is the best for me to reverse my decision to join its Board at the earliest possible time.

It has. For one thing, it's not "meteorology" anymore; it's about saving the planet - and you can't do that without breaking a few eggheads. After The Times *of London ran a front page story on Bengtsson's defenestration, Mann sneeringly Tweeted[2]:*

REAL story via @NafeezAhmed 'Murdoch-owned media hypes lone meteorologist's #climate junk science'" ...#denial

So to Michael Mann Lennart Bengtsson is now "junk science"? Over the years, the two of them have collaborated on scientific conferences[3]. But a half-century of distinguished service to climate science - the directorships, the prizes, all the peer-reviewed papers, the shared platforms with the great Dr Mann - is swept into the garbage can of history, and Bengtsson is now just another "denier" peddling "junk science".

---

[2] https://twitter.com/MichaelEMann/status/467310861237760000
[3] http://www.ecowho.com/foia.php?file=0374.txt

XI

Mann hole

STUCK WITH THE STICK

A model is such a fascinating toy that you fall in love with your creation... Every model has to be compared to the real world and, if you can't do that, then don't believe the model.[1]

PROFESSOR FREEMAN DYSON

"CLIMATE DISASTERS, SAFE NUKES AND OTHER MYTHS" (2009)

---

[1] http://www.scientificamerican.com/blog/post/freeman-dyson-and-the-irresistible-2009-04-30/

I N 2010 MICHAEL E MANN gave an interview to the BBC, which Britain's *Daily Telegraph* reported under an hilarious headline:

Michael Mann Says Hockey Stick Should
Not Have Become 'Climate Change Icon'[2]

Professor J Huston McCulloch of Ohio State University couldn't resist commenting:

Let's see, who was lead author of the TAR chapter on paleoclimate that iconized Mann's HS? Wasn't it the same Michael Mann?[3]

Indeed it was. Fancy that! As Professor John Christy explained, as an IPCC Lead Author Mann sat in judgment on what work would make it into his chapter and chose to "promote his own result" and exclude "studies that contradicted his". That was his decision as Lead Author.

But Mann has prospered in the years since thanks to an impressive ability to say whatever he needs to get him through the moment, no matter how ridiculous. As the *Telegraph* reported:

Speaking to the BBC recently, Professor Mann, a climatologist at Pennsylvania State University, said he had always made clear there were 'uncertainties' in his work.

'I always thought it was somewhat misplaced to make it a central icon of the climate change debate,' he said.

---

[2] http://www.telegraph.co.uk/news/earth/environment/climatechange/7849441/Michael-Mann-says-hockey-stick-should-not-have-become-climate-change-icon.html
[3] http://wattsupwiththat.com/2010/06/29/mann-says-hockey-stick-icon-is-misplaced/

As Professor McCulloch might say: Let's see, would this Michael Mann suddenly going on about "uncertainties" be the same Michael Mann who declared with respect to Keith Briffa's post-1960 tree-ring "decline"..?

> *I don't think that doubt is scientifically justified, and I'd hate to be the one to have to give it fodder!*[4]

No room for "uncertainties" there: Mann's priority was that "the skeptics" should not have "a potential distraction/detraction from the reasonably concensus [sic] viewpoint we'd like to show". The point of the hockey stick is it communicates more certainty more simply than anything else. It is not, technically, a "climate model", in that it does not attempt to project its trend line into the future. But, as a practical matter, it functions as a climate model. Its use to the IPCC and Al Gore is that that temperature line disappearing out the top right-hand corner of the graph and through the ceiling prompts the reaction: "Holy cow, the whole powder keg's about to blow! We gotta do something..." It enabled the climate establishment to promote the subtle, nuanced and highly scientific line: "Give us all your money or the planet's gonna fry."

But the planet didn't fry, the powder keg didn't blow. Instead, from the very moment Mann joined the global-warming A-listers, the actual, real-world temperature flatlined and his hockey stick got the worst case of brewer's droop since records began. By 2015, Big Climate had a far worse "divergence problem" than those tree rings: reality had diverged from the models; the climate had declined to follow instructions, and that's a decline that's far harder to hide. With a couple of Québécois trees, Mann could determine the entire meteorological course for hemispheres and half-centuries:

---

[4] http://www.di2.nu/foia/0938018124.txt

If only the real, actual third millennium had been as compliant as its predecessor.

In that sense, the hockey stick is the ultimate climate model: It became the model for climate science in the 21st century. It showed that keeping it simple and abolishing uncertainty worked - it worked for Al Gore, it worked for Rajendra Pachauri, it worked for the IPCC.

But it didn't work for science. Even "the end is nigh" has to be replicable if it purports to be science. As the blogger Iowahawk Tweeted:

> *Do all scientists keep their data & programs locked inside a boobytrapped Ark of the Covenant, or is that just a climate science thing?*[5]

If you read between the lines, many, many climate scientists understand that Mann's hockey stick has corrupted almost everything it touched, starting with the journal *Nature*, which has been damaged by its publication of Mann and by its refusal to acknowledge its error by publishing the short comment McIntyre & McKitrick submitted; the broader world of peer review, which was exposed as a joke and a racket; the IPCC, which catapulted the hockey stick to global celebrity; the school science teachers who inflicted this cartoon on their young charges; the Climatic Research Unit, founded by a truly great climatologist Hubert Lamb, whose life's work his successors trashed - and from within a building named after him - in order to hitch themselves to Mann's coattails.

But climbing off the hockey stick was easier said than done...

---

[5] https://twitter.com/iowahawkblog/statuses/467700833400782848

101

"I am particularly unimpressed by the MBH style of 'shouting louder and longer so they must be right'."

REFEREE FOR NATURE

The British publication *Nature* vies with its American cousin *Science* for the title of the world's most prestigious scientific journal. According to *Journal Citation Reports* in 2010, it was the most cited scientific journal on the planet. In 1998, it published the very first hockey stick by Mann, Bradley and Hughes.

In publishing the original hockey stick, Nature *fell for a hoax much as* Rolling Stone *did with their 2014 University of Virginia "gang-rape" story, which turned out to have a lack of gang and a lack of rape. Likewise, Mann's proxy reconstruction was deficient in both proxies and reconstruction. With* Nature *as with* Rolling Stone, *the story was, as they say, too good to check.* Rolling Stone *eventually came clean to its readers;* Nature *never has. In 2004 McIntyre & McKitrick submitted a short article to the journal pointing out errors in Mann's hockey stick. Here is the response of* Nature's *Referee Number One[1]:*

I find merit in the arguments of both protagonists, though **Mann et al (MBH) is much more difficult to read** than McIntyre & McKitrick (MM). Their explanations are (at least superficially) less clear and they cram too many things onto the same diagram, so I find it harder to judge whether I agree with them. [I am] uneasy about applying a standardisation based on a small segment

---

[1] http://www.uoguelph.ca/~rmckitri/research/fallupdate04/referees.mar.pdf

of the series to the whole series, if that is what is being done.

Referee Number Two said:

The technical criticisms raised by McIntyre and McKritrik (MM) concerning the temperature reconstructions by Mann et al (MBH98), and the reply to this criticism by Mann et al is quite difficult to evaluate in a short period of time, since they are aimed at particular technical points of the statistical methods used by Mann et al... A proper evaluation would require to redo most of the calculations presented in both manuscripts, something which is obviously out of reach in two weeks time... Therefore, my comments are based on my impression of the consistency of the results presented... In general terms found the criticisms raised by McIntyre and McKritik worth of being taken seriously. They have made an in depth analysis of the MBH reconstructions and they have found several technical errors that are only partially addressed in the reply by Mann et al.

And finally Referee Number Three[2]:

Generally, I believe that the technical issues addressed in the comment and the reply are quite difficult to understand and not necessarily of interest to the wide readership of the Brief Communications section of *Nature*. I do not see a way to make this communication much clearer, particularly with the space requirements, as this comment is largely related to technical details.

A lot of damage to climate science could have been avoided had Nature *behaved with even the grudging residual integrity of* Rolling Stone. *But the third referee prevailed over the other two, and so the stain on* Nature*'s reputation and long, distinguished history remains.*

---

[2] http://www.uoguelph.ca/~rmckitri/research/fallupdate04/referees.aug.pdf

102

"Very few paleoclimatologists agreed to the shape of the curve."

PROFESSOR PER HOLMLUND, PHD

Professor of Glaciology at Stockholm University. Member of the national committee of geophysics at the Royal Swedish Academy of Sciences, and if the International Meteorological Institute. Former Director of Tarfala Research Station, and member of many expeditions to the Arctic and Antarctic. Swedish member of the World Glacier Monitoring Service, the International Arctic Science Committee, the Scientific Committee for Antarctic Research, etc.

Eventually, Mann was forced to issue corrections to the two MBH papers in successive months in June 2004 (in Geophysical Research Letters*) and in July 2004 (in* Nature*). If the correction does "not contradict the original publication",* Nature*'s policy is to publish it as an "addendum". But, "if the scientific accuracy or reproducibility of the original paper is compromised", only a "corrigendum" can be published. Both of the above were "corrigenda" - yet Mann refused to accept the plain meaning of that word. In 2005 Professor Marcel Leroux wrote[1]:*

> After describing their errors, they still considered (2004) that "none of these errors affect our previously published results"! ...The corrigenda issued by Mann et al are "a clear admission that the disclosure of data and methods... was materially inaccurate."

At the IPCC there would not be even a corrigendum. Many serious paleoclimatologists were astonished by Mann's hockey stick, and then

---

[1] Leroux: *Global Warming: Myth or Reality? The Erring Ways of Climatology* (Springer-Praxis, 2005)

appalled at its adoption by the IPCC for the Third Assessment Report. For the Fourth Assessment Report, they attempted to restore some sanity. Reviewing the Second Order Draft, Professor Holmlund wrote[2]:

This remark concerns the handling of the Mann "hockey stick"... When Mann et al presented their hockey stick six-to-seven years ago they formatted paleodata in such a way that climate modellers could use it. But very few paleo climatologists agreed to the shape of the curve and nowadays we have much better data to use. It is therefore natural to describe the Mann curve in a history of science perspective, but not as a valid data set. A good example of a good modern curve is the one presented by Moberg et al... It has at least the variation seen in almost all paleo climate records for the past millennia. In the present IPCC text the view described is that we have the hockey stick and then later some scientists have raised critical voices. **The basic meaning is that the hockey stick is still the number one description of the past millenia. This is not flattering** and it certainly mis-credit [sic] the report. I believe that it is rather easy to go through the five pages and update the spirit of the text and perhaps make some adjustments in the figure captions.

But Mann's Hockey Team were still running the show and any suggestion that the IPCC acknowledge valid criticisms of the stick met with rejection. Professor Holmlund received the following response:

Rejected – the Mann et al curve is included for consistency and to maintain a historical context for the current state of the art.

In other words, we bought this thing and we're sticking with it.

---

[2] http://www.climateaudit.info/pdf/ipcc/sod/Ch06_SOD_ReviewCommentResponses2.pdf

103

"*I know that this is a sensitive issue...*"

PROFESSOR JAN ESPER, PHD

Professor and Head of Unit at Gutenberg University's Department of Geography. Head of Dendro Sciences at the Forest, Snow and Landscape Division of the Swiss Federal Institute of Technology. Author of peer-reviewed papers published in *Nature*, *The Journal of Hydrometeorology*, *Geophysical Research Letters*, *The Journal of Climate* and many more.

In the comments to the First Order Draft of the IPCC Fourth Assessment, Professor Esper tried to suggest, ever so delicately, that this might be an appropriate occasion to be just a wee bit more forthcoming about relying on a couple of Californian bristlecones to divine the temperature of entire hemispheres[1]:

I do believe that with this IPCC report, it would be useful to be a bit more precise and say that tree-ring data dominate the Mann et al 1999 record (at least) during the first half of the last millennium, and that the low frequency component is heavily weighted towards the bristlecone pine data from SW USA (as originally stated by MBH99). I know that this is a sensitive issue, but clearly stating this information seems much better then [sic] just saying that the record is "based on a range of proxy types". Some counts of the number of proxy types and locations integrated in MBH99 (and some other records) were recently

---

[1] http://www.climateaudit.info/pdf/ipcc/fod/Ch06_FOD_ReviewCommentResponses2.pdf

published (Esper et al 2004, EOS 85) that could be cited, if necessary. Further, given the dominance of tree-ring data in the earlier portion of MBH99, the reconstruction (as most others) is certainly weighted towards warm season temperatures back in time. Also, this point should perhaps be emphasized, given the heated discussion on this reconstruction.

But the IPCC was not, yet, ready to disown its biggest hit. The hockey stick's success had made it the model for all models, to the point where there was a not-so-subtle pressure to find other hockey sticks in other climate areas. It was such a simple, graspable snapshot, so why confine it only to temperature? As Dr Nils-Axel Mörner, former head of Stockholm University's Department of Paleogeophysics and Geodynamics, and former Chairman of the International Union for Quatenary Research's Commission on Sea Level Changes and Coastal Evolution, wrote in London's Spectator *in 2011[2]:*

> In 2003 the satellite altimetry record was mysteriously tilted upwards to imply a sudden sea level rise rate of 2.3mm per year. When I criticised this dishonest adjustment at a global warming conference in Moscow, a British member of the IPCC delegation admitted in public the reason for this new calibration: **"We had to do so, otherwise there would be no trend."**
>
> This is a scandal that should be called Sealevelgate. **As with the Hockey Stick, there is little real-world data to support the upward tilt.**

The transnational serpents had been tempted by Mann, and were disinclined to go back.

---

[2] http://www.spectator.co.uk/features/7438683/rising-credulity/

104

"I would rather that the whole 'hockey stick' debate were de-emphasised..."

DR TAS VAN OMMEN, PHD

Principal Research Scientist for ice cores and climate in the Australia Antarctic Division of the Department of the Environment. Lead investigator in the ICECAP airborne geophysical survey covering East Antarctica. Australian representative on the International Partnerships in Ice Core Sciences steering committee. Secretary of the Standing Scientific Group on Physical Sciences at the Scientific Committee on Antarctic Research. Member of the Australian Academy of Science National Committee for Earth System Science. IPCC contributing author.

In a sense, Mann's graph had been too successful for the IPCC. The most popular and recognizable shorthand for global warming, it had taken off like a rocket and climbing off the hockey stick was always going to be tricky. Nevertheless, by 2007, some scientists were willing to try. In a reviewer comment to the First Order Draft of the IPCC's Fourth Assessment Report, Dr van Ommen expressed a preference for burying Mann's hockey stick in a footnote[1]:

This has to be one of the most difficult sections of the chapter, because it so clearly attracts controversy. I would rather that the whole "hockey stick" debate were de-emphasised as **something that belongs 5+ years ago and is superseded by more current**

---

[1] http://www.climateaudit.info/pdf/ipcc/fod/Ch06_FOD_ReviewCommentResponses2.pdf

studies. Is it possible to de-emphasise this paragraph and get away from this entirely (footnote? box?)

A decade on, the cost of defending the hockey stick was taking its toll on climate scientists. In his lectures, Dr Richard Alley (a colleague of Mann's at Penn State) gave a hint of his frustration at the way one man's "icon" had swallowed whole his entire field. He relayed a conversation he claimed to have had with a Congressional staffer[2]:

> The staff member who has the Congress people's ear says: "I didn't take science in school. I don't know science. I don't like science. But you scientists are wrong, you don't know what you're talking about. Okay?" And then says, "Okay, I know that the basis for global warming is a hockey stick that's broken."

Dr Alley tried to explain to the poor chap:

> **The basis for global warming is physics... It's not hockey sticks, it's physics...** "You're basing global warming on a hockey stick." No, we're not.

Film of Dr Alley making this point, very forcefully, appears in a short Internet video by Peter Sinclair called "Climate Denial Crock of the Week". Following Dr Alley's calm explanation that the basis for global warming is physics, not that ol' broken hockey stick, Mr Sinclair then popped back up to insist in the show's finale that Mann's hockey stick is so totally not broken.

Dr Alley must sometimes wonder why he bothers.

---

[2] https://www.youtube.com/watch?v=uHhLcoPT9KM

105

"Using the notion 'hockey stick', even in quotes, is a mistake. Such an expression must not enter serious literature on climate change issues."

PROFESSOR THOMAS STOCKER, PHD

Professor of Climate and Environmental Physics and Co-Director of the Physics Institute at the University of Bern. Nominated to succeed the disgraced Rajendra Pachauri as IPCC chair. Recipient of the Hans Oeschger Medal from the European Geosciences Union, the Descartes Prize for Transnational Collaborative Research from the European Commission, and the National Latsis Prize from the Swiss National Science Foundation. Fellow of the American Geophysical Union.

In contrast to Dr van Ommen, Professor Stocker didn't want the words "hockey stick" to sully the document at all[1]:

I feel strongly that using the notion "hockey stick", even in quotes, is a mistake. Such an expression must not enter serious literature on climate change issues. The very wording of this sentence links "hockey stick" with the work of Mann et al (1999). This is not fair, as **this notion is now used as to discredit this work. IPCC should not adopt this language.**

Professor Stocker seems to be suggesting that there are two separate things here: a paper called "Mann et al (1999)", which is part of the "serious

---

[1] http://www.climateaudit.info/pdf/ipcc/fod/Ch06_FOD_ReviewCommentResponses2.pdf

literature on climate change issues", and some vulgar reductio "the hockey stick", which is "used to discredit this work". But Mann himself assiduously promoted the concept of "the hockey stick" on his rise to global stardom, and he continues to do so to this day - on his website, in his bio, in the very title of his book, The Hockey Stick and the Climate Wars.

Professor Stocker may be revolted by such ghastly populist simplicities as the term "hockey stick" sullying the IPCC, and he rightly discerns that there is something malodorous about it. But the notion that it's this label that is "discrediting" Mann et al (1999) is ridiculous. The problem is Mann et al itself.

Even his closest collaborators are stumbling on the Medieval Warm Period and "natural variability" everywhere they look. In 2012, The Holocene *published a paper, by Dr Thomas Melvin of the Climatic Research Unit, Professor Håkan Grudd of Stockholm University and - golly - even Keith Briffa himself, called "Potential bias in 'updating' tree-ring chronologies using regional curve standardisation"[2]:*

> We can infer the existence of generally warm summers in the 10th and 11th centuries, similar to the level of those in the 20th century... The results here imply a level of recent summer temperatures that is equivalent, though not yet as persistent over as long a period, to the warmth in medieval time.

He's a slippery fellow, this Medieval Warm Period. You find him in Scandinavia and South America and China and Indonesia ...but when Mann compiles it all together into one big picture, the poor chap vanishes every time.

---

[2] http://hol.sagepub.com/content/early/2012/10/26/0959683612460791.full. pdf+html

106

"It should never have been singled out ...and been promoted to such a position of superiority."

PROFESSOR RICHARD PELTIER, PHD

Professor of Physics and Founding Director of the Centre for Global Change Science at the University of Toronto. Scientific Director of the SciNet Facility for High Performance Computation, Canada's largest supercomputer center. Recipient of Canada's highest scientific award, the Gerhard Herzberg Gold Medal in Science and Engineering, and of the Bancroft Award of the Royal Society of Canada, the Milankovic Medal of the European Geosciences Union, the Bower Award of the Franklin Institute and the Vetlesen Prize of the G. Unger Vetlesen Foundation of New York. Fellow of the Norwegian Academy of Science and Letters and Leiv Erikson Fellow of the Norwegian Research Council.

A decade after it soared to scientific superstardom, even longtime believers in anthropogenic global warming recognized that resting the case on the hockey stick had been a terrible error. On March 27th 2012 Professor Peltier gave evidence to the Standing Senate Committee on Energy, the Environment and Natural Resources of the Parliament of Canada [1]:

As an add-on to this, it should be seen and acknowledged as a mistake by those who chose what to put in the summary for policy makers not to make it clear that the actual report did

---

[1] http://www.parl.gc.ca/content/sen/committee/411%5CENEV/18EVA-49441-e.HTM

contain this large number of different hockey sticks.

I believe it was an administrative mistake to take Michael Mann's more perfect looking hockey stick and put it in the summary for policy makers. If anything is to be faulted in the hockey stick story, it is that. It should never have been singled out because it was the best-looking hockey stick and been promoted to such a position of superiority by appearing alone in the summary for policy makers. **It was a big mistake on the part of the IPCC.**

Ten months after Professor Peltier spoke to Canadian parliamentarians, Dr Peter Stott of the Met Office gave evidence to the House of Commons at Westminster. Both Peltier and Stott are part of the "97 per cent consensus" on global warming. But, whereas the Canadian was willing to acknowledge the IPCC's promotion of the hockey stick, his English counterpart denied they'd given it any emphasis at all[2]:

I think it is important to put the Paleo information in context. The IPCC assessment is based on multiple lines of evidence looking right across the climate system, from the instrumental data, warming of the ocean, changes in the water cycle, and sea level rise. All this wealth of evidence builds into this picture and robust comprehensive assessment, as I say, based on multiple lines of evidence of which the Paleo reconstructions with the uncertainties that are involved with inferring global temperatures from indirect proxies of temperature play their part but **a relatively small part in the overall assessment.**

Funny how it didn't seem like that at the time.

---

[2] http://data.parliament.uk/writtenevidence/WrittenEvidence.svc/EvidenceHtml/5743

258

107

"We were aware of these proxy climate reconstructions, but did not give them much weight... because the statistical methods used were (and arguably still are) rather opaque."

PROFESSOR MYLES ALLEN, PHD

Head of the Climate Dynamics Group at the University of Oxford's Atmospheric, Oceanic and Planetary Physics Department. Professor of Geosystem Science in the School of Geography and the Environment, and Fellow of Linacre College. Recipient of the Appleton Medal from the Institute of Physics. Member of the US NOAA/Department of Energy International Advisory Group on Anthropogenic Climate Change. Formerly with the UN Environment Programme, the Rutherford Appleton Laboratory and the Massachusetts Institute of Technology. IPCC Lead Author.

In 2012 Professor Allen wrote to the "skeptics" at the Bishop Hill website to bemoan their strange obsessions[1]:

The public are kept distracted by a debate over the Medieval Warm Period, which has only ever featured in one of the lines of evidence for human influence on climate (and **not, in my view, a particularly strong one**)... My fear is that by keeping the public focussed on **irrelevancies**, you are excluding them from the discussion of what we should do about climate change.

---

[1] http://bishophill.squarespace.com/blog/2012/5/26/myles-allen-writes.html

Notice that, even as he dismisses the hockey stick as an "irrelevancy" and "not a particularly strong" line of evidence , even at this late date, a sense of self-preservation obliges him not to mention Mann or his stick by name. Professor Allen is a loyal supporter of the climate "consensus", and therefore for many years of Mann and the CRU. However, by 2013, in evidence before the British House of Commons Select Committee looking into the IPCC's Fifth Assessment Review, he argued (somewhat risibly) that the hockey stick had never been terribly important[2]:

I can also confirm that the particular reconstruction of Northern Hemisphere temperatures over the past millennium (the so-called "Hockey Stick"), which subsequently came in for considerable criticism, was **not in any way central to the conclusions of the 2001 Assessment** regarding attribution of causes of recent warming. We were aware of these proxy climate reconstructions, but did not give them much weight in the attribution assessment because the statistical methods used were (and arguably still are) rather opaque. I remember specific discussions among the attribution chapter authors questioning the error budgets of those reconstructions, and concluding that **it would be premature to rely on them too heavily.** With the benefit of hindsight, these discussions seem remarkable prescient, and confirm the importance of scientific judgment in the IPCC process.

This is a near Soviet level of historical airbrushing. When Mann's patron Sir John Houghton unveiled the Third Assessment Report to the world in Shanghai, he did so with a giant blow-up of the hockey stick behind him. And for years afterwards Sir John continued to feature a prominent display of Mann's stick in his public speeches and lectures.

---

[2] http://data.parliament.uk/writtenevidence/committeeevidence.svc/
evidencedocument/energy-and-climate-change-committee/ipcc-5th-assessment-
review/written/4280.pdf

108

"Given the extensive use the IPCC made of it in the past... this absence is peculiar"

PROFESSOR PHILIPPE DE LARMINAT, PhD

Former head of research at CNRS, the French National Center for Scientific Research, professor at the University of Nantes and at INSA, the National Institute of Applied Sciences, at Rennes.

Eventually, however, if never formally disowning it, the IPCC simply ceased all reference to Mann's stick. Chapter Three of Philippe de Larminat's book Changement climatique: identification et projections *is called "The War of the Graphs". Professor de Larminat regrets having to bring up the subject[1]:*

Such a chapter should not be found in a scientific work. It is necessary, however, given the controversial context unsettling the climate change issue.

Professor de Larminat performs a technical analysis of competing climate reconstructions and is not impressed by Mann's work:

The hockey stick curve, which ignores large climatic events, seems to have come straight from another world.

Just so. But, by 2014, it had apparently gone back to its home planet. Commenting on its absence from the Fifth Assessment Report, Professor

---

[1] de Larminat: *Changement climatique: identification et projections* (Éditions ISTE, 2014)

de Larminat writes on page 32 of his book:

This Chapter 5 in question does not make the slightest mention of the famous publication from M Mann et al ...neither in the text nor among the some 1,000 specific bibliographical references in this chapter. Given the extensive use that the IPCC made of it in the past (cited six times in the Third Assessment Report), and the controversy it still causes, this absence is peculiar.

The IPCC's airbrushing of its monster does not erase the damage it did. Professor de Larminat adds in a footnote:

According to Google Scholar, Mann (1999) is quoted 1,681 times in scientific literature, Moberg 1,008 times, Ljungqvist 103 times and Loehle 56 times (for their respective reconstructions).

In his own book, Heaven and Earth, *Professor Ian Plimer observed[2]:*

In the next IPCC report, the Medieval Warming and Little Ice Age mysteriously reappeared.

This suggests that **the IPCC knew that the "hockey stick" was invalid.** This is a withering condemnation of the IPCC. The "hockey stick" was used as the backdrop for announcements about human-induced climate change, it is still used by Al Gore, and it is still used in talks, on websites and in publications by those claiming that the world is getting warmer due to human activities. Were any of those people who view this graphic told that **the data before 1421 AD was based on just one lonely alpine pine tree?**

No. For Nature, *for the IPCC, for Al Gore, you can't see the tree for the big global millennial forest.*

---

[2] Plimer: *Heaven and Earth: Global Warming - The Missing Science* (Quartet, 2009)

109

"The fundamental conflict is of what (if anything) we should do about greenhouse gas emissions ...not what the weather was like 1,000 years ago."

DR GAVIN SCHMIDT, PHD

Director of NASA's Goddard Institute for Space Studies. Recipient of the American Geophysical Union's Climate Communications Prize, for among other things his co-founding of the pro-Mann RealClimate blog. Author of peer-reviewed papers in *Proceedings of the National Academy of Sciences* and other journals.

In February 2011 Professor Jerry Ravetz, with the help of some funding from the European Commission and the Gulbenkian Foundation, hosted a conference in Lisbon that was intended to help reconcile the climate-consensus crowd with those who oppose them. Skeptics such as McIntyre & McKitrick and Steve Mosher were invited, as were climate scientists such as Hans von Storch and James Risbey. Dr Schmidt, one of the few scientists willing to defend Mann with enthusiasm, declined to attend, and explained why[1]:

Thanks for the invitation. However, I'm a little confused at what conflict you feel you are going to be addressing? The fundamental conflict is of what (if anything) we should do about greenhouse gas emissions (and other assorted pollutants), not what the weather was like 1,000 years ago... None of the

---

[1] http://www.newscientist.com/blogs/shortsharpscience/2011/02/climate-sceptics-scientists-at.html

seemingly important "conflicts" that are "perceived" in the science are "conflicts" in any real sense within the scientific community... No "conflict resolution" is possible between the science community who are focussed on increasing understanding, and people who are picking through the scientific evidence for cherries they can pick to support a pre-defined policy position.

You would be much better off trying to find common ground on policy ideas... than trying to get involved in irrelevant scientific "controversies".

So much for that. But his crack about "what the weather was like 1,000 years ago" was revealing. Shortly after the conference, Robert Goebbels (no relation, one assumes), a Luxembourg socialist, asked the following question in the European Parliament[2]:

According to *the New Scientist* magazine, the Commission organised a meeting in early February in Lisbon between scientists defending the IPCC's theories on climate change and more sceptical scientists.

Is it true that, at this meeting, it was acknowledged that **the 'hockey stick theory', which denies the existence of climate variations over the last two millennia, was mistaken?**

The New Scientist *suggests this was a rare point of agreement between skeptics and believers. Dr Schmidt can sneer who cares "what the weather was like 1,000 years ago". Yet the hockey stick was not conjured into existence to determine the past, but to change the future. Schmidt is certainly free to mock those who pointed out the flaws in Mann's science, but the fact that he no longer wants to defend it is revealing.*

---

[2] http://www.europarl.europa.eu/sides/getDoc.do?type=WQ&reference=E-2011-001813&format=XML&language=EN

110

"There is a concern always if previous mistakes have been made, as in some cases, or maybe the accentuation of one view..."

PROFESSOR SIR BRIAN HOSKINS, CBE, FRS, PHD

Meteorologist and climatologist based at Imperial College, London and the University of Reading. Knight Bachelor, Commander of the Most Excellent Order of the British Empire, Fellow of the Royal Society, and chair of its Global Environmental Research Committee. Former President of the Royal Meteorological Society, and member of the Royal Commission on Environmental Pollution. Recipient of the Symons Gold Medal, the L F Richardson Prize and the Buchan Prize from the Royal Meteorological Society, the Vilhelm Bjerknes Medal from the European Geophysical Society, the Calf-Gustaf Rossby Research Medal from the American Meteorological Society, and the Chree Medal from the Institute of Physics. Member of the US National Academy of Sciences, Honorary Professor of the Chinese Academy of Sciences, and Fellow of the American Meteorological Society.

On January 28th 2014 Sir Brian gave evidence on the IPCC's Fifth Assessment Review to the Energy and Climate Change Committee of the British House of Commons[1]. He was asked by the chairman if he thought that "controversies" such as the hockey stick had damaged the

---

[1] http://data.parliament.uk/writtenevidence/WrittenEvidence.svc/EvidenceHtml/5743

IPCC's credibility and replied with what A W Montford called "a wonderful sirhumphreyish locution[2]":

MR TIM YEO, MP: Do you have any anxiety that controversies that arose from previous reports - take the hockey stick graph that seems to be referred to quite frequently - may cast doubt on the conclusions reached in AR5?

PROFESSOR SIR BRIAN HOSKINS: There is a concern always if previous mistakes have been made, as in some cases, or maybe the accentuation of one view. It is a group of people, and mistakes will be made and that should not reflect on anything in the future for that body. Of course, we should all be sceptical - and we are all sceptical. the whole time. So probing, it must go on. It is not going to be taken as the Bible, but it should be taken as the view of a large group of scientists from the diverse range of where the scientists come from, and this is the consensus view given by them. That is what it is. There must always be a concern if then people can return to **a mistake made 20 years ago**, or an accentuation made 20 years ago, to down excellent work that has been done now. There must be a concern...

We'll take that as a yes.

---

[2] http://www.bishop-hill.net/blog/2014/4/20/celebrating-bad-science.html

XII

Mann overboard

THE FALL OF THE STICK

With the collapse of the 'hockey stick', and the recent failure of global temperature to follow its supposed script, the sole argument an increasingly desperate Intergovernmental Panel on Climate Change coterie is left with is the deployment of the results of unvalidated, speculative computer General Circulation Models.[1]

PROFESSOR ROBERT M CARTER, PHD

"FLACKS FOR ALARMISTS" (THE COURIER-MAIL, SEPTEMBER 6TH 2009)

---

[1] http://www.couriermail.com.au/news/flacks-for-alarmists/story-e6frerdf-1111114348783

MICHAEL E MANN is the bristlecone pine of scientists. Just as removing the bristlecones makes his hockey stick collapse, so removing Mann from the climate conversation would make a lot of the drama and hysteria and sheer unpleasantness disappear.

For example, why do we have leaders of advanced, prosperous societies talking like gibbering madmen escaped from the padded cell, whether it's President Obama promising to end the rise of the oceans or the Prince of Wales saying we only have 96 months left to save the planet. He started that countdown in 2009, by the way. The 96 months is up in July 2017. On the other hand, it gives us an extra 18 months on January 2016, which is the official final storewide-clearance date for Al Gore's 2006 prediction of the end of the world.

This sort of thing was once reserved for amiable lunatics with sandwich boards passing out leaflets in the street. What made it suddenly respectable for princes and presidents?

Answer: The declaration by the IPCC that this is the hottest year of the hottest decade of the hottest century since hotness began. And who provided the underlying "science" for that? Mann.

Another question: Why is Big Climate so weirdly defensive? To the point where an entire sub-discipline of junk science has sprung up in which supposed "academics" publish papers purporting to show that 99.99999 per cent of all scientists agree with them[2], and producing "studies" to prove that anyone minded to disagree is a conspiracy theorist who believes the moon landings were faked.[3] (In fact, two of the very few men who've set foot on the

---

[2] joannenova.com.au/2015/03/the-97-consensus-misrepresented-miscalculated-misleading/

[3] http://websites.psychology.uwa.edu.au/labs/cogscience/documents/

moon are, in Mann terms, climate deniers: Buzz Aldrin and Harrison Schmitt.)

Why are they doing this? Answer: They're playing by Mann rules. Don't address the argument, destroy the guy making it - he's a "denier", he's in the pay of the Koch brothers. Clearly this Buzz Aldrin kook is just some wackjob who believes the moon landings were filmed in Nevada.

Those who think that the very real disputes within climate science should nevertheless be debated within civilized norms have argued that, in Dr Richard Betts' words, "the whole climate conversation would be better off with the word 'denier' being dropped completely." But no climatologist promotes this witless slur as zealously as Mann: He lends a gang insult the imprimatur of science, and his thuggish acolytes have enthusiastically embraced it. Because what they're defending - the hockey stick - is indefensible, their best defense is a good offensiveness, remorseless and virulent.

Much has flowed from the decision to stick with the stick. You'll recall Professor Richard Tol's words a few pages ago:

> *Who does most damage to the climate movement? Michael Mann, Phil Jones, Jim Hansen, Peter Gleick, Al Gore, Rajendra Pachauri (not necessarily in that order).*

James Hansen was the most influential climate-change promoter pre-Mann. In June 1988 his dramatic testimony to the US Senate was reported by the following day's *New York Times* under the headline "Global Warming Has Begun". Certainly, the global-warming movement had begun. Hansen pushed the boundaries between scientist and propagandist, but, unlike Mann, he did not push the science itself into outright propaganda. Peter Gleick is a

LskyetalPsychScienceinPressClimateConspiracy.pdf

climatologist who stole the identity of a director of the (skeptic) Heartland Institute and released several confidential documents plus a "strategy" paper that he forged outright. He remains a respected figure in his field, and he and Mann are mutual admirers, with Mann comparing Gleick favorably to whoever "hacked" into the CRU. In reality, the Climategate emails were almost certainly leaked by a disgusted CRU employee - and are not forged.

But put Hansen and Gleick aside. Everyone else on Professor Tol's list of those who do "most damage to the climate movement" is a Mann promoter: Rajendra Pachauri was the head of the organization that made the hockey stick the most famous "science" graph of the 21st century; Al Gore is the climate crusader who made the stick the star of his Oscar-winning movie and the lodestar of a new school of cartoon science force-fed to a generation of western schoolchildren; Phil Jones is the older, respected scientist who put a distinguished institution in the service of hockey-stick science, colluded with Mann in obstructing legitimate requests for data, and would have been criminally prosecuted for breach of the Freedom of Information Act were it not for the statute of limitations.

In other words, take away Mann and the hockey stick, and a lot of the other bad stuff goes away, too. Embracing the stick corrupted the heart of climate science, from *Nature* to peer review to the CRU to the IPCC to government policy around the world. If scientists of integrity are not willing to, in Jonathan Jones' phrase, "publicly denounce the hockey stick as obvious drivel", they do need, in the interests of a fresh start for a very damaged brand, to acknowledge the damage it did. They owe it to their own integrity to repudiate the stick. In this section are some of the scientists who spoke up, without fear, very early.

111

"The 'hockey stick' concept of global climate change is now widely considered totally invalid and an embarrassment to the IPCC."

PROFESSOR DON J EASTERBROOK, PHD

Professor Emeritus of Geology at Western Washington University. Fellow of the Geological Society of America and past president of the Quaternary Geology and Geomorphology Division. Founding member of the American Quaternary Association, member of the Commission on Quaternary Stratigraphy of North America, and US representative to UNESCO International Geological Correlation Project. Associate Editor of *Geomorphology* and *The Geological Society of America Bulletin*.

In his book Evidence-Based Climate Science, *Professor Easterbrook put it very bluntly*[1]:

The Mann et al "hockey stick" temperature curve was so at odds with thousands of published papers... one can only wonder how a single tree-ring study could purport to prevail over such a huge amount of data. At best, if the tree-ring study did not accord with so much other data, it should simply mean that the tree rings were not sensitive to climate change, not that all the other data were wrong... The "hockey stick" concept of global climate change is now widely considered totally invalid and an embarrassment to the IPCC.

---

[1] Easterbrook: *Evidence-Based Climate Science: Data opposing CO2 emissions as the primary source of global warming* (Elsevier, 2011) pages 28-29

Surely many scientists thought as much all those years ago. And yet it took an extraordinary amount of time for them to speak up against a whole-hearted assault on the scientific method. One by one, disinterested parties who took the time to look at McIntyre & McKitrick's work came away feeling the two Canadian outsiders had the better case than Mann and his acolytes. In February 2005, Anthony Lupo, Professor of Atmospheric Science at the University of Missouri, Fellow of the Royal Meteorological Society, IPCC expert reviewer, and editor-in-chief of National Weather Digest, *was one of the first American climate scientists to contact the stick-slayers directly[2]:*

> I will confess that I was not aware of the details of Steve McIntyre and Ross McKitrick's critique of the "hockey stick" but after a cursory reading of the enclosed materials it seems that **the critics have valid points.**
>
> **I've been skeptical of the "hockey stick" for a long time** simply on the grounds that there is too much evidence that climate has been more changeable than the "hockey stick" would indicate... Also, having taken part in the IPCC review process for the 2nd and 3rd assessments, I was continually frustrated with drafts that had: [will include text later] [will insert figure here] riddled throughout them. Thus, I'm not surprised that some may have made errors in their science and then, for whatever reason fail to provide their methods.
>
> Again, I'm not an expert in tree ring studies, but Steve and Ross's work to me makes good points. I'm happy to see work like theirs get published.

His was a comparatively lonely voice in 2005. Not now.

---

[2] http://climateaudit.org/2005/02/08/mm-feedback-by-anthony-lupo/

112

"Claims based on the 'Mann hockey-stick curve' are by now totally discredited."

PROFESSOR PETER STILBS, PHD

Professor of Physical Chemistry at the Royal Institute of Technology in Stockholm. Fellow of the Royal Society of Chemistry, member of the American Chemical Society and the American Physical Society, and Docent of Physical Chemistry at Uppsala University and Åbo University. Member of the International Advisory Board for the RSC journal *Chemistry World*.

In September 2006 Professor Stilbs and the Royal Institute of Technology hosted 120 participants from 11 countries representing a wide spectrum of views at a conference on "Global Warming - Scientific Controversies in Climate Variability". At the conclusion of the meeting, he wrote[1]:

By the final panel discussion stage of the conference, there appeared to be wide agreement that:

1) It is likely that there has been a climate trend towards global warming underway since 1850...

2) There are many uncertainties in climate modeling...

3) Natural variations in climate are considerable and well-documented...

---

[1] http://gamma.physchem.kth.se/~climate/

4) There is no reliable evidence to support that the 20th century was the warmest in the last thousand years. Previous claims based on the "Mann hockey-stick curve" are by now totally discredited.

Bert Bolin, former head of the IPCC, agreed to attend this conference on the condition they waived his admission fee of approximately $25. (When one is part of the transnational climate jet set, one loses the habit of ever writing a personal check.) In the end, Professor Bolin stormed out on the first day after a presentation by Professor Tom Segalstad of the University of Oslo that concluded with a famous cartoon showing the inverse relationship between global warming and the size of bathing suits (from billowing bloomers to thongs). Bolin exploded with rage, told Professor Segalstad to read a text book, denounced the conference as garbage, and then walked out.² So the former IPCC chair was not part of that consensus on the "totally discredited" hockey stick.

As the host of one of the first conferences to push back against Mann's cartoon science, Professor Stilbs would not be surprised by the revelations that emerged in the years ahead. In 2011, rsponding to his colleague Pehr Björnbom, emeritus professor of chemical engineering at the Royal Institute of Technology, after Björnbom's inventory of "hide the decline", Professor Stilbs remarked sadly³:

Thank you, Pehr, for this thorough compilation of an organized scam. The climate scientists who do not renounce it lacks all credibility. Unfortunately, it seems to apply to most of them.

What Mann hath wrought.

---

² http://climateaudit.org/2006/09/19/kth-stockholm-conference/
³ http://www.klimatupplysningen.se/2011/11/18/hide-the-decline/

113

"The Mann curve does not hold anymore... It's not falsifiable, so it's not science."

PROFESSOR VINCENT COURTILLOT, PHD

Director of the Institute of Geophysics in Paris and Professor of Geophysics at the Paris Diderot University. Chevalier of the Légion d'Honneur, and Member of the French Academy of Sciences. Former Director of Research at the French Ministry for National Education, Research and Technology. Former editorial advisor to the journal *La Recherche*.

In December 2010 Vincent Courtillot gave a presentation to the International Energy and Climate Conference in Berlin, in which, inter alia, he expressed mystification as to why the British and Americans had sole charge of the global surface-temperature records - which means, in effect, according a monopoly to Mann's UK buddies (Phil Jones and a handful of others) and Mann's US buddies (Gavin Schmidt and another handful). So much for the "thousands of scientists from hundreds of countries". Professor Courtillot also managed to trump the "97 per cent consensus"[1]:

I'm pretty sure here that 99.9 per cent of the people - which if I round it up means everyone - is aware of the fact that the Mann curve does not hold anymore... It's not falsifiable, so it's not science.

---

[1] https://www.youtube.com/watch?v=IG_7zK8ODGA

As Professor Courtillot says in that lecture, he asked Hockey Team deputy captain Phil Jones for data, but, like McIntyre & McKitrick, was rebuffed. In 2008, Jones had written to James Hansen[2]:

Jim,

I see you're down for a meeting in London tomorrow and Friday. I have been having something of a run in with a French scientist called Vincent Courtillot. He is making Édouard Bard's life awful in French. If you're there on the Friday when Vincent is talking then tell him he's just completely wrong. He will likely say the climate isn't warming and even if it was it has little to do with greenhouse gases. So shouldn't be difficult!!

I'm lecturing here in Norwich to students so can't make it to London.

If you're not there on the Friday, just make sure one or two reasonable scientists are aware that they have invited a bit of rogue!

Cheers

Phil

The French climatologist Jean Jouzel took a less hostile position on Professor Courtillot. He said[3]:

If the [warming] plateau continues for another ten years, Courtillot will be right ...but in ten years it will be too late.

Dr Jouzel said that in 2005. On his terms, Courtillot is right.

---

[2] http://www.ecowho.com/foia.php?file=4184.txt
[3] http://www.bvoltaire.fr/yannsergent/conference-climat-paris-2015-offrons-des-vacances-m-hulot,149370

114

"This lack of scientific rigor has totally discredited the curve."

PROFESSOR ISTVÁN E MARKÓ, PHD ET AL

István Markó is Professor of Organic Chemsitry at the Catholic University of Louvain, Chairman of the European Chemical Society, and the man in whose honor the chemical reaction the Markó-Lam deoxygenation was named. Alain Préat is Professor of Geology at the Free University of Brussels. Henri Masson is a professor at Maastricht University and former vice-president of SRBII, the Royal Belgian Society of Engineers and Industrialists. Samuele Furfari is Professor of Energy Geopolitics at the Free University of Brussels and a longtime senior advisor on energy to the European Commission.

In 2013, in a country where acceptable opinion on "climate change" is even narrower than in the anglophone world, Professors Markó, Préat, Masson and Furfari received a rare invitation to give a half-dozen well-attended lectures on the subject at the Royal Academy of Belgium. Among their conclusions[1]:

1)   The climate has always changed. This was true during ancient times and it has also been true since the beginning of the modern era. These climate changes have always been, and still are, independent of the concentration of CO_2 in the atmosphere;

2)   During Roman times and the Middle Ages temperatures were observed well in excess of those currently experienced. From

---

[1] http://www.contrepoints.org/2013/04/30/123047-conference-a-lacademie-belge-des-sciences-deux-poids-deux-mesures-sur-le-climat - English version here: http://www.thegwpf.com/belgian-scientists-double-standards-climate-change/

the 16th till the 19th century a cold period referred to as the "Little Ice Age" predominated. All these changes took place without mankind being held responsible...

3)   The so-called "abnormally rapid" increase in global temperatures between 1980 and 2000 is not unusual at all. There have in fact been several such periods in the past, during which temperatures rose in a similar manner and at comparable rates, even though fossil fuels were not yet in use;

4)   Temperature measurements do not necessarily correlate with a building up or a decrease in heat since heat variations are energy changes subject to thermal inertia. Apart from heat many other parameters have an influence on temperature. Moreover the measurement of temperatures is subject to numerous large errors. When the magnitude and plurality of these measurement errors are taken into account, the reported increase in temperatures is no longer statistically significant;

5)   **The famous "Hockey-stick" curve, known as the Mann curve and presented six times by the IPCC in its penultimate report, is the result among other things of a mistake in the statistical calculations and an incorrect choice of temperature indicators, i.e. proxies.** This lack of scientific rigor has totally discredited the curve and it was withdrawn, without any explanation, from subsequent IPCC reports...

Professor Masson has also said[2]:

We remember the famous curve in the shape of a hockey stick... However, **no serious scientist still gives it the least credit.**

---

[2] http://www.contrepoints.org/2012/03/10/72535-interview-exclusive-de-henri-masson-sur-les-modeles-du-giec-aberration-statistique

115

"A shoddy stick"

PROFESSOR MARCEL LEROUX, PHD (1938-2008)

Director of the Laboratory of Climatology at Jean Moulin University, Lyon. Knight of the Ordre des Palmes Académiques. First proponent of the Mobile Polar High, a new concept explaining the meridional air mass and the worldwide propagation of paleoclimatic changes.

In 2005 Professor Leroux wrote a book published in English as Global Warming: Myth or Reality? The Erring Ways of Climatology. *The section beginning on page 215 is headlined "A shoddy stick"[1]:*

So the "hockey stick" has had its day, and, as Corcoran[2] (2004) puts it, "is about to get swept away as a piece of junk science". However, this saga has had its uses, and in more than one way, because:

~It is symptomatic of the state of mind of the IPCC, whose scientific rigour and credibility seem rather tenuous; it appears to be preoccupied with using "scientific reasoning" only to facilitate propaganda. It comes as no surprise that it was [Sir Robert] Watson, true to form in his capacity as IPCC president [chairman], who proclaimed at the Hague in November 2000 that "the Earth's surface temperature this century is clearly warmer than in any other century during the last 1,000 years"!

---

[1] Leroux: *Global Warming: Myth or Reality? The Erring Ways of Climatology* (Springer-Praxis, 2005)
[2] Terence Corcoran in *The National Post* of Canada, July 13th 2004

~It highlights just how far some "scientists" are prepared to go to gain recognition, to be seen as original, even to curry favour with some existing or hoped-for sponsor, or otherwise to seek benefits for themselves and their groups.

~It reveals the degree to which scientific journals (or those considered as such) can "follow the fashion" and adopt the methods of the "media types", or just deliberately adopt the *parti pris* of the IPCC. An editorial team can, by selecting the "right" referee, launch onto the market any so-called "scientific" idea, just as if it were some kind of washing powder or fizzy drink, and then shamelessly block any corrections, for the most feeble of reasons!

All this represents an obvious danger to science, and to its credibility.

Professor Leroux was right. But as he wrote on page 209 of his book, "We are certainly no longer moving in the realms of science here!"

Earlier, the Nobel Laureate Ivar Giaever compared the hockey stick to a Hans Christian Andersen fairy tale. Alas, in the new version of The Emperor's New Clothes, *the little boy points out that His Majesty is naked, and the enraged courtiers and the more fevered members of the crowd club him to a pulp yelling, "Don't you know? The clothing is settled!"*

And so, almost two decades into the global-warming "pause", Mann & Co were still insisting that the climate models are all in agreement, so it's reality that must be wrong - and we need to find a way to bring a flawed reality into line with our flawless models. Professor Leroux was right: We have departed the realm of science, and we have yet to return.

116

"The charlatan Michael Mann and his infamous hockey stick."

DR WALTER STARCK, PHD

Marine biologist whose half-century of reef studies has led to the discovery of dozens of hitherto unknown species of fish, as well as corals, shells and crustaceans. A pioneer in the use of scuba diving for marine research and reef biology, whose decade-long project beginning in 1958 in the Florida Keys resulted in the collection of over 20,000 scientific specimens and what remains the greatest number of fish ever recorded in any single locale in the New World - some 517 species, 60 of which had never been found in US waters and 19 of which were entirely unknown to science. Developer of the optical dome port for wide-angle underwater photography and of the electrolung, which enabled him to explore deep reefs where no man had gone before and which has since been taken up by NASA, the US Navy and many others.

At the end of 2014, Dr Starck surveyed the state of the climate wars in the Australian magazine Quadrant[1]:

The ultimate arbiter, climate itself, has made clear its decision by ceasing to warm for over 18 years. Despite the ongoing use of fossil fuels, a proclaimed 95 per cent certainty of 97 per cent of scientists and the high-powered projections of the world's most advanced climate models, the climate has refused to pay the slightest heed...

   The debate... is also unique in that **the alarmists refuse to directly address their opponents, preferring to ignore, censor and personally denigrate them...** All who disagreed were

[1] https://quadrant.org.au/opinion/doomed-planet/2014/11/climate-scams-meltdown/

deemed to be fools, knaves and/or in the pay and pocket of Big Energy... Self-serving publicity releases were regurgitated undigested beneath the by-lines of environmental "reporters", who eagerly reduced themselves to unquestioning stenographers.

Yet even as the alarmists received kid-glove treatment in the mainstream media, the Internet has been a very different story... Think here of how WattsUpWithThat[2] demolished the charlatan Michael Mann and his infamous hockey stick, and the Climategate emails revealed **the lengths professional warmists are prepared to go in order to silence sceptics, not least by debasing the conventions of the peer-review process.**

Scoffing at the way the same people who told us the science was "settled" are now latching onto ever more desperate alternative explanations - the missing heat is hiding at the bottom of the ocean; the trade winds are monkeying with the sea thermometers - Dr Starck continued:

The core alarmist proponents only comprise a few dozen, mostly third-rate academics whose scientific reputations are minimal outside of climate alarmism. They co-opted the niche, little known interdisciplinary field of climatology, proclaimed themselves to be the world authorities, declared a global crisis, received lavish funding to research it and gained global attention. They have been aided and abetted by sundry fellow travellers who see advantage for various other agendas...

Although climate itself is presenting its irrefutable opposing argument, failed prophets never willingly concede defeat until their mouths are stopped with the dust of reality... Until the crunch comes, the rent-seekers and their useful idiots in the press will rant and rage without pause.

_____

[2] The widely read climate website run by Anthony Watts

117

"It is difficult to fathom how the main players and proponents of the Hockey Sticks are still able to act as experts."

DR SEBASTIAN LÜNING, PHD

Geologist and co-author of *Die Kalte Sonne* - or *The Cold Sun*. Former Visiting Professor at the University of Vienna. Contributor to *The Encyclopedia of Geology*. Author of peer-reviewed papers published by *The Journal of Petroleum Geology*, *Sedimentary Geology* and others.

How long can Mannworld continue in defiance of reality? In 2012, Dr Lüning and his colleague Professor Fritz Vahrenholt wrote[1]:

Leading representatives of the IPCC tried for years to have policymakers and citizens believe the pre-industrial temperature history was more or less uneventful and was the ideal climate condition that we should all strive to maintain. The warming of the 20th century, on the other hand, was completely unusual, something dangerous. However, as we now know, the page turned a few years ago and the notorious Hockey Stick chapter

---

[1] http://www.kaltesonne.de/mittelalterliche-warmeperiode-und-kleine-eiszeit-als-lokales-nordatlantisches-phanomen-seit-wann-liegt-japan-am-atlantik/ - translation by Pierre Gosselin here: http://notrickszone.com/2012/06/17/hockey-stick-was-refuted-before-its-fabrication-study-ignored-ipcc-and-mann-took-world-on-a-10-year-joyride/#sthash.dECihEG6.dpbs

ended. **The flawed curve was taken off the market** and the Medieval Warm Period and Little Ice Age reappeared.

As is often the case in history, it is in retrospect difficult to comprehend how this historical joyride could have happened to begin with. It started at the end of the 1990s with a doctoral thesis by Michael Mann, and did not end until about ten years later – thanks to the discovery of the scientific scandal by Steve McIntyre and Ross McKitrick... Today it is difficult to fathom how the main players and proponents of the Hockey Sticks are still able to act as experts and public opinion shapers.

One of the main excuses used back then was that the Medieval Warm Period and Little Ice Age in Europe and North America were local phenomena. At other locations on the planet the temperature anomalies were more than evened out (e.g. Stefan Rahmstorf, Gerald Haug). For years we had to listen to their tales and we had to trust these "specialists" for better or for worse. Moreover, we paid them with our tax money so that they could deal exclusively with the climate and carry out the tedious work all this entails.

As Drs Lüning and Vahrenholt point out, there were numerous pre-Mann studies - a 1995 Japanese paper from Geophysical Research Letters, *etc - that provided plenty of evidence for worldwide medieval warming greater than today:*

The Medieval Warm Period and the Little Ice Age as a local North Atlantic phenomenon? **A nutty claim.**

118

"In many fields of endeavour, Mann would have been struck off the list of practitioners."

PROFESSOR IAN PLIMER, PHD

Professor Emeritus of Earth Sciences at the University of Melbourne and Professor of Mining Geology at the University of Adelaide. Recipient of the Sir Willis Connolly Medal from the Australasian Institute of Mining and Metallurgy, the Clarke Medal from the Royal Society of New South Wales, the Eureka Prize from the Australian Museum, the Centenary Medal from the Government of Australia, and the Leopold von Buch Plakette from the German Geological Society, Fellow of the Australian Academy of Technological Sciences and Engineering, the Australian Institute of Geoscientists, the Australasian Institute of Mining and Metallurgy, and honorary fellow of the Geological Society of London. Member of the Royal Society of New South Wales, the Royal Society of South Australia, the Royal Society of Victoria and the Geological Society of Australia. Co-editor of *The Encyclopedia of Geology*. In 2009 a new phosphate mineral was named "Plimerite" in honor of his contributions to the geology of ore deposits.

It is, indeed, *"difficult to fathom"* how Mann and his Hockey Team are still able to pose as experts. Ian Plimer took up the same theme - albeit somewhat more forcefully expressed than Doctors Lüning and Vahrenholt On page 97 of his book Heaven and Earth *(2009)*, Professor Plimer summarizes Mann's behavior[1]:

In many fields of science, this would have been considered as

---

[1] Plimer: *Heaven and Earth: Global Warming - The Missing Science* (Quartet, 2009)

fraud. In many fields of endeavour, Mann would have been struck off the list of practitioners. In the field of climate studies, he was thrashed in public with a feather and still gainfully practises his art.

The damage is not to one third-rate computer modeler but to science itself:

After reading the history of the 'hockey stick' no one could ever again trust the IPCC or the scientists and environmental extremists who author the climate assessments. The IPCC has encouraged a collapse of rigour, objectivity, and honesty that were once the hallmarks of the scientific community.

The 19th century polymath Charles Babbage (half of whose brain is on display at the Science Museum in London, the other half at the Royal College of Surgeons) built some steam-powered mechanical computing machines, any of which would have done a better job than whatever contraption Mann runs his numbers through. On page 473 of Heaven And Earth, *Professor Plimer reminds us of Babbage's identification of the three forms of scientific dishonesty:*

(i) Trimming (the smoothing of irregularities to make data look extremely accurate);

(ii) Bias (retention of data that fits the theory and discarding data that does not fit the theory); and

(iii) Forging (inventing some or all of the data).

And then Professor Plimer adds, with immense restraint:

Some science supporting human-induced global warming (most notably the "hockey stick" of Mann) fulfills **at least** two of these criteria.

119

"Has he shown that there's no hockey stick..? The answer is yes."

PROFESSOR CLAUDE ALLÈGRE, PHD

Emeritus Professor at the Institute of Geohysics in Paris. One of the most highly cited researchers, according to the Institute for Scientific Inforemation. Former Minister of National Education, Research and Technology in the French Government, under the Socialist Prime Minister Lionel Jospin. Recipient of the William Bowie Medal, the Gold Medal of the French National Centre of Scientific Research, the Wollaston Medal of the Geological Society of London, the Crafoord Prize for Geology from the Royal Swedish Academy of Science and the V M Goldschmidt Award. Member of the French Academy of Sciences, Foreign Honorary Member of the American Academy of Arts and Sciences, and Foreign Associate of the US National Academy of Sciences.

Throughout all his self-inflicted travails of the last decade, Mann has insisted that he speaks for science and he takes the blows for science. But increasingly scientists from across the spectrum - from "alarmists" to "deniers" via "skeptics", "lukewarmers" and "realists" - agree at least that whatever their taste in climate science it doesn't include Mann. In 2010, upon the publication of his book L'imposture climatique, *Claude Allègre got into a public spat with the Swedish paleoclimatologist Håkan Grudd over the use the former made of the latter's landmark 2008 paper. In a sense, it was an argument about the precise degree of their antipathy to Mann and his hockey stick. Nevertheless, as Professor Allègre wrote[1]:*

---

[1] http://www.pseudo-sciences.org/spip.php?article1399 - English translation by the editor

Does Mr Grudd establish that historic temperature variations are underestimated in the tree-ring data used by Mann?

The answer is yes.

Has he shown that there's no hockey stick in the temperatures he estimated?

The answer is yes.

Has he shown that [per Mann] current temperatures are hotter than the historical periods?

The answer is no.

"Has he shown that there's no hockey stick?" Yes - but it should never have taken so long. Way back when Doctorandus Hans Erren wrote that first Yahoo forum post[2], on Sunday January 26th 2003 at 10.27 pm, he pointed out that, for a "proxy reconstruction", both Mann's proxies and reconstruction seemed a wee bit off. Mr Erren noticed that Mann had calibrated his North American tree rings with the Northern Hemisphere temperature record. Hmm. Why wouldn't you first calibrate the North American tree rings with the North American temperature record?

Because they don't match. So Mann decided that North American trees, which can't tell us the temperature of the continent they're planted on, can somehow tell us the temperature of the planet.

And thus, when the same tree rings that can't tell the temperature of their own backyard fail to show any medieval warming, that means that it's safe to wipe the Medieval Warm Period off the global temperature graph.

And voilà!

And the hockestick [sic] was born.

Mann still has no honest answer to the questions one curious Dutch scientist posed in a Yahoo web group.

---

[2] https://groups.yahoo.com/neo/groups/climatesceptics/info

120

"It's time to let Michael Mann sink or swim on his own."

DR JUDITH CURRY, PHD

Professor and former Chair of the School of Earth and Atmospheric Sciences at the Georgia Institute of Technology. Member of the National Research Council's Climate Research Committee and the NASA Advisory Council Earth Science Committee. Recipient of the Henry G Houghton Research Award from the American Meteorological Society. Co-editor of *The Encyclopedia of Atmospheric Sciences*.

On February 22nd 2014, in an extraordinary statement at her website, Dr Curry laid bare the appalling damage that Mann's Warmano style has done to climate science[1]:

The key issue regarding academic freedom is this: no scientist should have to fall on their sword to follow the science where they see it leading or to challenge the consensus. I've fallen on my dagger (not the full sword), in that my challenge to the consensus has precluded any further professional recognition and a career as a university administrator. That said, I have tenure, and am senior enough to be able to retire if things genuinely were to get awful for me. I am very very worried about younger scientists, and I hear from a number of them that have these concerns.

That's an astonishing admission, but not unjustified. Away from the world of academic tenure, the reaction of hockey-stick defenders to even the mildest criticism is to get the guy sacked. Willie Soon, co-author of

---

[1] http://judithcurry.com/2014/02/22/steyn-et-al-versus-mann/

one of the first papers to take issue with the hockey stick, is still the target of Mannworld's ire over a decade later. Greg Laden, one of Mann's most loyal hitmen, spent early 2015 trying to talk up a petition to put Dr Soon on the breadline[2]. As one of Mann's Twitter followers put it[3]:

> Patrick @Cyclonebuster Mar 2
> @MichaelEMann Willie Soon be fired?

Destroying lives seems to be what Mannworld enjoys, and what it will do in its death throes. But, as Dr Curry concluded, in a profound sense Michael E Mann and science have parted company:

For the past decade, scientists have come to the defense of Michael Mann, somehow thinking that defending Michael Mann is fighting against the 'war on science' and is standing up for academic freedom. It's time to let Michael Mann sink or swim on his own. **Michael Mann is having all these problems because he chooses to try to muzzle people that are critical of Mann's science, critical of Mann's professional and personal behavior, and critical of Mann's behavior as revealed in the climategate emails. All this has nothing to do with defending climate science or academic freedom.**

The climate science field, and the broader community of academics, have received an enormous black eye as a result of defending the hockey stick and his behavior. It's time to increase the integrity of climate research particularly with regards to increasing transparency, calling out irresponsible advocacy, and truly promoting academic freedom so that scientists are free to pursue research without fear of recriminations from the gatekeepers and consensus police.

---

[2] http://gregladen.com/blog/2015/01/willie-soon-fire-him-soon/
[3] https://twitter.com/michaelemann/status/572420646208061440

POSTSCRIPT

The case for Mann

Stubborn audacity is the last refuge of guilt.
SAMUEL JOHNSON
A JOURNEY TO THE WESTERN ISLANDS OF SCOTLAND (1775)

MICHAEL E Mann may believe *le climat, c'est moi*, but, as we noted at the beginning, although he claims to be taking a stand for science, science is increasingly disinclined to take a stand for him. It would be unfair, however, to say he has no scientific associates. He's just picky, as he told Irish science journalist John Gibbons in an exclusive interview:

JOHN GIBBONS: Our leading climate scientist, Prof John Sweeney had to actually boycott a recent TV programme, on the grounds that this type of 'debate' (giving oxygen to known climate deniers) is feeding the problem - you've experienced this..?

MICHAEL MANN: If we allow that sort of 'false balance' approach, it does a disservice to the public. If you as a scientist share the stage with an industry-funded denier, you are implicitly telling the audience that these are two equally credible voices – and they're not[1].

That's why Mann won't appear with "serial climate disinformer Judith Curry" or "climate denier Roy Spencer".

John Gibbons is best known to Irish readers for his idiosyncratic understanding of temperature:

Just in case you're not familiar with the basic science... the current global average surface temp. is c14.5C. Add 4C to that in half a century and you have increased the average surface temp by over 25 per cent.[2]

Er, no. That wouldn't be Centigrade, so much as Percentigrade. But Mr Gibbons rather touchingly believed that, if it's 10° Celsius today, and 15° Celsius tomorrow, it means it's 50 per cent warmer. Whereas, if it's 50° Fahrenheit today, and 59° Fahrenheit tomorrow, it's only 18 per cent warmer - which would seem one easy way to reduce the rate of climate change.

So Mann won't share a stage with notorious "#AntiScience" types like Dr Curry, but he will give an exclusive interview to a chap who thinks the thermometer measures percentages.

Surely John Gibbons can't be the only man of science to speak up for the beleaguered hockey captain? Well, we scoured around and found one or two more...

---

[1] http://www.villagemagazine.ie/index.php/2014/04/5706/
[2] https://skepteco.wordpress.com/2012/01/22/climate-change-will-the-real-deniers-please-stand-up/

i

"Mann and his colleagues are distinguished, independent scientists."

DR RAJENDRA PACHAURI, PHD

Chair of the Intergovernmental Panel on Climate Change until his resignation in 2015 following charges of sexual abuse currently before the High Court in Delhi. Ranked fifth in the Top 100 Global Thinkers by *Foreign Policy* magazine for "ending the debate over whether climate change matters". Recipient of the Order of the Rising Sun (Gold and Silver Star) from His Imperial Majesty The Emperor of Japan for his contribution to the country's policy on climate change, and likewise endowed with the Legion of Honor (France), the Order of the White Rose (Finland), and the Newsmaker of the Year award from the peer-reviewed journal *Nature*. Member of the honor committee of the Jacques Chirac Foundation to promote world peace. Former Indian Railways engineer at the Diesel Locomotive Works in Varanasi. Author of the romantic fiction *Return to Almora*, acclaimed as the world's first warmographic novel .

In 2005 the prestigious journal Nature *interviewed Dr Pachauri, the head of the IPCC, about the stick and other matters[1]:*

NATURE: Was it unwise to give Mann's "hockey stick" so much prominence in the IPCC's summary for policy-makers?

DR RAJENDRA PACHAURI: No. It is no exaggeration and it doesn't contradict the rest of the IPCC assessment. Of course you can always argue about details. But we assess all the available literature, and we found the hockey stick was consistent with that... Mann and his colleagues are distinguished, independent scientists who are able to explain their points of view.

[1] http://www.nature.com/nature/journal/v436/n7047/full/436007a.html

In 2015, Pachauri resigned as IPCC chair. When Mann launched his latest defamation suit, it was because of a "knowingly false comparison" between Mann's approach to data and sexual molestation. (The author, Rand Simberg, was speaking metaphorically - a literary device apparently unknown to Mann.) If you had said at the time that the head honcho of the Big Climate elite would turn out to be an actual sexual molester, most observers would have thought it statistically improbable. Bu that's why Pachauri, facing a criminal complaint at the Delhi High Court, was obliged to step down from the IPCC. From one of Dr Pantsdowni's accusers:

> I and many other female colleagues and friends who have worked at the same organisation as the complainant at/in different points of time and capacities during the last ten years have either been through similar harassment at his hands or have known someone who did.

Oh, my. Another 97 per cent consensus. After Mann claimed in court that the defendants had committed the hitherto unknown crime of "defamation of a Nobel prize recipient", the Nobel Institute announced that he is not, in fact, any kind of Nobel Prize winner. Mann's initial reaction to being called on his lie was to dig in deeper: how come, if he wasn't a Nobel Prize winner, he had one of these official Nobel Prize awards on display in his very office, huh?

If you win a real Nobel Peace Prize, you get invited to Oslo to meet the King of Norway and receive a Nobel Medal.

If you win a fake Michael E Mann Nobel Prize, you wind up like Mann with a piece of paper run off at the IPCC branch of Kinko's signed by a sexual abuser. Dr Mann's original complaint argued that it's totally unacceptable to compare a Nobel Prize winner with a sex fiend. But in fact he has the only "Nobel Prize" ever handed out by a sex fiend. What are the odds of that?

ii

"The 'hockey stick' graph that the IPCC so touted has... been debunked as junk science."

RESPONDENT TO THE CONSENSUS ON THE CONSENSUS

The Consensus on the Consensus: An opinion survey of earth scientists on global climate change was conducted by Margaret R K Zimmerman, MS, and published by the University of Illinois in 2008.

Aside from his support from Dr Pantsdowni, Mann often claims the imprimatur of "settled science": 97 per cent of the world's scientists supposedly believe in catastrophic anthropogenic global warming requiring massive government intervention. That percentage derives from a survey conducted for a thesis by M R K Zimmerman. The "survey" was a two-question, online questionnaire sent to 10,257 earth scientists, of whom 3,146 responded.

Of the responding scientists, 96.2 per cent came from North America.

Only 6.2 per cent came from Canada. So the United States is overrepresented even within that North American sample.

Nine per cent of US respondents are from California. So California is overrepresented within not just the US sample: it has over twice as large a share of the sample as Europe, Asia, Australia, the Pacific, Latin America and Africa combined.

Of the ten per cent of non-US respondents, Canada has 62 per cent.

Not content with such a distorted sample, the researchers then selected 79 of their sample and declared them "experts". Of those 79 scientists, two were excluded from a second supplementary question. So 75 out of 77 made it through to the final round, and 97.4 per cent were found to agree with "the consensus". That's where the 97 per cent comes from.

So this is a very Michael Mann "reconstruction": just as a couple of Californian bristlecones can determine the climate for a millennium, so a couple of dozen Californian scientists can determine the consensus of the world.

Nonetheless, the compilers also invited comments from respondents and published them in the appendices. In terms of specific scientific material, the hockey stick attracted three comments - one blandly positive, the other two not so much[1]:

I will note that **Mann's "hockey stick curve" has been demonstrated to be incorrect.**

And again:

The "hockey stick" graph that the IPCC so touted has, it is my understanding, been debunked as junk science. While they've never admitted this to be so, it's my understanding that **the graph has disappeared from IPCC publications.**

So what's that? A 67 per cent consensus from The Consensus on the Consensus *that Mann's stick is "incorrect" "junk"?*

---

[1] http://www.lulu.com/us/en/shop/m-r-k-zimmerman/the-consensus-on-the-consensus/paperback/product-4281091.html

iii

Mann "is distorting evidence to prove his point" and "should be fired from the university".

THE OTHER 97% CONSENSUS

Dr Donald Mikulecky, PhD is Professor Emeritus and Senior Fellow of the Center for the Study of Biological Complexity at Virginia Commonwealth University, and was formerly a Visiting Lecturer in Biophysics at Harvard Medical School, and a Visiting Professor at the Max Planck Institute for Biophysics and the University of Paris.

On March 9th 2012, Dr Mikulecky wrote a post at the acclaimed left-wing website The Daily Kos with the headline "Michael Mann is a Modern Hero and we need to acknowledge that!"[1]:

I just finished a very moving experience reading *The Hockey Stick and the Climate Wars*... So I will devote this diary to trying to convince you that this Mann is a hero... He has become a symbol for what our future is all about and he did not chose his role. No sane person would have... I will try to paint a broad picture of how much is at stake and give you a perspective on how this one Mann has focused on the threat to all of us... It is the scariest story ever written as a straightforward narrative of modern history. We can tell which way the wind is blowing by reading this weatherman!

At which point, Dr Mikulecky's readers were invited to respond to a poll

---

[1] http://www.dailykos.com/story/2012/03/09/1072828/-Michael-Mann-is-a-Modern-Hero-and-we-need-to-acknowledge-that#

offering the following options:

Michael Mann...

a) did not choose to became a symbol

b) has been attacked in many of the same ways that the President and John Kerry were

c) Is an outstanding scientist and human being

d) all of the above

e) is distorting evidence to prove his point

f) should be fired from the university

A week later, Professor Luboš Motl chanced to happen on the poll and reported the results[2]:

97% of DailyKos readers: Mann is dishonest

He was right:

Michael Mann...

a) did not choose to became a symbol 10 VOTES

b) has been attacked in many of the same ways that the President and John Kerry were 3 VOTES

c) Is an outstanding scientist and human being 8 VOTES

d) all of the above 36 VOTES

e) is distorting evidence to prove his point 2,341 VOTES

f) should be fired from the university 819 VOTES

So, indeed, 97 per cent of Daily Kos readers think Mann is dishonest. We have a consensus!

The good news is that, just over three years later, only 96 per cent of readers thought he was dishonest. At this rate of progress, Mann will be respectable to the Kos crowd around the year 2156 - if he can find an unmelted ice floe to do a celebratory macarena on.

---

[2] http://motls.blogspot.com/2012/03/97-of-dailykos-readers-mann-is.html

iv

"No researchers in this field have ever, to our knowledge, 'grafted the thermometer record' onto any reconstruction... The instrumental record (which extends to present) is shown along with the reconstructions, and clearly distinguished."

DR MICHAEL E MANN, PHD
Self-conferred Nobel Laureate, and personal climatologist to Jessica Alba.

In 2004, Mann and his friends put a lengthy post up at their Real Climate site correcting various "myths" about his hockey stick. Longtime reader John Finn expressed a reservation[1]:

> The practice of grafting the thermometer record onto a proxy temperature record – as I believe was done in the case of the 'hockey stick' – is dubious to say the least.

Mann himself responded:

---

[1] http://www.realclimate.org/index.php/archives/2004/12/myths-vs-fact-regarding-the-hockey-stick/

No researchers in this field have ever, to our knowledge, "grafted the thermometer record onto" any reconstruction. It is somewhat disappointing to find this specious claim (which we usually find originating from **industry-funded climate disinformation websites**) appearing in this forum. Most proxy reconstructions end somewhere around 1980, for the reasons discussed above. Often, as in the comparisons we show on this site, the instrumental record (which extends to present) is shown along with the reconstructions, and clearly distinguished from them (e.g. highlighted in red as here). Most studies seek to "validate" a reconstruction by showing that it independently reproduces instrumental estimates (e.g. early temperature data available during the 18th and 19th century) that were not used to "calibrate" the proxy data. When this is done, it is indeed possible to quantitatively compare the instrumental record of the past few decades with earlier estimates from the proxy reconstruction, within the context of the estimated uncertainties in the reconstructed values (again see the comparisons here, with the instrumental record clearly distinguished in red, the proxy reconstructions indicated by e.g. blue or green, and the uncertainties indicated by shading).

-mike

Mann is right: No respectable researchers have ever grafted apples onto oranges without distinguishing them.

But Mann does - on the front cover of his own book. The Hockey Stick And The Climate Wars *has a full color jacket that nevertheless shows both the proxies and the thermometer record as one continuous yellow line.*

...and don't forget

"A disgrace to the profession"
Volume II

featuring much more from
THE WORLD'S SCIENTISTS
~ in their own words ~
ON MICHAEL E MANN,
HIS HOCKEY STICK,
AND THEIR DAMAGE TO SCIENCE

coming soon from

STOCKADE
BOOKS

INDEX OF SCIENTISTS

Wallace, John **151**
Wang, HuanYe **211**
Wang, Zheng **211**
Warrilow, David 121, 122
Way, Robert 66, **71**, 74, 208
Wegman, Edward 74, 153, 154, 171
Wigley, Eirik **47**
Wigley, Tom 47, **111**, 113, 225

Wilson, Rob 216, **217**, 233, 235
Woodruff, Jonathan 204
Wyner, Abraham 5, **49**, 203
Zhang, Zhihua 204
Zhao, Cheng **211**
Zidek, James **67**, 156
Zimmerman, Margaret 295
Zorita, Eduardo **23**, 144, 214

BOLD TYPE indicates principal entry

also from Stockade Books

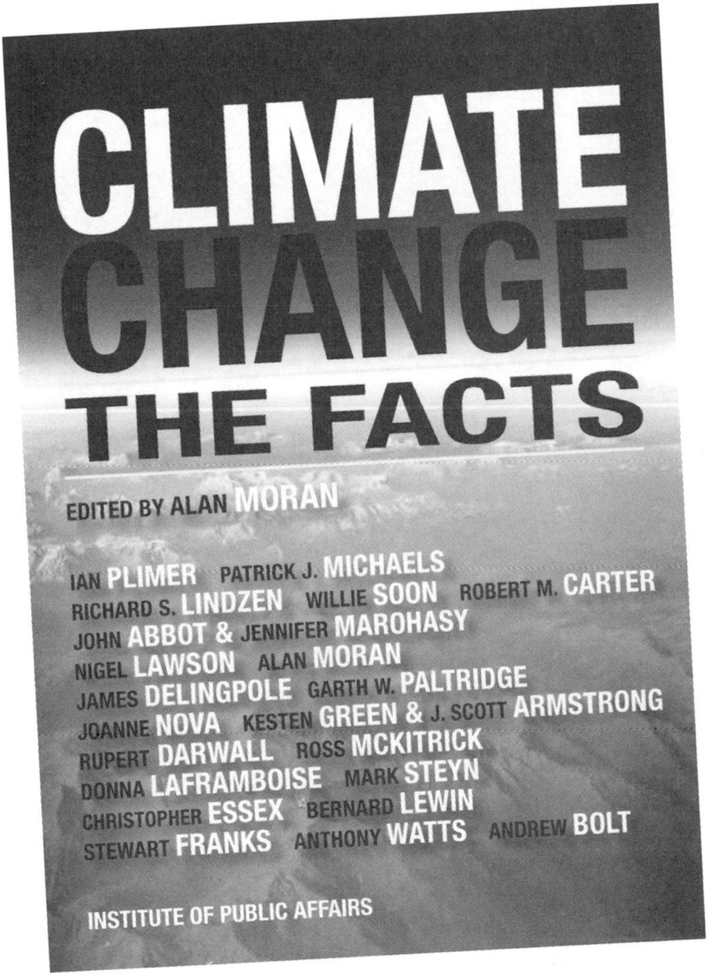